INVINCIBLE AND RIGHTEOUS OUTLAW

INVINCIBLE AND RIGHTEOUS OUTLAW

The Korean Hero Hong Gildong in Literature, History, and Culture

MINSOO KANG

University of Hawai'i Press

HONOLULU

Printed in the United States of America
25 24 23 22 21 20   6 5 4 3 2 1

Library of Congress Cataloging-in-Publication Data

Names: Kang, Minsoo, author.
Title: Invincible and righteous outlaw : the Korean hero Hong Gildong in
    literature, history, and culture / Minsoo Kang.
Description: Honolulu : University of Hawai'i Press, [2018] | Includes
    bibliographical references and index.
Identifiers: LCCN 2018013969 | ISBN 9780824874421 (cloth ; alk. paper)
Subjects: LCSH: Hong, Kil-tong. | Hŏ, Kyun, 1569–1618. Hong Kil-tong chŏn.
Classification: LCC PL989.27.K9 Z73 2018 | DDC 895.7/32—dc23
LC record available at https://lccn.loc.gov/2018013969

ISBN 978-0-8248-8431-4 (pbk.)

Cover art by Liam Cassidy

Dedicated to the memory of

Ambassador Kang Sung Ku (1931–2011)

my last king

my insurmountable mountain

my beloved father

Contents

Acknowledgments

Before I began writing this book, I completed a new translation of *The Story of Hong Gildong*, which was published as a Penguin Classic in 2016. The essential help I received from a number of people for the project made this book possible. My first and the greatest acknowledgment goes to Professor Lee Yoon Suk (Yonsei University, emeritus), a leading expert on classic Korean literature. He not only provided me with the digital files of various variant manuscripts of *The Story of Hong Gildong* that I worked with, but he also arranged for me to visit Yeonsei University to give talks to scholars and students about the progress of my work. As he continues to offer me invaluable help and support, most recently for my new translation project on the classic Korean novel *Record of the Virtue of Queen Inhyeon, Lady Min*, I cannot adequately express my gratitude to him for the great generosity in time and effort he has shown me.

The translation of *The Story of Hong Gildong* first appeared in the journal *Azalea: Journal of Korean Literature & Culture*, which was made possible by its editor, Professor Lee Young-Jun (Humanitas College, Kyung Hee University), who also provided me with significant help and advice, as he continues to do. Sam Raim, the editor of Penguin Classics who published the translation, gave me many insightful comments during the process of editing the translation and its introduction. They proved to be extremely helpful when I began putting this book together. Thanks also to Andrea Lam for her publicity work, which got the word out about *The Story of Hong Gildong*. Ken Chen organized a memorable event at the Asian American Writers' Workshop on the translation. I am grateful to him and to the two other participants at the event, the wonderful novelists Marie Myung-

Ok Lee and Min Jin Lee, for their appreciation and inspiration that renewed my enthusiasm for this project.

Thanks also to Yi Jongsik, who did great work for me as a researcher; to Heinz Insu Fenkl, for his continuing friendship and sage advice on all things literary; and to my indefatigable agent, Christopher Vyce, for his unflagging support of my work. John Dalton read the first draft of the translation, and Francis Grady, Suzanna Love, and Daron Dierkes read early versions of this manuscript at different points in its editorial process—I am grateful for their effort and comments. Thanks to Carla Nappi for the enjoyable interview I did with her for the New Books Network podcast. And thanks to my editor, Stephanie Chun, for guiding this book to publication.

Introduction

Despite significant reservations, I have to admit that the easiest way to introduce the subject of this book, the classic Korean work of fiction *The Story of Hong Gildong* (*Hong Gildong jeon*), is to describe it as the narrative of the Korean Robin Hood. For those unfamiliar with the story, the reference provides an immediate impression of an intrepid outlaw who, though a criminal in the eyes of the authorities, is on the side of the oppressed and the impoverished. The description also points to the cultural importance of the figure, given the fact that Robin Hood is famous not just in England but across the world, even to people who have never read any of the medieval and Renaissance ballads about him or seen the films starring Douglas Fairbanks, Errol Flynn, an animated fox, Kevin Costner, or Russell Crowe.[1] Likewise, every modern Korean knows Hong Gildong and can picture him as a sturdy youth in a blue vest, flying through the air on a cloud. He is an invincible warrior of uncanny powers and ingenious stratagems, the leader of fearless bandits who obey him with unshakeable loyalty.

The Robin Hood–Hong Gildong analogy may be useful as an initial introduction, but it is also a problematic one. Because the English figure enjoys such worldwide fame, it may distort the reader's perception of the Korean character as merely an Asian "version" of Robin Hood, one with idiosyncratic cultural differences. This would result in a skewed reading of his story. The examination of cross-cultural parallels may yield interesting insights into the iconic figure of the heroic outlaw, but it is also important to comprehend an individual narrative in its specific historical and cultural contexts, whether it tells the story of Robin Hood of England,

Song Jiang of China, Nezumi Kozō of Japan, Juro Jánošik of Slovakia, Salvatore Giuliano of Sicily, Ned Kelly of Australia, or Jesse James of Missouri.

So yes, Hong Gildong is the Korean Robin Hood, but also, no, he is a unique Korean character, the protagonist of an essential work of premodern fiction. He, furthermore, holds the distinction of being the most famous and beloved literary character in Korea, rivaled only by Chunhyang, the icon of young love and fidelity.[2] Through countless movies, television shows, children's books, comic books, and revisionist works of literature, the vast majority of Koreans who have never read the original text of *The Story of Hong Gildong* are familiar with this story of an illegitimate son of a nobleman who becomes a righteous outlaw.

One piece of evidence indicating the figure's importance to modern Korean culture is the ubiquitous use of his name as the generic cognomen, in the manner of "John Doe." Instructions on how to fill out forms use "Hong Gildong" to indicate where one's name should be written. I also discovered recently that the English-language Wikipedia article on "Korean Names" features an illustration with "Hong Gildong" in both Korean phonetic script (홍길동) and Chinese ideograms (洪吉童). The name may also ring a bell for those familiar with the history of the Vietnam War. It is little known in the United States that over three hundred thousand South Korean troops participated in the conflict.[3] The largest mission conducted by the Korean contingent, a forty-eight-day military action in Phu Yen Province launched in July 1967, was dubbed Operation Hong Kil Dong.[4]

I first became interested in writing about *The Story of Hong Gildong* when I was an undergraduate, in a course I took on the introduction to cultural history. One of the required texts was Eric Hobsbawm's classic 1969 work *Bandits*. In the fourth chapter of the book, he discusses the "noble robber," a legendary figure found in many cultures around the world and recognizable by the following nine characteristics:

> First, the noble robber begins his career of outlawry not by crime but as a victim of injustice or through being persecuted by the authorities for some act which they, but not the custom of his people, consider criminal.
> Second, he "rights wrongs."
> Third, he "takes from the rich to give to the poor."
> Fourth, he "never kills but in self-defense or just revenge."
> Fifth, if he survives, he returns to his people as an honorable citizen and member of the community. Indeed, he never actually leaves the community.
> Sixth, he is admired, helped, and supported by his people.

Seventh, he dies invariably and only through treason, since no decent member of the community would help the authorities against him.

Eighth, he is—at least in theory—invisible and invulnerable.

Ninth, he is not the enemy of the king or emperor, who is the fount of justice, but only of the local gentry, clergy, or other oppressors.[5]

This description immediately reminded me of Hong Gildong, not from the text of *The Story of Hong Gildong*, which I had never read, but from the children's books and cartoons that had been part of my childhood in Korea. I subsequently wrote my final paper for the class on the figure, applying Hobsbawm's ideas and using Marshall Pihl's 1968 translation of the work.[6] I no longer possess the paper and have only a scant memory of what I wrote in it, but I do remember noting that some of Hobsbawm's nine characteristics of the noble robber were not applicable to my subject (for details, see chapter 3). I also pointed out that unlike the stories of many figures discussed by Hobsbawm that were transmitted orally among the people as folktales, the text of *The Story of Hong Gildong* is not a product of popular imagination. While the narrative was inspired by a real-life bandit who was captured by authorities in the year 1500, the work was written by Heo Gyun (1569–1618), a writer and statesman from an illustrious noble family. I speculated that in the century or so between the time of the historical Hong Gildong and the writing of the story, legends about the figure had been passed down among common people until Heo Gyun gathered them into a coherent narrative, elevating it to the level of high literature by adding many learned allusions to ancient history, classic literature, Confucian philosophy, and Daoist magic.

I was, however, dissatisfied with the Pihl translation's truncated feel of the narrative, as many of the episodes seemed to unfold in a hurried manner that left many loose ends. In that last year as an undergraduate, though I decided to pursue a PhD in European history, I promised myself that one day I would undertake a new translation of *The Story of Hong Gildong*. I imagined that reintroducing that beloved tale from my childhood to English readers would be a rewarding as well as entertaining way of bringing greater awareness of Korean culture and literature to the West.

After the passage of more years than I care to dwell on, having completed my tenure book on the history of the automaton in the European imagination, I decided that it was high time I fulfilled the promise I had made to myself as an undergraduate. I thought it would be a challenging but concise project that would require perhaps a year's work, a relief after wrestling for so long with the massive undertaking of my previous endeavor.

But when I began to read up on recent scholarship on *The Story of Hong Gildong*, I realized that the task was going to be much more complicated than I had thought.

In the last decades, scholars of classic Korean literature have cast doubt on almost everything known about the history of the work. For instance, it now seems highly unlikely that Heo Gyun was the author of the extant text, which was probably written as late as the middle of the nineteenth century. That alone requires a complete reassessment of its place in the history of Joseon-dynasty literature. There is the additional problem of the existence of no fewer than thirty-four different manuscripts of *The Story of Hong Gildong*, some of them merely abbreviated texts but others featuring unique passages and significant thematic differences. In the course of my research, I realized that the Marshall Pihl translation felt incomplete because it was rendered from the *gyeongpan* 24 version of the work, which was considered authoritative at the time but is now known to be an abbreviation of the *gyeongpan* 30 text.

As I delved further into the matter, both fascinated and intimidated by the prospect of venturing into unfamiliar scholarly territory, I realized that the very nature of my project had to change if I hoped to give a full and proper account of the work's significance. What I originally envisioned as a fairly simple translation-and-introductory-essay project turned into a full historical investigation into the development of a set of cultural and historical myths surrounding *The Story of Hong Gildong*, including the myth of its authorship, the myth of its status as the first work of fiction written in the native Korean script of *hangeul*, the myth of the radical political message of the narrative, and the myth of its protest against the Joseon dynasty's policy on the status of secondary offspring. It would be useful at this point to lay out the work's basic plot, the nature of its variant manuscripts, and the history of previous English summaries and translations.

THE PLOT OF *THE STORY OF HONG GILDONG*

The numerous variants of the work tell the same three-part story of the heroic outlaw Hong Gildong in varying levels of realism and fantasy. The first part, the most realistic, takes place entirely within the family compound of a Joseon-dynasty government minister and relates the conception of the minister's illegitimate son Hong Gildong, his childhood, and the circumstances under which he ends up leaving home. In the second part, Hong becomes the leader of a band of outlaws with whom he causes havoc across the country. The last and most fantastic part narrates his adventures in foreign lands, where he defeats monsters and conquers a kingdom. Most versions have the story take place during the reign of King Sejong the Great (r. 1418–1450), but one points to the reign of Sejo (1455–1468), and the longest and probably the oldest variant (*pilsa* 89) refers to a fictional king named Seonjong.[7] There are many other differences in details among the different manuscripts, so the following summary is from the *pilsa* 89 variant, the longest and most complete version.[8]

Minister Hong, a renowned statesman from an illustrious noble family, has a daytime dream in which a dragon appears in a beautiful land. Upon waking, he realizes that it presages a great fortune to come and goes to his wife to have intercourse with her. When she refuses him out of embarrassment, he leaves her presence in frustration. In his own quarters, a household maid named Chunseom arrives to serve him tea. He lies with her, and she becomes pregnant. The minister is impressed with the girl's modesty and loyalty, so he elevates her to one of his concubines. Their child turns out to be extraordinary in strength and intelligence, but the minister laments that his prospects for advancement in the world are dim given his status as an illegitimate child. Although the boy, named Gildong, grows up to become a person of heroic qualities, he is filled with sorrow at the fact that he is barred from entering government service because he is lowborn. In fact, he is not even allowed to address his father as Father and older half-brother (the legitimate son of the minister by his wife) as Brother.

A senior concubine named Chorang, a wicked woman and a former courtesan, comes to hate Hong Gildong because she is childless. She plots with a shaman and a physiognomist to slander the boy to Minister Hong, suggesting that he is destined to bring great calamity to the family, and then arranges for an assassin named Teukjae to murder him in the middle of the night. Hong Gildong, through his studies of ancient texts, has become a master magician, so he is able to foresee the coming of the killer and thwart him. When he discovers the truth about the plot against him, he kills Teukjae, the shaman, and the physiognomist but spares Chorang, since she is his father's beloved concubine. He realizes then that he can no longer stay in the family compound and takes leave of his parents. Minister Hong tries to dissuade him from going, but when he realizes that the boy is set on his course, he gives him permission for the first time to call him Father. After Hong Gildong leaves, the minister has the dead bodies disposed of, commands everyone in the household not to reveal what has occurred, and throws Chorang out of the house.

In the second part, Hong Gildong wanders the land until he stumbles upon the mountain lair of bandits. Through a show of his incredible strength, he assumes the leadership of the group. His first act as the chief of the outlaws is to raid the famous Buddhist temple of Haein, stealing all its treasures and eluding government soldiers by bringing his men safely back to their lair using his magical powers. Afterward, he gives the name of Hwalbindang (League of Those Who Help the Impoverished) to the bandits and declares that they will only take the ill-gotten wealth of the corrupt and leave the property of the common people alone. Following another successful raid on the administration center of Hamgyeong Province, he comes to the attention of the king of Joseon, who offers a great reward for his capture. Hong Gildong makes eight straw men and uses his magic to animate them. They look so much like their creator that no one can distinguish them from Hong. Gildong sends them out to lead bandits' raids in all eight provinces of the kingdom, so it seems as if he is committing his criminal acts in multiple places at once, which confounds the king. When Yi Heup, the head of the Police Bureau, goes forth to capture him, Gildong appears in the guise of a young scholar and lures him to his lair, where he humiliates him before releasing him. He further aggravates the king by dressing up as a government official and punishing corrupt magistrates, then sending reports of his deeds to the monarch.

When the king finds out that Hong Gildong is the illegitimate son of a former government minister and the half-brother of a current official, he summons them both and threatens to punish them if they do not bring the outlaw in. Gildong's half-brother, newly appointed as the governor of Gyeonggi Province, writes a public notice begging Gildong to surrender himself for the sake of the Hong family. Eight identical Gildongs give themselves up to the authorities, only to reveal themselves to be straw men when they are brought before the king. The real Hong Gildong surrenders to his half-brother and allows himself to be put under arrest and sent to the capital. After he makes another spectacular show of escaping through the use of magic, the king and his officials discuss how to get rid of him once and for all. Hong promises to leave Joseon if he is pardoned of his crimes and given an important position in the government, so the monarch makes him the minister of military affairs. Some of the officials, however, decide to ambush him when he comes to accept the appointment. When Hong Gildong faces the king, he tells his sovereign that all he ever wanted was to serve him as a loyal and righteous official but was barred from pursuing his ambitions because of his status as an illegitimate son. That is what drove him to commit criminal actions as the leader of outlaws, though he tried to act righteously by only targeting the greedy and punishing the corrupt who have abused their powers. He then thanks the monarch for relieving him of his life's frustration by appointing him as a minister and informs him that he will leave the kingdom. He flies into the sky and disappears, leaving the king to wonder what great things such an extraordinary person could have achieved if he had been allowed to work for the country.

The third part unfolds over ever more fantastic episodes. First, Hong Gildong flies across the sky to inspect two islands where he can settle his outlaws and their families. He then returns to see the king of Joseon one last time, to ask him for many sacks of rice that will feed his people in their new home. With the king's generous gift, Hong takes his men and their families across the sea, to an island called Jae, which turns out to be a good place for them to settle down. He then flies to China, where he encounters magical monsters called *uldong* in a mountain. When Hong sees that they have kidnapped a human woman, he eradicates them with his magic. After he returns the woman to her parents, he marries her and also makes concubines out of two other women he has rescued. He settles down happily with his new family on Jae Island, until he realizes through his astrological insight that his father is dying. He returns to Joseon too late to see him before his death, but his half-brother allows him to choose the gravesite. The body is brought all the way to Jae Island, where Hong takes charge of the funeral arrangements.

Once the mourning period for his father is over, he conceives a great plan to invade the neighboring island of Yul, which is ruled by a powerful king with a great army. Hong Gildong becomes a military strategist and leads his men to battle, ultimately defeating the king of Yul and raising himself as the new monarch of the realm, which he names Annam. In the years that follow, the king of Annam sends an envoy to the king of Joseon to express his gratitude for his past generosity, buries his stepmother and mother on Jae Island upon their passing, and sees the birth of three sons by his queen and concubines. At the age of sixty, he abdicates in favor of his oldest son and moves into a mountain, where he practices the way of immortal spirits. One day, he and his wife disappear, having transcended themselves to a higher realm of being.

THE VARIANT MANUSCRIPTS OF *THE STORY OF HONG GILDONG*

When I set out to produce a new translation of *The Story of Hong Gildong*, I was faced with the problem of the existence of thirty-four extant manuscripts, featuring textual differences of varying degrees. The most complete version of the work (*pilsa* 89) is almost five times longer than the shortest (*gyeongpan* 17). Some texts feature extended passages not found in others, like an anti-Buddhist passage and more elaborate descriptions of the final battle in the *wanpan* versions. And there are numerous minor variations in details—for example, the *gyeongpan* texts identify the highest government post gained by Hong Gildong's father as the minister of personnel (*ijo panseo*), the *wanpan* texts as the state councilor of the left (*jwa uijeong*), and the *pilsa* texts as the state councilor of the right (*u uijeong*). The existence of so many variant manuscripts points to the great popularity the work enjoyed in the late nineteenth and early twentieth centuries.

Of the thirty-four known texts, twenty-five were handwritten and nine printed. The printed texts were produced in the three centers of the printing industry—Gyeongseong (today's Seoul), Wanju (today's Jeonju in North Jeolla Province), and Anseong (in Gyeonggi Province, south of Seoul). So the texts are referred to as *gyeongpan*, *wanpan*, and *anseongpan*, combining the first syllable of the cities where they were published and *pan*, which denotes a wooden or metal printing plate. The numerals attached to each text indicate the number of sheets in the volume, providing a general idea of the length of the narrative. For example, the *gyeongpan* 24 is a printed text of twenty-four sheets that was published in Gyeongseong, and the *wanpan* 36 is thirty-six pages and was published in Wanju. The handwritten (*pilsa*) manuscripts are referred to by the name of the person who owns a particular text or the institution where it is housed, followed by the sheet count. For example, the Park Sunho 86 is a handwritten text of eighty-six sheets in the private collection of Park Sunho, and the Tōyō bunko 31/31/33 is a work in three volumes of thirty-one, thirty-one, and thirty-three sheets each housed at the Tōyō bunko (Asian studies) library in Tokyo, Japan.

A major obstacle to the determination of the time of the original composition of *The Story of Hong Gildong* is that only fifteen manuscripts feature dates of publication, ranging from 1893 to 1936.[9] Lee Yoon Suk, however, has made an exhaustive study of the extant texts, coming to the conclusion that the *pilsa* 89 version is the oldest.[10] In the nineteenth and early twentieth centuries, printers did not solicit original works from authors but published print versions of handwritten works that were already popular. Once a work proved to be successful, both copiers of handwritten texts and publishers of printed texts produced abbreviated versions of the work in order to cut down on the cost of production, especially of paper. Given such practices, the longer handwritten texts can generally be regarded as older, with shorter, printed versions as later variants. Since the Kim Donguk 89 is the longest extant version in handwritten form, it can reasonably be regarded as either a copy of the original work or the one closest in content to the ur-text. (For more details on the extant variants, see the appendix.)

ENGLISH SUMMARIES AND TRANSLATIONS OF
THE STORY OF HONG GILDONG

The story of Hong Gildong was first introduced to the West by the American doctor, missionary, and diplomat Horace Newton Allen (1858–1932). During his years in Korea from 1884 to 1905, Allen played a significant role in the modernization of the country. He established the first Western-style hospital under King Gojong's patronage and arranged for American companies to build the first electric networks and railway systems in the peninsula. In 1889, he published a book entitled *Korean Tales*, with the purpose of correcting the impression in the West that the Koreans are "a semi-savage people."[11] Along with the four standard *pansori* narratives (*The Story of the Rabbit, The Story of Heungbu and Nolbu, The Story of Chunhyang,* and *The Story of Simcheong*), he told the story of a righteous outlaw under the title of "Hong Kil Tong, or The Adventures of an Abused Boy."[12]

There are indications in the text that it is based on a *gyeongpan* text, but Allen's narrative cannot be considered a translation of *The Story of Hong Gildong*, because he freely adds explanatory passages that are not in the original, and he does away with the last part of the narrative dealing with the conquest of Yul Island. The first sentence begins with a historical error—"During the reign of the third king of Korea . . ."[13] Allen must have mistaken King Sejong as the third monarch (he was actually the fourth). He also made alterations to the plot and inserted explanations mainly for the purpose of making Hong Gildong seem more of a moral exemplar. The hero subdues the assassins (plural in this story, unlike the single one in the original work) sent to murder him at home, but he spares their lives, after making them promise not to harm another person (he kills the assassin in the original).[14] Also, at the beginning of the episode in which Hong leads his men to attack the Buddhist temple of Hein, Allen adds his own explanation of why the place is targeted.

> As was the rule, this temple in the mountains was well patronized by officials, who made it a place of retirement for pleasure and debauch, and in return the lazy, licentious priests were allowed to collect tribute from the poor people about, till they had become rich and powerful.[15]

Likewise, before the assault on the provincial capital of Hamgyeong, Allen explains that its governor "was noted for his overbearing ways and the heavy burdens that he laid upon his subjects. He was very rich but universally hated, and Kil Tong decided to avenge the people and humiliate the Governor, knowing that his work would be appreciated by the people."[16] Allen also changed the magical monsters called *uldong*, whom Hong Gildong fights on Mangdang Mountain in China, into mundane robbers described as shaggy-looking barbarians.[17] The story generally follows the plot of *The Story of Hong Gildong*, and the work as a whole is a laudatory introduction to the popular Korean work, but it takes too many liberties with the narrative to qualify as a proper translation.

From the publication of Allen's *Korean Tales* in 1889, seventy-nine years had to pass before an actual English translation of *The Story of Hong Gildong* appeared. Marshall Pihl's rendering was first published in *Korea Journal* in 1968 and reprinted in Peter H. Lee's 1981 *Anthology of Korean Literature*.[18] It is generally a faithful translation of the *gyeongpan* 24 version, though there are a number of minor errors. For instance, Pihl assumes "Jang Chung's lowborn son Gilsan" to be a reference to Chinese figures and translates the two names into the Chinese "Chang Chung" and "Chi-san."[19] Jang Gilsan was actually a real-life Joseon-dynasty bandit who operated in the 1670s and 1680s, decades after the death of Heo Gyun, the purported author of *The Story of Hong Gildong*. Since the authorship of Heo was largely unquestioned at the time, Pihl must have assumed that the reference was to some obscure Chinese figure. Also, at the end of the narrative when Hong Gildong's stepmother and mother die, the hero undergoes *"samnyeon sang"* on both occasions, which Pihl renders as "three prescribed annual mournings" and "Three mournings, once a year."[20] Actually, the words signify not three mourning rituals that were performed every year but a three-year mourning period (technically, twenty-seven months) in which a bereaved son had to live in a simple hut built next to the grave and avoid social company. But such minor mistakes in the otherwise competent work are not the main reason a new translation was called for.

As previously mentioned, among the different versions of *The Story of Hong Gildong*, Marshall Pihl naturally chose the one thought to be authoritative at the time—a printed text of twenty-four sheets that is one of the shortest variants. In hindsight, it seems odd that scholars could not see that it must be an abbreviated version of a longer text. Not only are episodes like Gildong's first encounter with the mountain bandits and his exploits on Yul Island told in a rather hurried manner, but there are plot elements that are introduced but then never mentioned again. For instance, when the hero tells his men that he will go see the king, he explains to them that he will ask the monarch to grant him a thousand *seok* (approximately 180 liters, or forty gallons) of rice.[21] In the subsequent dialogue with the king, however, he makes no mention of it.

In 2000, the Korean Classical Literature Institute published a bilingual edition of the *gyeongpan* 30 version, with a modernized Korean text facing an English translation. The narratives in both are complete, but the quality of the English is substandard throughout the text, with grammatical mistakes and awkward stylistic constructions in virtually every sentence. For instance, the hero's lament at his condition as a lowborn child is rendered as follows:

> Generally, if a man who was born in the world can't follow the example of Confucius and Mencius, he had better learn strategy and tactics, as a commander, by conquering here and there, perform a meritorious deed for the country, so that he could make himself famous—that would be a delight of man. But Alas! All I feel is loneliness and though I have father and brother but can't call them by father, brother. This drive me to lament with heartbreak.[22]

The passage replicates the Korean phrasing in the original, including what appears as a run-on sentence in English. It is, however, clearly unacceptable as a proper translation.

In 2013, I completed the translation of the *pilsa* 89 version of *The Story of Hong Gildong*, which appeared in *Azalea: Journal of Korean Literature & Culture.*[23] It was subsequently published as a Penguin Classic, which was especially gratifying for me, as it was the very first work translated from Korean to be included in the prestigious series. In the introduction to both, I summarized the findings of my research on the work's origin and significance. Given the complexity of the issues surrounding its history, however, it became apparent that it would require a book-length study to explicate them fully. Readers having some familiarity with the text would be especially interested in why it appears implausible now that *The Story of Hong Gildong* was written in the early seventeenth century by Heo Gyun and why recent scholars think that it was probably composed around the middle of the nineteenth century by an anonymous writer of secondary or commoner status.

The present volume is divided into two parts. The first, consisting of chapters 1 through 3, deals with the text of *The Story of Hong Gildong* itself, detailing the history of its production, its central themes, and the many myths surrounding its significance. The second part, chapters 4 through 6, discusses the many modern adaptations of the Hong Gildong story in the diverse media of fiction, comics, cinema, and television, from the Japanese colonial period to the present day. The two parts are disparate in nature; the first features a detailed literary and historical analysis of the text, while the second is a descriptive survey. As such, they may read like two different types of scholarship in one book. For the purpose of fully demonstrating the significance of *The Story of Hong Gildong*, I felt it necessary to provide in one volume both a thorough analysis of the work as well as a demonstration of how its story has influenced modern Korean culture. While I hope the first part to be a definitive assessment of the work in English, the second part is an invitation for future scholars to write more detailed studies on the many works I describe and analyze.

Chapter 1 offers a detailed account of various myths about *The Story of Hong Gildong*, which most Koreans today still believe to be factual, having to do with its dating, authorship, and significance. Chapter 2 looks into what actual historical evidence reveals about the myths and discusses the problematic nature of commonly held views on the work, many of which originated in the 1930s, from the writings of the literary scholar Kim Taejun. In chapter 3, I examine the themes of the narrative in the context of current scholarship on the actual era of its production. I then offer my own analysis of the text in the context of Korean history and literature. From the detailed examination of *The Story of Hong Gildong*, I move to the ways in which the work has influenced Korean culture in the modern era. Chapter 4 covers the Japanese colonial era (1910–1945), when the story was translated into Japanese and loosely adapted for two films. Chapter 5 looks at numerous new versions of the narrative in literature, film, and comics, in both North and South Korea from 1947 to 1986. Chapter 6 continues the survey in the most recent works from South Korea. The appendix provides detailed information on the thirty-four extant manuscripts of *The Story of Hong Gildong*.

A Note on Romanization

Throughout this book I use the new revised romanization system introduced by the Republic of Korea's Ministry of Culture, Sports, and Tourism in 2000, rather than the older McCune-Reischauer. Since the revised system has become the standard in South Korea, it is high time that professors, academic journals, and presses allow scholars and students to utilize the system each finds best and let future generations naturally decide the matter through usage (as it happened with the replacement of the Wade-Giles system of romanizing Chinese characters by the pinyin system after it became the international standard in 1982). I commend the University of Hawai'i Press, a major venue for scholarly works on Korea, for allowing me the option.

I have, however, maintained the old spelling of the names of well-known modern figures like Syngman Rhee, Park Chung-hee, and Kim Jong-il, as well as the two most popular family names Kim and Yi, as per standard practice. I have also adopted the general policy of using the revised system for the names of figures who flourished mostly before the official establishment of North and South Korea in 1948 (two-syllable personal names written as one word with only the first letter capitalized and without the use of hyphens—for example, 태준 as Taejun rather than Tae Jun, Tae-jun, or Tae-Jun) but have maintained the spelling of those who were active after 1948 as they appear in English-language publications or according to their individual preferences (I do not want to change my name to Gang Minsu). Inconsistencies, hopefully, have been kept to a minimum.

PART I

THE STORY OF HONG GILDONG, ITS HISTORY AND MYTHS

CHAPTER ONE

The Phantom of Hong Gildong
in the Fog of Myth

The importance of Hong Gildong to Korean culture is evidenced in most modern Koreans' familiarity with the character's general story, even though the vast majority of them have never read the original text of *The Story of Hong Gildong*. Especially well known are the hero's lament that as an illegitimate son he is not allowed to address his father as Father and his older brother as Brother and his exploits as the leader of righteous outlaws. At school, young Koreans also learn four things about the work, which are taught as historical facts: First, that *The Story of Hong Gildong* is the first work of prose fiction to be written in the native Korean script (*hangeul*) rather than in literary Chinese. Second, that *The Story of Hong Gildong* was written by the Joseon-dynasty writer and statesman Heo Gyun (1569–1618). Third, that Heo Gyun was an intimate friend to illegitimate sons of noblemen and wrote *The Story of Hong Gildong* to bring attention to their plight in Joseon society. And fourth, that as a politician Heo Gyun was an idealistic reformer who sought to create a more egalitarian society in Joseon through a revolution but failed in the attempt and was executed for treason.

These four "facts" are widely believed notions about *The Story of Hong Gildong*, but the historical evidence they are based on is questionable at best and implausible in many cases. In a sense, they are more myth than fact. I fully explain their problematic nature in the next two chapters, but it is necessary to begin with an account of the received ideas themselves as they are perpetuated to this day through textbooks and popular works of history and literature. Four moments in Korean history provide the essential contexts of the making of the myth of *The Story of Hong Gildong*:

first, the announcement of the creation of *Proper Sounds for the Education of the People* (*Hunmin jeongeum*) by King Sejong the Great in late 1443 or early 1444; second, the capture of the historical outlaw Hong Gildong in 1500; third, the arrest of Heo Gyun for treason in 1618; and fourth, the publication of Kim Taejun's pioneering work *History of Joseon Fiction* (*Joseon soseolsa*) in 1930–1931.

For readers with no preexisting knowledge of Korea during the Joseon dynasty, I begin with a brief description of the period.

JOSEON DYNASTY SOCIETY, CULTURE, AND POLITICS

"Korea" is a distortion of Goryeo, a dynasty that ruled the peninsula from 918 to 1392. It has been speculated that Persian merchants in China became aware of the place after the founding of the dynasty and spread its name throughout Eurasia. As a result, the country is known outside of East Asia by some variation of Korea or Corea. In 1392, General Yi Seonggye completed his coup d'état of Goryeo by ascending the throne as the first monarch of the Joseon dynasty. For the rulers of the new kingdom, their most urgent task was to solidify their power by centralizing political authority to the new capital of Hanseong (today's Seoul, also referred to during the period as Hanyang, Jangan, Janganseong, Gyeongsa, and Gyeongseong). They also enacted social policies based on strict application of principles of Neo-Confucianism (that is, Confucian philosophy systemized by the Song-dynasty philosopher Zhu Xi, 1130–1200).[1]

Society as a whole was divided into four status groups,[2] which were largely determined by family lineage[3] and set up to make social mobility extremely difficult. At the top of the hierarchy were the noble *yangban*, who monopolized political power and much of the wealth of the country. In the second tier was a group best described as nonaristocratic elites, who are commonly referred to as *jungin* (middle people). The term actually signifies within the status only one set of people, those who fulfilled low-level bureaucratic functions in the government or held specialized jobs the *yangban* considered beneath them, such as translator, physician, astrologer, and geomancer. While *jungin* suggests their middle position between the aristocracy and commoners, it apparently originated from the fact that many of them resided in the central part of the capital city. The historian Kyung Moon Hwang uses the term "secondary status" to denote them and others in the group, including the *hyangni* (provincial hereditary clerks), the *muban* (military officers), the illegitimate offspring of *yangban* and lower-status women, and elites of the northern provinces who found it difficult to participate in political life at the capital because of prejudice against the people of the region.[4] The third status group, the *sangmin*, consisted of the vast majority of common people: peasants, artisans, and merchants. At the bottom of the social hierarchy were the *cheonmin*, the lowborn, mostly slaves but also people in occupations regarded as especially lowly, like butchers and tanners (because they engaged in killing animals and handling their corpses and blood), itinerant entertainers, shamans, and courtesans (*gisaeng*, comparable to the Japanese geisha).

One of the many social changes that occurred in the Goryeo–Joseon transition that is essential to understanding *The Story of Hong Gildong* has to do with laws concerning marriage. In the previous dynasty, polygamy was legal and widely practiced by elites who could afford to do so. In Joseon, however, Neo-Confucian ideas on family life dictated that a man could only have one legitimate wife (*cheo*). Wealthy *yangban* men continued to bring extra women into their households as concubines (or secondary wives, *cheop*), but they and their children were placed in an inferior status. When a Goryeo man died, all of his wives and their children were eligible to receive a part of his property, but in Joseon the children of concubines could claim none or only an insignificant portion of the inheritance.[5] This policy and many others concerning family organization, marriage, and social behavior made life for women, even those of noble families, much more restricted than it was in Goryeo. The illegitimate children of the *yangban* and their concubines were called *seoeol* or *seoja* (secondary offspring), and their numbers grew rapidly in the course of the dynasty's history as all of their descendants were placed in the secondary social status. This put *seoja* men in a difficult situation. They grew up in *yangban* households, became intimate with *yangban* men who were their fathers, half-brothers, and friends, and had access to education, but they were not accorded the rights of nobility. As a result, despite their privileged upbringing and elite education, they often had to depend financially on their relatives or engage in the occupations of commoners to live.

Yangban men married women from other noble families but took commoner or lowborn women as concubines. No self-respecting nobleman would allow his legitimate daughter to be taken in as a concubine, except in the case of the king. Powerful men, in fact, competed fiercely to have one of their daughters become a royal concubine (*hugung*), which was not only a great honor but also an opportunity for rapid advancement in political standing. A royal concubine could be elevated to the position of a royal consort (*bin*) or even queen (*bi*) if the previous one died or was deposed. Even if she remained a concubine, her son could become the next ruler if the queen failed to produce an heir. The Joseon monarchs Gwanghae, Gyeongjong, Yeongjo, and Sunjo were the sons of concubines, and a number of others were born of women who were initially concubines but later became queens.

The *yangban* monopolized political power until the last decades of the dynasty's history, but the Confucian principle of practicing meritocracy in the appointment of government officials was followed through the institution of civil examinations (*gwageo*).[6] The system existed in previous eras, but it became much more important in Joseon after the first kings of the dynasty successfully centralized power to the capital by curtailing the privileges of provincial elites and forcing ambitious men to pursue careers in the government. The word *yangban* literally means "two orders," signifying the choice of two paths men from noble families were expected to take. They could either take the literary examinations (*mungwa*), to enter into civil service, or the military examinations (*mugwa*), to join the ranks of military officers. A third type of "miscellaneous" examination (*japgwa*) was for secondary-status *jungin* pursuing technical occupations such as clerks, translators, physicians, astrologers, and geomancers. The *mungwa* was a grueling series of tests held in several stages in both the provinces and ultimately in the capital, challenging students on their mastery of the Confucian classics and their composition skills in essay writing. Because of the difficulty of the examinations, *yangban* men spent most of their childhood and youth at the reading desk, memorizing texts and practicing composition. Theoretically, most men of noble, secondary, and commoner status were allowed to take the examinations, but few who were not *yangban* had the economic wherewithal to provide their sons with the resources, including books, writing implements, and tutors, to devote many years to studying. Even when someone from a non-noble background managed to pass the examinations and gain a government post, he found himself stuck in junior positions, denied promotion because of prejudice against his background. The eligibility of the *seoja* (secondary son) to take the examinations was a controversial issue throughout the dynasty and was reflected in a number of changes to the laws.

Once a candidate successfully passed the various stages of the literary examinations, he entered into the hierarchy of government service, which was divided into nine grades (*pum*), each of which was subdivided into the senior (*jeong*) and the junior (*jong*), for a total of eighteen ranks, the lowest being junior ninth and the highest senior first. A retiring statesman was considered to have had a highly successful career if he had served as the head of a ministry (the central bureaucracy was composed of the six ministries of personnel, taxation, rites, military affairs, punishments, and public works), a position of senior second rank, or as the director of a special institution like the Office of the Inspector General (*saheunbu*) or the Office of the Royal Secretariat (*seungjeongwon*), at senior third rank. The positions at the apex of government service, at senior first rank, were the three highest councilors of the State Council (*uijeongbu*), who served as the closest advisors to the king and were honored with the special title of *jaesang* (high minister). The actual power wielded by state councilors was different from one period to another and the reign of one monarch to another. Their authority was greater early in the dynasty, when the heads of the six ministries had to report to them rather than directly to the king, but later on the positions became largely honorary posts awarded to those at the end of meritorious careers.

Of the two ways a nobleman could advance himself in society, the civil service route through the literary examinations was seen as more prestigious than the military. The highest positions in the Joseon military, including the minister of military affairs, were usually assigned to statesmen of civil service background. This policy reflected the Confucian principle of keeping the military order subordinate to the civilian, as countries ruled by their warrior class, like those of the Japanese, the Mongols, and the Jurchens, were regarded as barbaric. It was also a way to prevent the repetition of events during the twelfth and thirteenth centuries, when the Goryeo dynasty was hijacked and ruled by a series of military strongmen who reduced the monarchy to a figurehead position.[7] Eugene Park has traced the decline of the prestige of the military examinations from the seventeenth century onward, the central reason for which is relevant to a detailed look at the status of secondary offspring in Joseon society.[8]

At the beginning of the dynasty's history, laws were promulgated during the reign of King Taejong (r. 1400–1418) prohibiting the *seoja* from taking the civil examinations.[9] In the course of the following centuries, in response to periodic requests by high officials and secondary sons themselves, incremental progress was made in improving their lot, though usually under strict conditions and with limited actual effect. During the reign of King Myeongjong (r. 1545–1567), the grandson of a *yangban* man was allowed to take the civil examinations, provided that his mother and grandmother were commoners of good standing. In other words, the second-generation offspring of a noble-commoner

union were admitted, but those of noble-lowborn union, like Hong Gildong, were not. After the great Japanese invasion of 1592–1598, an enormous calamity, there was a need to recruit people to leadership positions
from a wider talent pool, especially in the military. As a result, the military examinations became increasingly open to people of secondary and
commoner status, including the *seoja*, and the tests also became progres-
sively easier to pass. During the reign of King Injo (r. 1623–1649), great-
grandchildren of noble-lowborn unions were allowed to enter the civil
service through the literary examinations, although with restrictions on
promotions that kept them at junior ranks. Finally, King Yeongjo (r. 1724–
1776), himself the son of a lowborn palace maid who became a royal consort, removed all restrictions against secondary sons taking the
examinations, with explicit permission for them to address their fathers
as Father and older brothers as Brother.[10] Even then, however, they faced
considerable obstacles to advancement through promotions because of
prejudice against their status.

The issue of allowing secondary sons access to positions of authority in the government was part of a larger dilemma facing the *yangban*,
a problem for the elites of any country. As people inculcated in Confucian principles, every statesman paid lip service to the importance of
practicing meritocracy, but they were also aware that elevating talented
people regardless of their background could undermine their own
privileged position. Many noblemen had genuine sympathy for the
plight of secondary offspring and found occasions to push for moderate
reforms to improve their condition. But the *yangban* as a whole was resistant to any policy that would increase social mobility and weaken
their hold on power. It was only in the last decades of the nineteenth
century, when the dynasty began to collapse, that people of secondary
status like the *seoja* found opportunities to play significant roles in society and politics.[11]

When it comes to the political history of Joseon, it is crucial to understand the essential role played by factional conflicts among government
officials and noble families. Since the beginning of the dynasty, there
were groups of allied statesmen who worked relentlessly to dominate the
government by bringing about the ouster of their opponents, but it was
during the reign of King Seonjo (r. 1567–1608) that factions were first formalized into the Eastern (*dongin*) and Western (*seoin*) groups, named for
the areas of the capital where the leaders of the cliques lived. In the course
of the following centuries, the two factions split and subdivided into an
increasingly complex array of groups (the Eastern splitting into the Southern and the Northern, the Northern dividing into the Greater and the

Lesser, the Western splitting into the Old Learning and the New Learning, and so on). In the reigns of kings who were not forceful or clever enough to keep the factions under control, their conflicts often led to gridlock or disastrous policies for the country as a whole. To give one famous example, on the eve of the Japanese invasion in 1592, King Seonjo sent a diplomatic mission to Japan to assess the recently unified country's military threat. Upon its return, Ambassador Hwang Yungil reported that the Japanese were preparing for war and that Joseon should ready itself for their imminent attack, but Deputy Ambassador Kim Seongil claimed that they were not a danger to Joseon. Because the two men were from opposing factions, most of the officials in the Western group felt obligated to support Hwang's view, while those of the Eastern group supported Kim.[12] The Easterners were in ascendance at the time, so the king decided to bury his head in the sand by heeding their position, resulting in catastrophe when the invasion came. Interestingly, the official recorder of the diplomatic mission was Heo Sang, the father of Heo Gyun, the putative author of *The Story of Hong Gildong*. Even though Heo Sang was a member of the Eastern faction, he believed Hwang Yungil's position to be the correct one and took a courageous stance in supporting the Westerner's view on the matter.

For the study of such political conflicts in the Joseon dynasty, the *Veritable Records* (*Sillok*) of the royal court is an invaluable resource. Historian-officials who worked at the Office of Royal Decrees (*yemungwan*) kept detailed daily records of everything of any importance that occurred inside the court and the country as a whole.[13] Upon the death of a monarch, a committee was formed to gather all available records and write the official annals of the reign. It would be naïve to regard any historical document as free of the cultural, social, and political prejudices and biases of its author and its time, but the *Sillok*, in general, is remarkably objective in its impersonal and unadorned reporting of events.

The entire *Sillok* survives today in 1,893 volumes, which stands as the longest continuous record of any single period in world history. A translation into the Korean script was made in North Korea during the 1980s and published in four hundred volumes, while in South Korea a new version in modern Korean was completed in 1993, digitized in 1995, and made available online by the National Institute of Korean History in 2005. The website for the latter is a remarkable resource for historians. The full text of the entirety of the *Sillok* in both literary Chinese and Korean translation is now available, with a search function to aid research.[14]

In the course of compiling the official history of a deceased king, one essential matter that had to be decided on was the posthumous temple name of the monarch. All Joseon monarchs are referred to in history books by their temple names, which end with either *jo,* meaning "progenitor" used for those who initiated something (for example, Taejo, the temple name of Yi Seonggye, who founded Joseon; and Seonjo, who rebuilt the country after the devastation of the Japanese invasion), or *jong,* meaning "ancestor." Two Joseon monarchs were denied temple names because they were forcibly removed from the throne, so they are known to this day by their princely titles of Lord Yeonsan and Lord Gwanghae (Yeonsan *gun* and Gwanghae *gun*—to avoid confusion, I refer to them as King Yeonsan and King Gwanghae). Other kings were pushed out of power, like Jeongjong (r. 1398–1400) and Danjong (r. 1452–1455), but they received temple names because their falls were engineered within the royal family (Jeongjong losing out to his younger brother Taejong, Danjong deposed by his uncle Sejo), and they complied with their successors in making shows of voluntary abdication.[15]

Despite devastating invasions by two neighboring countries (the Japanese in 1592–1598 and the Manchus in 1627 and 1636–1637), destructive internal conflicts by political factions, and murderous succession bids by royal princes, Joseon proved to be a remarkably resilient and stable dynasty that lasted over five centuries through the reigns of twenty-six kings, one of the longest continuous rules by a single clan in world history. It began to collapse in the second half of the nineteenth century under the overwhelming pressure of encroaching foreign powers that the country was ill-equipped to deal with after decades of corrupt and inept rule by the rapacious families of queens to a series of boy kings. In the course of the long history of the dynasty, the characteristics of the country changed significantly from one period to another—the early era of 1392 to 1592, the crisis of 1592 to 1674, the stable period of 1674 to 1800, and the decline from 1800 to 1897.

To comprehend fully the significance of *The Story of Hong Gildong,* it has to be placed in proper historical context, to discern the concerns of a particular time, to explicate the workings of the literary practices of the era, and to explore the influence of the work in the period of its origin and thereafter. The determination of when the writing was produced is, therefore, of central importance to the task. Unfortunately, the traditional dating of *The Story of Hong Gildong* is based on a series of myths, and this has created a major obstacle to the scholarly pursuit of its historical significance. In the exploration of the myth, special attention needs to be paid to three specific historical events, the first of which is the invention of the native phonetic script in the fifteenth century.

PROPER SOUNDS FOR THE EDUCATION OF THE PEOPLE

The Twelfth Lunar Month of the Twenty-Fifth Year of the Reign of King Sejong the Great (December 1443 or January 1444)

In the historical imagination of the Korean people, no one comes close to rivaling King Sejong in his reputation as the country's greatest monarch. After the bloody and despotic reign of his father, King Tae-jong (r. 1400–1418), who succeeded in firmly establishing the foundation of the new dynasty by eliminating all rivals and crippling threats to the central power of the capital, Sejong ascended the throne in a time of peace and stability. In addition to a long record of enacting judicious and benevolent policies that significantly enhanced the well-being of the common people, this particularly intellectual monarch stimulated a great flowering of learning in the royal court. This led to innovations in an astounding array of subjects, including philosophy, history, literature, cartography, astronomy, calendar study, musicology, mathematics, printing, physiology, pharmacology, and comparative linguistics.[16] The last area was of special interest to him. Among his many achievements, the one that modern Koreans point to as his greatest and most famous is the invention of a new phonetic script, today called *hangeul*.

The royal announcement of its introduction was made in the last lunar month of the twenty-fifth year of Sejong's reign. Since the exact date is not provided in the *Sillok* records, by modern reckoning it occurred sometime between December 21, 1443, and January 19, 1444.[17] It described the monarch having personally created a set of twenty-eight phonetic letters designed to be combined to form syllable units. The new writing system was given the name of *hunmin jeongeum*—"Proper Sounds for the Education of the People." In 1446, a text was published that explained the forms and sounds of the letters and demonstrated their use. It was supplemented by a work called *Explanations and Examples of the Proper Sounds for the Education of the People* (*Hunmin jeongeum haerye*) written by the court scholar Jeong Inji, the king's chief aide in the project.

As Gari Ledyard has detailed in his comprehensive work on the subject,[18] there were multiple reasons Sejong committed himself to the task, including the purely scholarly one of furthering his study of comparative linguistics and the more practical one of creating an easy method of teaching standardized pronunciation of Chinese characters. But the most famous motivation, the one routinely pointed to as the greatest example of his benevolence, can be found in Sejong's introductory remarks to *Explanations and Examples of the Proper Sounds for the Education of the People,* which most Koreans are familiar with from their schooldays because it is often quoted in textbooks.

> Our country's language is different from that of China, and so it cannot be easily communicated in Chinese characters. For this reason there are many unlearned people who cannot properly articulate what they wish to express. I have taken pity at their plight, so I have created these twenty-eight letters. All I wish is for every person to learn them easily and to use them comfortably through all of their days.[19]

From time immemorial, Koreans used literary Chinese despite the fact that the native language was of a completely different linguistic order. The sequence of words in even the simplest expressions is different in the two languages, and Korean is replete with suffixes and connective sounds that do not exist in Chinese. As a result, writing something down often amounted to taking thoughts and utterances in Korean and approximating them in Chinese, while abandoning idiosyncratic sounds, ways of expression, and rhythms particular to Korean. In the ensuing debates in the court on the new script, a point of contention was its use to improve the kingdom's judiciary, since adopting a more accurate method of recording people's statements in legal cases could prevent miscarriages of justice. The traditional solution to this problem was the use of systems that allowed a writer to reorder Chinese characters to reflect spoken Korean better and to use certain characters for their sounds alone to represent Korean suffixes. But these systems, called the *hyangchal* and the *idu*,[20] provided only a partial solution to the essential problem of linguistic difference.

As is well known, Chinese writing is composed of ideograms, each of which is a discrete symbol that directly represents a concept, so one has to memorize at least three thousand characters to be considered basically literate. The sheer difficulty of learning literary Chinese made it feasible only for the *yangban* and the more privileged among secondary- and commoner-status people who had the time and the resources for long-term education. Jeong Inji explains in *Explanations and Examples of the Proper Sounds for the Education of the People* that the new phonetic script, which requires the memorization of the sounds of only twenty-eight letters and learning how the syllable units are put together, could be mastered by an educated person in one morning or by a commoner within ten days.[21] Several former students of mine from Missouri who worked as English teachers in Korea confirmed to me that they were able to learn the sounds of Korean writing in three or four days.

Much of the intellectual, scientific, and technological innovations of Sejong's reign came out of the Hall of Assembled Worthies (*jiphyeonjeon*), a research and educational institution that was operated by younger scholars of noted intellectual talents. As a result, it has been assumed by many historians that the phonetic script was a product of the academy. Sejong did draw people like Jeong Inji from the place to aid him in the work, but Ki-Moon Lee has made a convincing case that the initial invention of the script was largely the achievement of the king himself.[22] In fact, a significant faction of officials at the hall, led by the senior scholar Choe Malli, put up a vociferous opposition to its adoption.

Even before the publication of the explanatory text in 1446, King Sejong faced resistance to his effort. Only months after the initial announcement of the phonetic script, Choe Malli presented a memorial to the monarch that articulated the reasons he considered it an unwise enterprise. Choe thought it would offend the Chinese if they got wind of it, which was a serious consideration, given that Joseon paid fealty to the Ming emperor; it would discourage the learning of Chinese classics, with a detrimental effect on the intellectual level of the country; it would bring down the level of the kingdom's civilization because only barbarians used phonetic scripts; it was unnecessary, since the *idu* system sufficiently dealt with the linguistic gap between spoken Korean and literary Chinese; and since Koreans had been using Chinese writing from time immemorial, they should not take the unprecedented step of adopting a new writing system just because it is easy to learn and more convenient to use.[23] It is also apparent that Choe was deeply concerned about how the script could encourage social mobility.[24] If it were adopted by the kingdom, he argued, less educated men who are not versed in Confucian philosophy and other classics would find it easier to advance themselves in society. What that objection reveals is that the difficulty of learning literary Chinese worked to the advantage of the *yangban* in maintaining their elite status because it ensured that literacy remained the skill of a privileged minority. Just as in the case of the problem of secondary offspring, the nobility was highly resistant to granting people of lower status opportunities for social advancement, out of the fear that it would lead to the erosion of *yangban* power and prestige.

Modern reverence toward King Sejong as the inventor of the phonetic script is somewhat ironic, since his effort to spread literacy among the common people ended in failure. He ordered major projects to encourage its use, including the translation of Chinese classics, the creation of dictionaries with pronunciation guides for Chinese characters, the commission of original works like the eulogistic poetry cycle *Songs of Flying*

Dragons,[25] and the compiling of Buddhist scriptures. Overt objections by government officials to the new writing ceased after the publication of the 1446 text, but the *yangban* managed to thwart the monarch's purpose by simply refusing to use what they began referring to as *eonmun* (vulgar script), continuing to write in Chinese for both official and literary purposes. So the dream of transforming the kingdom through the use of the script was not realized. Yet the opponents of the writing were not completely victorious either, as it was utilized in limited but enduring ways in certain sectors of Joseon society.

Despite the nobility's initial contempt for the vulgar script, it did not die out after the reign of its inventor for the simple reason that it was indeed so easy to learn and practical to use. The people who adopted it most readily were those who had some access to education and time for intellectual pursuits but were not *yangban* scholar-officials. Just as Choe Malli speculated, the secondary-status *jungin* found it eminently useful, especially those who worked as translators, because they now possessed a method of accurately representing sounds of different languages for both scholarly and teaching purposes. Also, upper-status women began using it for personal writings and communications, which resulted in the word *amgeul* (women's script) becoming another derogatory term for the writing. One of the finest examples of such writing by a Joseon woman is the set of memoirs by Lady Hyegyeong (1735–1815), the wife of Crown Prince Sado.[26] Even the *yangban*, who outwardly rejected *eonmun*, consulted phonetic dictionaries with definitions and pronunciations of Chinese characters, which young noblemen who were studying for the civil examinations found too useful to abjure. And in the later Joseon period, from the seventeenth century on, some *yangban* wrote private letters in the script especially to women in their lives, as did certain monarchs. JaHyun Kim Haboush has shown that during the Japanese invasion of 1592–1598, King Seonjo sent out pronouncements to the common people in the phonetic writing, urging them to remain loyal to the kingdom and to carry on the fight against the invaders.[27] In the second half of the eighteenth century, a period of peace and prosperity under the reigns of King Yeongjo and King Jeongjo, a noticeable increase in literacy led to the flowering of literary production in the native script, including a genre of prose fiction involving extraordinary heroes who embark on fantastic adventures.

But over five centuries had to pass before King Sejong's dream was fully realized. When the Joseon dynasty went into decline during the last decades of the nineteenth century, many progressive nationalists of secondary and commoner status advocated the adoption of the script as the official writing of the nation. It became a major issue for those who wanted the country to free itself of foreign political and cultural influences. The writing did become recognized during the Gabo Reforms of 1894, with *eonmun* given the more dignified name of *gukmun* (national script). In the following year, the nationalist organization Independence Club published the first newspaper in the script, *Dongnip sinmun* (The independent).[28]

King Gojong officially brought an end to Joseon in 1897 by renaming the country Daehan Jeguk (Great Han Empire—or Empire of Korea) as a way of signaling its independence from China after the defeat of the Qing in the First Sino-Japanese War (1894–1895). The newly adopted term Han (signified by the ideogram 韓, which is pronounced in a similar way but written differently from the "Han" of the Chinese dynasty and the majority ethnic group of China—漢) for the nation was a reference to the Samhan (Three Han) period of early Korean history (c. 100 BCE–350 CE), when the three kingdoms Mahan, Jinhan, and Byeonghan ruled over the southern and central part of the peninsula. The name was revived because it was thought that the Han kingdoms had never paid fealty to a foreign power.[29]

With the expanding popularity of the phonetic script in the new era, there was a need to update and standardize its use. The task was taken on by Ji Sigyeong (1876–1914), a linguistics scholar and fervent nationalist of secondary-status background from the northern province of Hwanghae.[30] In the first decade of the new century, as the country fell haplessly toward subjugation by the Japanese, Ji produced a series of pioneering works on the modern usage of the script before his untimely death in 1914. He was the one who coined the new term *hangeul* (Han script) for what began as King Sejong's *Proper Sounds for the Education of the People.*[31]

During the colonial era, the first generation of modern fiction writers, like Yi Gwangsu, Yeom Sangseop, and Kim Dongin, made a point of writing in *hangeul*, but nonfiction works tended to be written in combination with Chinese characters, usually with proper names and titles, technical concepts, and esoteric terms in the latter. After liberation from Japan and the splitting of the country into two nations in 1948, the communist north adopted the phonetic script exclusively, calling it *joseongeul* (Joseon script). In South Korea, Chinese characters were still used in scholarly nonfiction works, but they were gradually phased out. One can make a reasonable guess on the decade of an academic work's publication by seeing how much of the text is in Chinese characters.

Recently, the leadership of a minority ethnic group in Indonesia called the Cia-Cia, who live on Buton Island, became concerned that their native tongue might become extinct. Although the Latin alphabet is used throughout Indonesia, they found *hangeul* a better tool to express sounds in their language. In 2009, they adopted it as their official writing system, the first time a non-ethnic Korean group has done so.[32]

The justifiable pride Koreans feel at the brilliance of King Sejong's invention and the important place the writing system played in the history of modern Korea is a major part of the Hong Gildong myth. I will return to its relevance when I detail the circumstances under which *The Story of Hong Gildong* became designated as the first work of prose fiction to be written in *hangeul*.

THE CAPTURE OF THE BANDIT HONG GILDONG

The Twenty-Second Day of the Tenth Lunar Month of the Sixth Year of the Reign of King Yeonsan (1500)

After the idyllic days of King Sejong the Great, the social and economic stability achieved by the founding rulers of Joseon began to deteriorate as laws regarding land ownership and taxation began to be abused. An effective way the new regime centralized power to the capital was by placing most of the country's arable land under direct taxation by the government, instead of by regional elites.[33] The system was based on the idea that all lands of the kingdom belonged to the king, and his officials were to be paid for their service to the state through temporary lordship over specially designated properties close to the capital called "rank lands." When an official died, the property was supposed to return to the government so that it could be granted to newly appointed officials. This did not signal the end of all private ownership of land, but the policy placed most of the kingdom under direct state control and uniform taxation.

Over the second half of the fifteenth century, however, the system became degraded to the verge of utter collapse. Rather than returning rank lands to the state, increasing numbers of *yangban* took advantage of both legal loopholes and illegal methods to keep the land in their families. This forced the government to designate more land in the central and southern provinces as rank lands, causing a significant loss of revenue. Also, from the beginning of the dynasty, kings granted "merit lands" to people who performed extraordinary service, usually in helping them gain the throne, which stayed in their families permanently. The violent paths the monarchs Taejong and Sejo took in attaining kingship in the first half of the fifteenth century necessitated the rewarding of such lands to those who had taken risks and committed bloody acts on their behalf. Powerful *yangban* also found ways of circumventing laws that restricted the expansion of private property, gaining significant estates that they lorded over like the fiefdoms of old. This situation not only weakened the state via a steadily decreasing tax base but also brought a great deal of suffering to the common people. Unable to bear the burden of arbitrary taxation by local landowners and tax collectors, many peasants simply abandoned their farms to wander the land as groups of vagrants, some of them resorting to banditry, which caused further hardship on the people.[34] Then in 1494 a mad king ascended the throne.

While King Sejong is commonly regarded as the greatest ruler of the dynasty, the most eligible candidate for the worst is Yeonsan. When the future king was a young boy, he was taking a walk in the grounds of the royal palace with his father, King Seongjong, when the monarch's pet deer came up and licked the boy's hand. He flew into a rage and viciously kicked the animal, and his father severely reprimanded him for the wanton cruelty. After he became king, one of his first acts was to find the deer and kill it with an arrow. His violent and lascivious behavior has been explained by his troubled childhood. He was taken away from his mother when he was three years old and raised by a stepmother who showed him little affection. It was only after he ascended the throne that he learned his mother had been exiled and ultimately executed for scratching the king's face in a fit of jealousy. The discovery led to the slaughter of everyone Yeonsan held responsible for her demise, including two of his father's concubines, whom he personally beat to death.

In addition to enacting two major purges of officials, which Edward Wagner has interpreted as part of his effort to establish a true absolute monarchy,[35] he ordered the removal of people from a significant area of the capital so that it could be turned into his personal hunting ground and drove the country to the verge of bankruptcy with lavish parties. The neglect of his kingly duties brought essential works of the state to a standstill, and courageous officials who remonstrated with him were dismissed from their positions, exiled, or executed. When a palace eunuch begged him to change his ways, Yeonsan shot him with an arrow, chopped up his body, and saw to the eradication of all his relatives. The appearance of an anonymous public notice that criticized his behavior, written in King Sejong's *hunmin jeongeum*, prompted Yeonsan to ban the use of the writing and order the burning of books in the script.

During his misrule, it was announced on the twenty-second day of the tenth lunar month of the sixth year of his reign (1500) that a bandit leader by the name of Hong Gildong had been caught. The seriousness of the disturbance he had caused is apparent from the fact that the three high ministers of the State Council reported the event directly to the king, bidding him to take advantage of the development to arrest everyone in his gang, since "there is no task more important than ridding the country of poison." A record from the time of Yeonsan's successor, King Jungjong, indicates that the size of Hong Gildong's gang was significant. In 1523, a discussion took place in the royal court on the handling of sixty people who had been arrested, probably for banditry, since they are described as having caused "harm to the common people from their hiding places."[36] An official informed the king that all those who had participated in the crimes were likely several times the number already in custody. He suggested that instead of imprisoning all of them in one place, they should be divided into small groups and spread across facilities in several towns, because "the sight and talk of so many prisoners filling the streets would be unseemly." That, the official claimed, "would mirror the situation at the time of the prosecution of Hong Gildong."

While there are eight more records of Hong Gildong in the *Veritable Records (Sillok),*[37] those who are seeking the real-life model for the fictional character will be disappointed. No information can be found on where he came from, what his social status was, what his motivation was for becoming an outlaw, how he became a bandit leader, or how long he was active as one. In the immediate aftermath of his capture, his name comes up mostly in connection to another criminal, Eom Gwison, whose case was much more serious, since he was a high-ranking official. Eom was accused of having provided shelter and supplies to Hong Gildong and his band for which he was paid with goods stolen by them. His guilt was not in doubt, but he must have had significant influence in the government since his case was brought up four times, with some officials objecting to the harshness of his punishment (a hundred blows of flogging, then exile).

Despite the scarcity of information on Hong Gildong in the *Sillok,* two aspects of the real-life bandit stand out in relation to the fictional character. The first is the fictional hero's penchant for dressing up as a high-ranking official to commit his thefts, which was seen as a particularly outrageous crime in Joseon's extremely status-conscious society. The *Sillok* records indicate that the real-life bandit disguised himself similarly. An official named Han Chihyeong from the Office of the Deliberation of Forbidden Affairs (*uigeumbu*), the state tribunal that dealt with the most serious crimes against the state, informed King Yeonsan that Hong Gildong dressed himself up in the jade-decorated hat and red robe of a high official so that he could freely take armed men in and out of provincial administrative facilities.[38] It was Han's opinion that the bureaucrats there must have known of such activities but did not report them, so they should be dismissed and exiled. Just the fact that the Office of the Deliberation of Forbidden Affairs was involved in the investigation indicates how seriously they took the travesty of a bandit going about in the guise of an official. Over thirty years after Hong Gildong's capture, King Jungjong, while considering the case of another bandit, Seon Seok, noted that the outlaw and his gang were in possession of jade-decorated hats of high-ranking officials.[39] The monarch thought that they had used them for the same purpose as Hong Gildong.

The second interesting point of comparison between the historical and the fictional Hong Gildong is one of contrast. It has been speculated that the heroic portrayal of *The Story of Hong Gildong*'s protagonist may have been based on folk legends about the outlaw, though no evidence of oral storytelling about him has been found. Even if such a preliterary tradition existed, the idea of Hong as a righteous champion of the oppressed and the impoverished could only have developed significantly after the actual bandit's activities, since it is apparent that his initial reputation was a negative one. There are indications not only of the great suffering he inflicted on the common people through his criminal acts but also of him being regarded as a hated villain by them.

As officials discussed the appropriate punishment for the bandit's collaborator Eom Gwison, one of them described the situation in this way: "Cruel and vicious wretches formed a band and did great harm to the common people, so that everyone has been aroused to indignant fury."[40] This is, of course, the perspective of the state, which had an interest in maintaining the status quo by suppressing outlaws. But there is evidence of significant damage to the welfare of the common people, which supports the claim of anger on the part of the larger populace toward the criminals. The first mention of where Hong Gildong operated, the southwestern province of Chungcheong, can be found in a record from 1513. The Ministry of Taxation informed King Jungjong that given a number of circumstances, including several bad harvest seasons, a *yangjeon* had not been started despite the fact that it was well past time to do so.[41] A *yangjeon* was a comprehensive survey of all arable lands in the country conducted once every twenty years, primarily for the purpose of determining expected tax revenues. The ministry official claimed that the need for the survey was particularly urgent in the cases of the provinces of Gyeonggi and Chungcheong, since there were major obstacles to the collection of taxes from both. In Gyeonggi, it was difficult to take account of the population because there were so many empty and unclaimed houses in areas that had been cleared of residents through the abusive policies of the deposed monarch (Yeonsan). In Chungcheong, "the problem of widespread homelessness that was caused by the thievery of Hong Gildong has not yet been solved." This was thirteen years after the outlaw's capture, providing evidence of the considerable and long-term damage done to the common people.

The awareness of his mischief was recorded no less than eighty-eight years after his capture, in a revealing passage about his reputation. A *Sillok* entry on the twenty-first year of the reign of King Seonjo (1588) reads:

> In the time of the previous king, there were many able candidates to the position of high minister, and the ways of the people were righteous and fair with no disturbance to the Three Bonds and the Five Relationships, except those caused by Hong Gildong and Yi Yeonsu. So theirs were the only names that everyday people evoked when they cursed. But nowadays, with no good candidates for high minister, the deterioration of people's morals, and constant disturbances to the Three Bonds and the Five Relationships occurring everywhere, the names of Hong Gildong and Yi Yeonsu are becoming forgotten.[42]

At the center of Confucian social philosophy, utmost importance was placed on the harmony of the Three Bonds (between king and subject, parent and child, and husband and wife) and the Five Relationships (father and son, king and subject, husband and wife, old and young, and friend and friend).[43] The government was supposed to enact policies that supported the harmony of the relationships, and it was also thought that the moral qualities of those in positions of authority directly affected the virtues of all people of the land. Hong Gildong, presumably, was guilty of disrupting the true relationship between the king and his subjects through his crimes, while Yi Yeonsu, a well-known figure who committed the particularly heinous crime of patricide, perverted the connection between father and son. But the fact that theirs were the only names spoken of in the curses of the people is presented as evidence that the reign of the previous king was largely a time of peace and harmony. The passage goes on to complain that the contemporary period is one in which such unrighteous and unseemly acts occur so frequently, with the lack of competent and virtuous high officials seen as a cause, that criminals like Hong and Yi are no longer exceptional and so are disappearing from the collective memory of the people (a mistake was made in thinking that Hong Gildong operated during the time of King Jungjong, when the outlaw was actually captured in the reign of Yeonsan). Given the negative reputation of the outlaw, it would have taken a significant time for the villain who caused so much suffering to the common people to be transformed into their righteous champion in the popular imagination.

The historical Hong Gildong is sometimes referred to as one of the Three Great Bandits (*samdae dojeok*) of the Joseon dynasty, along with Im Kkeukjeong and Jang Gilsang. Records on Im are also sparse but more numerous than those on Hong, so we know that he was originally a low-born laborer and that he conducted his criminal activities in the northern province of Hwanghae starting from around 1559 (twenty-five records in the *Sillok*). He and his band of disgruntled peasants caused enough problems for local authorities that the government dispatched military troops. The outlaws evaded them for almost three years, before they were finally put down in 1562, when Im was captured and executed. Even less is known about Jang Gilsan, originally an itinerant entertainer who operated in the northern provinces of Hwanghae and Pyeongan around 1679 (three records starting in the eighteenth year of Sukjong). Unlike Hong and Im, there is no record of his arrest, so it is possible he was never caught. Despite the paucity of historical information about them, all three became figures of heroic legends, with novels written and dramas produced about them in the modern era.[44] An interesting discussion of the Three Great Bandits can be found in the writings of the philosopher Yi Ik (1681–1763), a major figure of the reformist *silhak* (practical learning) movement. While he relates famous stories about the exploits of Im Kkeukjeong and Jang Gilsang, he mentions Hong Gildong only to say that the bandit's acts are unknown to him because "they occurred so many generations ago."[45] Yi mentions, however, that the outlaw is evoked when merchants swear oaths to one another. As the *Sillok* entry just quoted shows, it was known in the late sixteenth century that the name of Hong Gildong was once uttered as a curse, in remembrance of the devastation he caused. Yi does not specify how exactly merchants used the name of Hong Gildong in their oaths (did they swear by him as a moral exemplar, or did they mean that one who breaks the oath is a lowly criminal like Hong Gildong?), but it is possible that by that time, two centuries after his capture, the bandit's reputation had undergone enough of a transformation that commoners were making pledges in his name.

To summarize, historical records point to the real-life Hong Gildong as an outlaw leader who operated in Chungcheong Province. His activities were part of the late fifteenth- and sixteenth-century phenomenon of widespread banditry that resulted from the deterioration of the "rank land" system and the expansion of the *yangban*'s private estates, which brought a great deal of hardship on the common people. Many commoners, unable to bear the oppressive demands of local landowners and tax collectors, left their homes to become vagrants and bandits. Apparently Hong Gildong and his band caused significant damage through their criminal activities, given that he was remembered in people's curses. It is impossible to ascertain exactly when and how his reputation may have changed to that of a righteous outlaw, but that could only have occurred long after the memory of his actual deeds had faded. As for the connection between the historical figure and the fictional version of him, a single literary reference that connects Hong Gildong to a statesman and writer named Heo Gyun has created much confusion about the origin of *The Story of Hong Gildong*.

THE ARREST OF THE SIXTH STATE COUNCILOR HEO GYUN

The Seventeenth Day of the Eighth Lunar Month of the Tenth Year of the Reign of King Gwanghae (1618)

Heo Gyun (1569–1618) is best known today by Koreans as a literary figure, but toward the end of his life he managed to rise to the near pinnacle of political power before falling precipitously to his doom.[46] As a powerful member of the Greater Northern (*daebuk*) faction of officials, which was firmly in control of the state after supporting the ascendance of King Gwanghae to the throne, he served as the minister of punishments (*hyeongjo panseo*) before being promoted to sixth state councilor (*jwachamchan*), a position of senior second rank. In addition, arrangements were being made for his daughter to become a concubine to the crown prince, since the royal heir's wife had failed to produce a child. If all had gone well for him, he could have become the grandfather of a king. Unfortunately, everything fell apart when he was arrested in 1618 for treason.

The seed of his downfall was planted eight months earlier, when an official by the name of Gi Jungyeok, an assistant section chief at the Ministry of Rites, submitted a secret report to the royal court that detailed the crimes of Heo Gyun. His charges were threefold: first, that he was the inspiration for a criminal incident that had occurred five years before that became known as the Arrest of Seven Secondary Sons; second, that he had fabricated evidence in the controversy that was being debated in the government on the ouster of the queen dowager; and third, and most seriously, that he was planning to overthrow the king to take control of the state himself. The first accusation, on Heo's involvement with the notorious seven secondary sons, has a rather complicated history.

In late 1607, Heo Gyun was appointed as the magistrate of the city of Gongju in Chungcheong Province. During his time there, he took three men and some of their family members into his household. People spoke of his having established three "*yeong*" in his home because the names of the dependents all ended in the same syllable—Yi Jaeyeong, Sim Uyeong, and Yun Gyeyeong. Of the three, Yi and Sim were secondary sons of *yangban* fathers. Also, Heo had been a student of Yi Dal, a renowned scholar and poet of *seoja* background about whom Heo wrote a reverent biographical sketch.[47] As a result, Heo was reputed to be a particular friend to secondary sons and thought to be sympathetic to their plight. In his treatise "Essay on Discarded Talent" (*Yujaeron*), Heo decried the discrimination against people of lower status that prevented the state from making use of their talents, which can be disastrous for a small country like Joseon.[48] "In the whole wide world, since time immemorial, it has been unheard of until now that a good person is discarded just because he was born of a concubine, and the talent of another is not utilized just because his mother remarried."[49]

Soon after Gwanghae ascended the throne in 1608, Heo Gyun's friend Sim Uyeong and six other men who were all secondary sons of prominent statesmen submitted a memorial to the court, asking the new ruler to end discrimination against the *seoja*, including the removal of prohibitions against the pursuit of official positions in the government. When their request was denied, it was reported that the disgruntled seven moved out of the capital, obtained property at Yeonju County in Gyeonggi Province, and built a communal home there. They then engaged in a series of criminal acts to maintain their community, including dressing up as merchants and wandering the land to commit theft as opportunities arose. This all culminated in the murder of a silver merchant by Bak Eungseo, one of the seven secondary sons, in the spring of 1613. Once the authorities were alerted and witnesses brought forth, all seven were arrested and interrogated until they confessed to everything. The fairly straightforward case of murder and theft became a much more serious matter when Yi Icheom, the most powerful official in the government as the leader of the Greater Northern faction, decided to use the incident for political purposes.

The Northern faction of officials was originally of the Eastern faction, which had split into the Southern and Northern groups in 1589 over political and ideological issues. The Northern faction then split further into the Greater and the Lesser in 1599, after which the Greater Northern faction managed to achieve dominance by throwing their support behind Gwanghae for succession to kingship. The power of the faction and its leader Yi Icheom was very much tied to the new ruler, so they had an interest in making sure that the monarch remained safely on the throne. The problem was that Gwanghae had become king under controversial circumstances, which left at least two viable candidates as replacements for those who might want to see him overthrown.

Gwanghae was born of King Seonjo's concubine, but he was designated as the crown prince in 1591 because the queen was constantly ill and unable to conceive a child. He was also chosen over an older brother, Lord Imhae, who was rejected as a possible heir because he was notorious for his evil temper. The succession question became more complicated when the queen died in 1600 and King Seonjo married a nineteen-year-old woman two years later. In 1606, the new queen (known today by her posthumous name Inmok) gave birth to a son who was given the title of Grand Lord Yeongchang. In the following years, the Lesser Northern faction urged the king to change the designation of crown prince to the new son, while the Greater Northern officials pressed him to keep Gwanghae as his heir. In the face of the serious dilemma, Seonjo delayed making a decision, ultimately following the wish of the Greater Northern faction while constantly beseeching his officials to take good care of the younger prince.

Even though Yi Icheom and his group won when Gwanghae became king, they felt that their power would not be completely secure as long as their sovereign's older brother, Lord Imhae, the king's half-brother, Grand Lord Yeongchang, and the queen dowager (Inmok) were still alive. Within a year, Lord Imhae was exiled and quietly executed. The boy prince was the next target.

At some point in the interrogation of the seven secondary sons who were accused of having committed theft and murder, it was made known to them that they would be treated with mercy if they confessed to an even greater crime. Under torture, some of the accused, though not all of them, stated that they had done their foul deeds to gather money for a treasonous act that was being planned by those who sought to dethrone the king and to replace him with his half-brother. The queen dowager was involved, as well as her father, Kim Jenam, and officials of the Lesser Northern faction. In the purge that followed, many who posed a threat to the Greater Northern faction were disposed of, including the young prince, who was deprived of his royal title, taken away from his mother, exiled, and murdered a year later. In the course of the interrogations of the prisoners, Heo Gyun's name came up once as a person who might have been involved in the affair, but the possibility was dismissed because of inconsistencies in the testimony.

The trial of the seven secondary sons occurred in 1613, and Gi Jungyeok's accusations against Heo Gyun came four years later. Gi pointed to Heo's close associations with men of secondary-son status in general and with Sim Uyeong in particular before claiming that Heo was the inspiration for their criminal activities. Gi further asserted that Heo had allied himself with the leader of the Greater Northern faction, Yi Icheom, to protect himself from the consequences of being associated with the criminal secondary sons; that Heo, at the behest of Yi, had fabricated a note that spoke of an upcoming revolt against the king that was currently being used against the queen dowager in the effort to oust her; and that Heo's actions were part of his long-standing plan to take control of the state himself.

After the secret report was submitted, officials discussed whether to take its charges seriously for eight months. During that time, Gi resubmitted the report twice, and Heo replied to his accusations on both occasions. Heo seemed to have been confident that it would come to nothing, as he was a close ally of Yi Icheom, and his daughter was soon to become the crown prince's concubine. He was also sure that the king would support him because he had played a significant role in Queen Dowager Inmok's ouster, which was underway at the time.

In the eighth month of 1618, Heo Gyun was arrested along with his accuser Gi Jungyeok, who had to answer for the crime of not reporting his knowledge of Heo's treason sooner. Heo was not interrogated, but some of his friends and servants who were arrested and tortured made confessions that confirmed his crimes. On the twenty-fourth day of the month, Heo and his accused co-conspirators were executed.

Historians have debated whether Heo Gyun had been actually guilty of all, some, or any of the crimes he was accused of. Characterizations of him in history books run the gamut from an idealistic revolutionary who sought to create a society devoid of social hierarchy to a hapless and maligned victim of political machinations. Those who regard Heo as a revolutionary point to his work "Essay on the Heroic Person" (*Hominron*). It begins with the assertion that the ruler of a country should fear nothing more than the wrath of his common subjects.[50] Heo then describes three types of people in the world: those who obey without question (*hangmin*), those who grumble in discontent (*wonmin*), and those who rise up under the right circumstances to fulfill their ambitions (*homin*, heroic person). It is the third group of people that those in power should fear.

A *homin* keeps his eye on the state of the country until the time comes when he can realize his will. He then rolls up his sleeves, stands atop a raised path between fields, and lets out a mighty shout. The *wonmin* then gather around him from the sound alone and join together in a unified shout without discussion. Finally, even the *hangmin*, wishing to preserve their lives, see no choice but to pick up hoes and spears and follow the others in killing those who have acted without morals.[51]

Heo feels that the state of Joseon in his own time is ripe for such an occurrence because of the abusive treatment the common people frequently receive at the hands of the corrupt and the greedy.

> Out of all the taxes the common people pay, only a fifth end up in the government, the rest becoming scattered chaotically among conniving people. There is, furthermore, no reserve wealth at the state, so whenever a disaster falls upon the country, taxes have to be collected twice in one year. Town magistrates often take advantage of such a situation to take away goods by the basketful, such cruel deeds knowing no end. That is why the common people have greater worry and harbor greater resentment than they did during the Goryeo dynasty.[52]

Given the sorry state of the country, it is thought that Heo took it upon himself to be the heroic *homin* who would lead the people to a revolution and to the building of a better country.

Heo Gyun was not only a statesman who moved among the most powerful people in the royal court but also a well-respected literary figure known especially for his great erudition and profound understanding of Chinese and Korean poetry. As a result, he had many students who sought his guidance on literary matters. One of them was Yi Sik (1584–1647), who would not only have a successful career in government service but emerge as one of the most renowned poets and essayists of his time. In his celebrated collection of writings, he discusses the nature of his former teacher Heo Gyun, describing him in a decisively negative manner. Yi also makes a claim about Heo's authorship of a story about a famous bandit.

> It has been related that the author of *Suhoji* was cursed for having written the work since three generations of his family were struck deaf and mute. This was because the writing was much admired by outlaws.
>
> Heo Gyun, Bak Yeop, and their group were fond of the work, to the extent of giving one another the names of bandit leaders from the story and making much merry from it. Gyun also wrote *The Story of Hong Gildong* in imitation of *Suhoji*. People of the group like Seo Yanggap and Sim Uyeong acted out deeds from the tale in real life, resulting in the destruction of an entire village, and Gyun himself committed treason

which ended in his execution. Those are harsher fates than being struck deaf and mute.[53]

Suhoji is Korean for *Shihuzhuan* (translated into English as *Water Margin* or *Outlaws of the Marsh*), an epic Chinese novel that relates the adventures of over a hundred bandits who gather at Liangshan Marsh to attack and steal the wealth of corrupt officials and rapacious strongmen. Yi Sik makes it clear that he believes his former teacher to have been a traitor to the country. He also points to *Water Margin* not only as inspiration for Heo's crimes but also as evidence of his dissolute nature, connecting him to the seven secondary sons (two of whom are named—Seo Yanggap and Sim Uyeong) by their common fondness for the novel. Then there is the claim that Heo also imitated the Chinese work in writing a story about the bandit Hong Gildong. This accusatory statement that sought to shed light on the criminal nature of Heo and his *seoja* acquaintances is the one and only piece of historical evidence that scholars have pointed to in attributing the extant *The Story of Hong Gildong* to Heo Gyun. But there is a rather complicated history of when and how that attribution became firmly established in modern scholarship.

Given Yi Sik's fame as a literary figure, a number of Joseon intellectuals familiar with his work repeated his claim that Heo had written a story about the bandit Hong Gildong. There is, however, no evidence that anyone actually had read or even seen a work entitled *The Story of Hong Gildong* until the second half of the nineteenth century. And the idea that the extant work is the very writing that Yi Sik claimed was authored by Heo Gyun was not established until the 1930s, when a literary scholar named Kim Taejun published his pioneering and influential work on the history of Joseon-dynasty fiction. That was at a time when the country had become a colony of the Empire of Japan, and Korean intellectuals were trying desperately to preserve Korean identity in a time of subjugation and humiliation.

THE PUBLICATION OF KIM TAEJUN'S *HISTORY OF JOSEON FICTION (JOSEON SOSEOLSA)*

1930–1931

The modern Korean word for prose fiction is *soseol*, literally meaning "lesser narrative." Traditionally, it was used as a catchall term for various types of writing that could not be categorized under respectable literary genres like poetry, history, moralistic biography, literary criticism, and philosophical essay. During the Joseon dynasty, works that were referred to as *soseol* in a somewhat derogatory manner included prose fiction, records of myths and regional folktales, sensational historical anecdotes, and entertaining stories of everyday life. While *yangban* readers enjoyed reading classic Chinese novels like *Three Kingdoms* (*Sanguozhi*), *Water Margin* (*Shuihuzhuan*), and *Journey to the West* (*Xiyouji*), there was a great deal of ambivalence on the part of the literati toward the genre because they felt that there was something suspect and lowly about made-up stories filled with sensational elements that enticed the reader into its false dream. As a result, the Joseon dynasty can boast of an illustrious tradition of poetry, history, and philosophical essay, but its achievements in prose fiction are modest. And the vast majority of fictional works are of unknown or uncertain authorship.

In the early twentieth century, when the first generation of modern novelists began to produce works in *hangeul,* the genre they practiced was called *soseol,* the word taking on the significance of the new type of prose fiction they learned from their study of modern Japanese and Western literature. The word is commonly translated today as "'novel," but that is somewhat inaccurate. The English word not only denotes a fictional narrative in prose form but also one of certain length, as a writing that is shorter than a hundred pages or so is referred to as a novella or a short story. Since *soseol* carries no indication of length, a novel is referred to in modern Korean as *jangpyeon soseol* (full-length fiction) and the short story as *danpyeon soseol* (short fiction). For the first Korean practitioners of the modern literary form, one of their most important tasks was to give expression to the people, to preserve their historical and cultural memory at a time when they had lost their country to a foreign power.

Only eight years after King Gojong ended the Joseon dynasty proper by renaming the nation Daehan Jaeguk (Empire of Korea), a protectorate treaty with Japan (1905) allowed the establishment of the protocolonial administration of the Residency General. Two years later, after a failed attempt by Gojong to rally world opinion against Japanese encroachment by sending a secret envoy to the International Peace Conference at the Hague, he was forced to abdicate in favor of his son, Sunjong, the last royal ruler of Korea. Finally, in 1910, Japan annexed the peninsula outright.

Two decades later, a twenty-six-year-old scholar of Korean and Chinese literature by the name of Kim Taejun began to publish a series of articles for the newspaper *Donga ilbo* on the *History of Joseon Fiction* (*Joseon soseolsa*). The essays were later collected and published as a book in 1933. In the introduction to the work, Kim Taejun clearly states his nationalist agenda: to establish the legacy of a rich and vibrant literary tradition prior to Japanese colonization. Kim begins by considering the definition of *soseol* as modern fiction, quoting a scholar named Long (William J. Long, 1867–1952), who provides the following characterization: "By a true novel we mean simply a work of fiction which relates the story of a plain human life, under stress of emotion, which depends for its interest not on incident or adventure, but on its truth to nature."[54] On the basis of this quintessentially realist definition of the novel, Kim declares his purpose in writing his work.

> There was no *soseol* during the Joseon dynasty! Why? Because Joseon did not produce any work that described the internal thoughts and external circumstances of the people! I wish to respond to such a statement. It is true that until the cultural revolution that occurred around the time of the Gimi Movement, not one work that fits Long's definition of the novel [the English word "novel" is used here, transliterated into Korean] can be found. But there are many records of folktales, humorous stories, historical anecdotes, and other writings that can be described as romance, story, and fiction [the English words for all three are used here, with "story" and "fiction" in the Latin alphabet] which existed in abundance and are well-known enough that there is no need for me to mention them. In other words, countless works were written that are *soseol* in the sense that the people of the past understood the word.
>
> It is the purpose of this work to explore such *soseol* works through the previous era's conception of the genre, and to describe its path of progress. I assert that what the term *soseol* signified changed over time.[55]

The Gimi Movement refers to the events of March 1, 1919 (by traditional reckoning, the Yellow Sheep Year of Gimi), when massive protests demanding Korean independence erupted all across the country, a seminal moment of modern Korean history now referred to as the March First Movement.

For Kim Taejun, the best example of Joseon-dynasty fiction is *The Story of Hong Gildong.* He dedicates a subchapter to the work, discussing both the narrative and the life of Heo Gyun, whom he affirms as its author.[56] Kim, furthermore, portrays Heo as an idealistic and progressive thinker who dreamed of creating an egalitarian society devoid of the privileges and inequities of social status. Heo's attempt to realize the vision through a revolution failed, but the legacy of his lofty ambitions survives in his story of the heroic bandit, which is a narrative manifesto of his radical political ideas. In the highly subversive work, Heo borrowed the outlaw-as-hero motif from the Chinese novel *Water Margin* in order to criticize Joseon society. He made the protagonist a secondary son and depicted the frustrations of such a person to further expose class discrimination in the kingdom.

Kim Taejun's pioneering book, the first comprehensive study of classic fiction, became an essential text of singular importance on the subject, establishing the basic historical outline for all future scholarship. As a result, Kim's interpretation of *The Story of Hong Gildong* as a work of radical social criticism and his attribution of the writing to Heo Gyun, based on Yi Sik's claim that Heo wrote a work of that title, was uncritically accepted and continuously repeated by scholars. In the postcolonial era, every new publication of *The Story of Hong Gildong* identified Heo Gyun as its author, and the work was included in every new anthology of Heo's writings. The almost universal acceptance of the attribution, with only a handful of scholars casting doubt on the claim, also resulted in another assertion about the work's essential importance to Korean literature.

In the second half of the 1980s, a version of *The Story of Hong Gildong* in literary Chinese was discovered in Seongang University's library, which prompted some discussion about the possibility that it was the original work by Heo Gyun.[57] But given the late date of the text (1909) and the fact that all other extant manuscripts are in *hangeul*, it is seen by most scholars today as a later translation. Unless another such text is discovered that can definitively be proven to predate all other manuscripts, it will remain the general consensus that *The Story of Hong Gildong* was originally composed in *hangeul*. And if it was indeed authored by Heo Gyun in the early seventeenth century, the work could very well be the first work of prose fiction written in King Sejong's phonetic script. For the vast majority of scholars who accepted Kim Taejun's depiction of Heo Gyun as a radical egalitarian thinker, it made sense that he would write the subversive anti-feudal work in the script created for the benefit of the common people.

It must be noted, however, that Yi Sik never mentioned that Heo wrote it in *hangeul*, nor did Kim Taejun make such a claim. The assertion that *The Story of Hong Gildong* was the very first work of *hangeul* fiction does not appear until 1948, when the literary scholar Yi Myeongseon, in his book *History of Joseon Literature* (*Joseon munhaksa*), stated that Heo Gyun's work "was the first work of fiction written in the Joseon script."[58] Since Yi Myeongseon did not provide any evidence for the claim, it may have been based on a misreading of Kim Taejun's description of the writing as "the first Joseon work that is worthy of being called *soseol*."[59] But after Yi Myeongseon made the assertion, almost every major work on traditional Korean literature has repeated it.[60]

In the decades following the end of the colonial era, through continuous and uncritical repetition in scholarly writings, school textbooks, and popular works on Korean literature and history, it became firmly established in the national consciousness that the singular importance of *The Story of Hong Gildong* to Korean culture lay in the fact that it was the very first original work of fiction written in *hangeul*, authored by the radical statesman and writer Heo Gyun.

From the announcement of the invention of the *Proper Sounds for the Education of the People* by King Sejong the Great in 1443–1444, the capture of the notorious bandit Hong Gildong in 1500, the arrest and execution of the statesman and writer Heo Gyun in 1618, up to the publication of Kim Taejun's *History of Joseon Fiction* in 1930–1931, the various myths surrounding *The Story of Hong Gildong* coalesced as it became elevated as an essential work of classic Korean literature. To this day, Koreans appreciate the writing as the finest and most famous work of traditional fiction written in the phonetic script. The text also has the advantage of being an exciting story of a rebel and an adventurer, a secondary son of unparalleled talents who is initially treated with contempt and set upon by evil people but who emerges victorious at every turn eventually to become a respected leader, family member, and king. The narrative seemed to embody the hope for the retrieval of dignity, respect, and power to a nation that had suffered through the calamities and humiliations of colonization, division, devastating warfare, and authoritarian tyranny.

I further discuss the symbolic function of the character of Hong Gildong in chapter 3, but first, what will be explicated in the following chapter is the problematic nature of the historical narrative that I have described here as a myth. The authorship of Heo Gyun, the status of *The Story of Hong Gildong* as the first *hangeul* fiction, and its significance as a radical and subversive writing are, at best, questionable. As the phantom image of Hong Gildong in the fog of myth fades away, another manifestation of the outlaw in the historical imagination of the Joseon dynasty and modern Korea emerges.

CHAPTER TWO

Elusive Traces of Hong Gildong
in History

Contemporary scholarship on *The Story of Hong Gildong* bears a reverse-mirror-image resemblance to the so-called authorship question of the works of William Shakespeare. For the vast majority of mainstream Shakespeare scholars the issue is a settled one of no interest, but for over two centuries a few skeptics have cast doubt on the attribution, putting forward such figures as Christopher Marlowe, Francis Bacon, or Edward de Vere as the true writer of the revered plays and poems. As James Shapiro has shown, the preponderance of the evidence is on the side of the traditional attribution, yet persistent doubters have continued to make historical and literary arguments even though they have failed to change the scholarship in any significant way.[1] In the case of *The Story of Hong Gildong*, however, the vast majority of academic scholars as well as the general public hold ideas about the work based on evidence that turns out to be highly suspect when placed under scrutiny. The two most prevalent are Heo Gyun's authorship of the work and its status as the first work of fiction originally composed in *hangeul*.

In the 1960s, scholars including Yi Neungu and Kim Jinse first exposed major problems with the attribution.[2] Despite their findings and those of more recent critics, such as Lee Yoon Suk, Paik Sung-Jong, and Lee Pok-kyu,[3] academics have generally ignored the issue and repeated the received ideas in scholarly works and textbooks. This is the result of both indifference to new research in the field and reluctance to question the significance of a cherished literary work of national importance to Korean culture.

To conduct a full examination of the prevailing myths about the work, three specific historical questions need to be asked: (1) Yi Sik first made the claim in the seventeenth century that Heo Gyun wrote a work entitled *The Story of Hong Gildong* in imitation of the Chinese novel *Water Margin*. Can this assertion be substantiated by external evidence? (2) Even if Heo Gyun did compose a work called *The Story of Hong Gildong*, is it the extant work of the title? (3) Was Heo Gyun a revolutionary and a martyr to his dream of establishing an egalitarian society, and was *The Story of Hong Gildong* a kind of narrative manifesto of his radical political ideas?

After these issues are addressed through the analysis of historical sources, subsequent questions of the work's significance will be explored.

YI SIK'S ATTRIBUTION OF HEO GYUN TO A WORK ENTITLED *THE STORY OF HONG GILDONG*

The brief anecdote that Yi Sik tells about his former teacher Heo Gyun and his authorship of *The Story of Hong Gildong* is in the *Collected Works of Taekdang* (*Taekdang jip*—Taekdang was Yi Sik's literary name), the lauded collection of Yi's poetry and essays that was anthologized in 1674 and solidified his reputation as one of the greatest literary figures of the period. It is impossible to determine when exactly Yi wrote the passage, but its content makes it apparent that it was composed sometime after 1618, the eventful year in which both Yi resigned from his government post to protest the ouster of Queen Dowager Inmok and Heo Gyun was executed for treason. To quote the passage again:

> It has been related that the author of *Suhoji* was cursed for having written the work since three generations of his family were struck deaf and mute. This was because the writing was much admired by outlaws.
>
> Heo Gyun, Bak Yeop, and their group were fond of the work, to the extent of giving one another the names of bandit leaders from the story and making much merry from it. Gyun also wrote *The Story of Hong Gildong* in imitation of *Suhoji*. People of the group like Seo Yanggap and Sim Uyeong acted out deeds from the tale in real life, resulting in the destruction of an entire village, and Gyun himself committed treason which ended in his execution. Those are harsher fates than being struck deaf and mute.[4]

It is essential to examine every element of this passage as well as its historical context, for the crucial reason that if Yi Sik had not written it, no one ever would have associated Heo Gyun with the extant *The Story of Hong Gildong.*

As mentioned in the previous chapter, *Suhoji* is Korean for the classic Chinese novel *Shihuzhuan,* or *Water Margin,* which features the stories of over a hundred heroic bandits. There is a tradition that has attributed the work and that of another classic novel, *Three Kingdoms,* to a fourteenth-century figure by the name of Luo Guanzhong.[5] Luo may have written some of *Water Margin,* or he may have merely edited what was substantially authored by Shi Nai'an, about whom even less is known. Like the other epic novels of the Ming dynasty, it is actually the product of multiple writers and editors over the course of centuries, as evidenced by the existence of varying editions in seventy, one hundred, and 120 chapters.[6] When the Chinese novels were imported into Joseon in the late sixteenth century,[7] so was the attribution of *Water Margin* and *Three Kingdoms* to Luo, who was referred to by the Korean pronunciation of his name, Na Gwangjung. Joseon readers were also familiar with the legend of how three generations of Luo's descendants were struck dumb. According to Ch'ên Shou-yi, the cause of the curse was Luo's "overexpressiveness in divulging the basic mysteries of the universe."[8] Yi Sik, however, provides an alternate explanation, linking the curse specifically to *Water Margin* in claiming that it was divine punishment for writing a work that became admired by criminals. There is an ironic possibility that Yi might have learned this legend from his teacher Heo Gyun, who offered a similar explanation in his assessment of Chinese novels.

Yi's interpretation of the curse allows him to explain the fate of his former teacher, as he tells how Heo and his friends were admirers of *Water Margin,* implying that their fondness for the stories of heroic outlaws inspired them to commit crimes. The essential thing to understand about this passage is that Yi assumes that Heo was indeed guilty of two of the charges against him—first, involvement with the *seoja* criminals of the Arrest of Seven Secondary Sons incident of 1613, naming two, Seo Yang-gap and Sim Uyeong, who were friends of Heo; and second, hatching a plan to dethrone the king and usurp power for himself. Yi Sik is essentially offering an explanation of how Heo Gyun became involved in such illicit activities, pointing to the immoral influence of *Water Margin.*

For the modern historian, the task of determining if Heo had been guilty of all, some, or any of the crimes he was charged with is not an easy one. In various narratives of his life, he has been portrayed alternatively as a treasonous would-be usurper, an innocent victim of court machinations, and a forward-thinking revolutionary. The last view is a popular one, even though the idea of Heo Gyun as a political radical is entirely a twentieth-century invention. Before the issue can be tackled through the examination of historical evidence, Yi Sik's own role in the political conflicts of his time must be examined, for it reveals a motivation behind his negative portrayal of Heo Gyun.

As Heo Gyun's student, Yi Sik revered his teacher for his great erudition and profound understanding of classic literature. But their relationship became troubled starting in 1610, when Heo, who was serving as a judge in that year's final civil examination, was accused of favoritism in passing his nephew Heo Bo and his niece's husband Bak Hongdo. Officials were prohibited from judging people who were closely associated with them, including relatives, friends, and students, but the ban was frequently ignored. In this case, however, Heo and a number of other officials engaged in such a blatant act of corruption that it became necessary for the king himself to intervene. After an investigation by the Office of the Deliberation of Forbidden Affairs, Heo was singled out for punishment, and he was dismissed from his position, flogged, and exiled for eleven months. Other accused officials managed to evade prosecution by using their political influence, and only two people, Heo's nephew and a former monk named Byeon Heon, were deprived of their degrees. Some of those who passed the examination that year had to bear the suspicion of having qualified illegitimately because they were associated in some way with the corrupt examiners. Yi Sik was one of them, as he had been Heo's student.

Seven years later, their relationship became even more strained when they found themselves on opposite sides of the controversy over the ousting of Queen Dowager Inmok. While Heo took a leading role in advocating her removal, Yi became part of the faction trying to dissuade the king from that course. A year later, in 1618, when Inmok was deprived of her title and confined to West Palace (Deoksu Palace), Yi and many other officials felt obliged to resign their posts in protest. Even though Heo's effort on the matter came to fruition, he was subsequently arrested for treason and executed.

After King Gwanghae was dethroned in 1623 and the Greater Northern faction fell from power, Yi Sik returned to government service, ultimately attaining the lofty positions of the director of the Office of Special Councilors and the Office of Royal Decrees as well as the minister of personnel and the minister of rites. Despite his successes as both a statesman and a literary figure, he must have felt some insecurity, since his name was connected with an executed traitor who had been his teacher and who, some suspected, may have helped him pass the final examination. It also must have galled him to be associated with someone whose political actions he had come to despise.

Yi Sik had good reason to distance himself from Heo Gyun by denigrating him in his writings, but that does not mean that we must dismiss his view of Heo altogether. Yi may have truly believed that Heo had been guilty of all he had been accused of. There are, however, reasons to be skeptical about his claims that Heo's actions were inspired by his fondness for *Water Margin* and that he wrote a story entitled *The Story of Hong Gildong* in imitation of the Chinese work.

As it happens, Heo Gyun himself wrote an assessment of Chinese fiction, including *Water Margin*. In a postscript to the Chinese fantasy novel *Journey to the West* (*Xiyouji*), a picaresque epic about the adventures of a monkey with magical powers, Heo claims that he has read tens of such "dramatic works of entertainment."[9] With the exception of *Chronicle of the Three Kingdoms* and *Chronicle of the Sui and the Tang Dynasties*, however, he has nothing good to say about writings of that nature.

> I found *Yang Hanji* [*Chronicle of the Two Han Dynasties*] to be incoherent, *Jewiji* [*Chronicle of the Qi and the Wei Dynasties*] to be poor in quality, *Jandang odae yeonui* [*Chronicle of the Decline of the Tang Dynasty and the Five Dynasties*] to be unrefined, *Songtaejo yongho pungunhoe* [*Momentous Meeting of the Dragon and the Tiger in the Time of Taizu of Song*] to be undeveloped, and *Suhoji* [*Water Margin*] to be licentious and slyly deceptive.

Heo then attributes all those works to Na Gwanjung (Luo Guanzhong) and presents the legend of the curse upon his generation.

> None of these works possess sufficient value to instruct the reader in moral cultivation, and they all came from the hand of a single person. It is fitting, then that three generations of Na Gwanjung's descendants were afflicted with muteness.

This passage offers the intriguing possibility that Yi Sik may have learned of the legend from Heo, only to use it to explain his teacher's fall. But the more significant statement here is, of course, the denigration of *Water Margin* as an immoral and deceptive work, to the extent that Luo's descendants should be cursed for it. This goes directly against Yi's assertion that Heo was so fond of the novel that he wrote *The Story of Hong Gildong* in imitation. So either Yi lied or mistakenly reported a false story that Heo was an avid admirer of *Water Margin*, or Heo went out of his way to pour scorn on a work he secretly loved. Peter H. Lee has speculated that Heo "might have wished to deny his indebtedness to the Chinese work" in the composition of *The Story of Hong Gildong*.[10] It has to be pointed out, however, that Heo never mentioned *The Story of Hong Gildong* in any of his own writings. It is implausible, therefore, that he would worry that people might think that the work was derivative.

A more convincing case can be made that Heo's view of Chinese novels is indicative of the Joseon literati's ambivalent attitude toward the genre. *Yangban* readers consumed such works avidly, but they also generally held prose fiction in low regard. Proper scholars were supposed to devote themselves to the reading and writing of poetry, history, and essays on philosophical, moral, and political subjects. For that reason one can find many writings denigrating entertaining prose works as vulgar and corrupting, even as they remained popular as guilty pleasures.[11] In Heo Gyun's postscript to *Journey to the West*, he provides the reader with a brief summary of its plot but then calls the whole thing "tedious, obscure, and far from the telling of truth."[12] Yet he admits that he cannot help reading the work whenever he feels tired from studying proper works of moral cultivation, as the entertaining narrative helps him ward off sleep. So it is possible that Heo criticized *Water Margin* and other novels in order to present himself as a proper scholar of refined literary taste who was not taken in by the sensationalistic qualities of vulgar storytelling.

The question remains, however, whether we should believe Yi Sik's assertion that Heo Gyun admired *Water Margin* or Heo's claim that he found the work to be licentious, deceptive, and lacking in moral value. The absence of any further evidence pertaining to the matter makes the question impossible to settle, but most modern scholars have tended to accept Yi's view uncritically. This is the result of the assumption, which solidified after the 1930s, of Heo Gyun's authorship of the extant *The Story of Hong Gildong*. Yet even if we imagine that Heo Gyun was secretly fond of *Water Margin* and wrote his *The Story of Hong Gildong* in imitation, significant literary problems remain.

Paik Sung-Jong has pointed out that other than the single common theme of an intrepid outlaw's struggle against the authorities, there is no resemblance in plot, character, or narrative form between *Water Margin* and *The Story of Hong Gildong*.[13] The Chinese work is an epic novel of thousands of pages with over a hundred characters, while *The Story of Hong Gildong* is a concise narrative about a single protagonist. The Korean work is fantastic in nature, featuring Hong Gildong's magical powers, the appearance of supernatural monsters, and adventures on a faraway island. There are a few episodes involving magic in *Water Margin*, but they are rare. The vast majority of characters use mundane fighting skills and strategy, and none of them became outlaws because of their status as an illegitimate child. So other than the one commonality of both narratives being about heroic outlaws, it is difficult to point to any characteristic of *The Story of Hong Gildong* that could be regarded as having been influenced by the Chinese work.

In addition to the reasons Yi Sik had to distance himself from Heo Gyun, the conflicting testimony in Heo Gyun's view of *Water Margin*, and the lack of any substantial resemblance between *Water Margin* and *The Story of Hong Gildong*, there are two even more serious problems in using Yi's statement to attribute the extant text *The Story of Hong Gildong* to Heo. The first is that for well over two centuries after Yi Sik's lifetime, not a single piece of writing has been found in which someone demonstrates that he or someone he knows has actually read or even seen the work. As Yi himself does not provide any details about the work, we do not know if he saw the writing or was just relating a rumor. In other words, the very existence of the work prior to the mid–nineteenth century cannot be ascertained.

Recently, a scholar by the name of Seol Seonggyeong published a series of books detailing his quixotic search for the "historical Hong Gildong." As part of the effort, he amassed every reference to *The Story of Hong Gildong* he could find in Joseon writings.[14] All of them repeat Yi's attribution of the work to Heo Gyun. Sim Jae (1624–1693) writes that according to Yi Sik, "three generations of the descendants of the person who wrote *Water Margin* became deaf and dumb, and that outlaws thought highly of the work," and he recounts Yi's assertion that Heo Gyun wrote *The Story of Hong Gildong* in imitation of *Water Margin*.[15] The statement appears in almost the same exact wording in two anonymously written books of historical anecdotes, *Essential History of the Court and the People* (*Joya jipyo*, written around 1784) and *Record of Knowledge and Experience* (*Mungyeon chagi*, late nineteenth century).[16] Seol also found two mentions that do not explicitly refer to Yi Sik. Hwang Yunseok (1729–1791), in the work *Enlarged Edition of the Extraordinary Events of Haedong* (*Jeungbo Haedong ijeok*), relates that "Some people have said that the story [about Hong Gildong] made up by Heo Gyun cannot be trusted, so how can we believe the tale?"; the scholar Hong Hanju (1798–1868) states simply that "it has been related that *The Story of Hong Gildong* is also the work of Heo Gyun" but does not elaborate further.[17]

The references in the writings of Sim Jae and in *Essential History of the Court and the People* and *Record of Knowledge and Experience* are quotations of Yi Sik's claim, so they are not independent verifications of the work's existence at the time. In *Enlarged Edition of the Extraordinary Events of Hae-*

dong, which was completed in the late eighteenth century, Hwang Yun-seok relates an interesting legend about Hong Gildong and mentions people being skeptical of the veracity of Heo's story, but there is uncertainty in the language about whether the legend is from Heo's work. That could be regarded as evidence, albeit precarious, of the existence of a work about Hong Gildong that was considered to be Heo Gyun's. But that brings up further problems related to major discrepancies between the legend that Hwang relates and the content of *The Story of Hong Gildong.* This point will be discussed in detail in the next chapter.

In the late nineteenth century, the *hangeul* work entitled *The Story of Hong Gildong* became popular, as evidenced by the significant number of manuscripts, both handwritten and printed, that were produced at the time. The first independent mention of the story can be found in the introduction to an 1876 edition of *Record of the Black Dragon Year* (*Imjinrok*), a fictional narrative of the Japanese invasion of 1592–1598—"Tales of old that are widely known among the people are stories about characters like So Daeseong, Jo Ung, Hong Gildong, and Jeon Uchi. The contents of these books consist of the exploits of a single character . . ."[18] To reiterate, in the interval of over two hundred years between the time Yi Sik claimed that Heo Gyun wrote a work entitled *The Story of Hong Gildong* and this reference to the work's popularity in 1876, not a single piece of evidence has emerged of anyone having actually read or even seen the writing. It is also important to point out that while there are thirty-four extant manuscripts of *The Story of Hong Gildong* that were all produced in the late nineteenth or early twentieth centuries, not one of them bears the name of Heo Gyun as its author, not even in an afterword or as a marginal note.

Another major problem with uncritically associating Yi Sik's assertion of Heo Gyun's authorship of *The Story of Hong Gildong* with the extant work of the title has to do with the writing's supposed status as the first fiction to be written in *hangeul.* Heo Gyun knew how to use the phonetic script, which he would have referred to as "vulgar script" (*eonmun*), as he once wrote a poem for a Chinese diplomat in which each ideogram of the verse was preceded by a phonetic syllable, something that would have been an exotic curiosity to the foreigner.[19] The problem is that with the single exception of that poem, which really amounted to an exercise in experimental verse, Heo composed no writing in the phonetic script. The entirety of the significant collection of his poetry, essays, and memoirs was written in literary Chinese.

If Heo Gyun had indeed written *The Story of Hong Gildong* in the phonetic script and Yi Sik had seen the work, Yi would surely have commented on the fact. A *yangban* writer composing an extended work of fiction in *eonmun* at that time would have been such an unusual act of eccentricity that it would not have escaped Yi's attention. In the seventeenth century, literary works originally written in literary Chinese were sometimes translated into the phonetic script, mainly for the readership of noble ladies and secondary-status elites. Most *yangban*, however, continued to eschew the use of the vulgar script. Recently, scholars have cast doubt on the *eonmun*-composition tradition of the prose works *Nine Cloud Dream* (*Gu un mong*) and *Record of Lady Sa's Journey South* (*Sassi namjeonggi*), both attributed to Kim Manjung (1637–1692) based on uncertain evidence.[20]

Defenders of the traditional attribution of Heo Gyun as the author of *The Story of Hong Gildong* have argued that Heo had good reason to hide his authorship of the subversive work that he had written in the phonetic script for the benefit of the common people, perhaps to arouse them into action against the status quo.[21] To avoid the attention of the authorities, Heo never acknowledged the work nor included it in his collected writings. That theory points to a hidden history of the work's secret readership through two centuries of silence about the writing, until the political and social changes of the late nineteenth century made it possible for the dangerous work to be published and read openly. That may be an attractive and provocative tale, but one without a single shred of evidence to support it.

Despite all the reasons to doubt the veracity of Yi Sik's claims about his former teacher, it is within the realm of possibility that Heo did write a work entitled *The Story of Hong Gildong* about the notorious bandit who lived a century before his time, a text that has become lost. If Heo had done so, he would have written it in literary Chinese, like all his other writings. But it must be pointed out yet again that other than Yi Sik's questionable assertion, no historical evidence of such a lost work exists. For most modern Koreans, however, the idea of Heo Gyun as the author of *The Story of Hong Gildong* seems so plausible not just because his authorship has been presented as a fact for so long but also because of what they think they know about Heo Gyun himself. He is often portrayed in popular history books as a nobleman who sympathized with the plight of the powerless in Joseon society through his friendship with secondary sons and who eventually harbored radical political ideas of remaking the country into a utopian society devoid of status distinctions. At the end of his life, he attempted to take over the leadership of the kingdom through a revolution so that he could enact the reforms he dreamed of, but his purpose was discovered by the authorities, who arrested and executed him. Thus he died a martyr to his egalitarian ideals. Jae-Yung So, in a portrait of Heo's life and works, claims that his "conspicuous features which appeared in his life-long adventurers can be represented by his championship of the weak and the oppressed poor. He stood by them and suffered loss himself and he sympathized with other disappointed persons in grief"[22] Likewise, Kichung Kim asserts:

> Even though he was himself wellborn and rose rapidly to prominence as a scholar-statesman, Hŏ Kyun was deeply distressed by the plight of illegitimate sons. He befriended a number of them and tried in various ways to assist them in their futile effort to gain social and professional acceptance. It is therefore not surprising that he should have composed tales championing the cause of the illegitimate, misfit, nonconformist, and poor, exposing the self-destructive blindness of his own class and society. Perhaps it was his recognition of this narrowness that ultimately led him to turn against his class.[23]

And Tai-jin Kim has written:

> The arguments and propositions [Heo] advanced for reformation of various social systems were highly progressive ones, reflecting his high ideals for a better society.
> With the sensitivity of a poet, the progressive convictions of a revolutionary, and the broad and deep insight of a politician combined, he devoted himself to his great dream of rectifying the corrupt political system and protecting the helpless farmers and humble multitude.[24]

In the most recent biography of Heo Gyun (2002), by Heo Gyeongjin, in which the author assumes that Heo did plan an armed revolution, the section on the last part of his life is entitled "A Dream of Revolution" and the final chapter on the events that led to his execution, "The Failed Revolution."[25]

The problem with the depiction of Heo Gyun as a revolutionary harboring an egalitarian ideology is that no one regarded him as such until Kim Taejun invented that image of him in the 1930s. Previously, every assessment of Heo Gyun's life and character portray him either as a hapless victim of court machinations or a treasonous would-be usurper motivated by greed for power. Like Yi Sik, just about every Joseon commentator thought him a morally suspect character, a substandard statesman, and a political opportunist. Yet most modern Koreans have been taught to think of Heo as a heroic champion of the underclass of Joseon society and of *The Story of Hong Gildong* as a narrative manifesto of his radical ideas. It is essential to examine the reasons behind Kim Taejun's idealization of the controversial figure, but first we must attempt to take an objective accounting of Heo Gyun as a historical figure.

HEO GYUN: VICTIM, TRAITOR, OR REVOLUTIONARY?

The first misconception about Heo Gyun that has to be dismissed at the outset is that he himself was an illegitimate son of a nobleman, a notion that some have assumed to be true through his association with the famous story about a *seoja* hero. The mistake first appeared in a commentary on *The Story of Hong Gildong* in a 1937 collection of classical Korean fiction, and it has unfortunately shown up in a number of English-language sources.[26] The notion may have risen from confusion over the fact that Heo's mother was the second wife of his father, Heo Yeop. It is difficult to find detailed information about the vast majority of Joseon-dynasty women even from *yangban* families, but it is almost certainly the case that Heo Yeop's first wife died sometime before 1551, the year the oldest child by his second wife was born. Only one legitimate wife per man was recognized in Joseon, and Heo Gyun's mother was the daughter of Kim Gwangcheol, who was no less a personage than the minister of rites at the time. It should also be remembered that if Heo Gyun had been a secondary son by a concubine, he would have been barred from taking the civil examinations.

Heo Gyun was born into one of the most illustrious *yangban* families of Joseon. His father, Heo Yeop (1517–1580), had a brilliant career in government service and was one of the leaders of the Eastern faction when such alliances of noblemen became formalized during the reign of King Seonjo. Heo Yeop's son by his first marriage, Heo Seong (1548–1612), also had a successful career, ultimately attaining the position of the minister of personnel. Heo Yeop had two sons by his second wife, Heo Bong and Heo Gyun, and a daughter in the middle, Heo Chohui, who is a significant figure in the history of women's writing in the Joseon dynasty. She is one of the few female writers whose poetic works (written under the literary name of Heo Nanseolheon) have survived.[27] Despite his privileged background, Heo Gyun's early life was marked by a series of tragedies. When he was twelve years old, his father, after a lauded tenure as the governor of Gyeongsan Province, was returning to the capital to take up a ministerial position when he fell ill and passed away. Eight years later, his older brother Heo Bong, his first teacher and substitute father-figure, also died, followed by his beloved sister Heo Chohui a year later. In 1592, after the commencement of the Japanese invasion of Joseon, Heo Gyun's wife and son died from the hardships they underwent as war refugees.

He passed the preliminary stages of the civil examinations in 1589, when he fatefully became friends with Yi Icheom, the future leader of the Greater Northern faction, with whom he earned the privilege of studying at the National Confucian Academy (*Seonggyungwan*) for the final tests. The outbreak of the Japanese war delayed his progress, but he finally qualified in 1594. Three years later, when the once-a-decade special examination known as *jungsi* was offered, Heo not only retook the examination but also came first among the five people (of the initial seventy-one candidates) who passed the test, which allowed him to jump up to senior sixth rank in government position. From that point on, he had a career that could only be described as checkered, although he ultimately attained the position of sixth state councilor (*jwachamchan*) at senior second rank.

There are accounts of his first-rate intellect and impressive erudition, especially of Chinese and Korean poetry. Yet there are also numerous testimonies, often by the same people who praised his scholarship, of his lascivious and unprincipled character, incompetence as an official, and immoral opportunism. The most damning evidence that supports such negative characterizations is the number of times he was dismissed from various positions throughout his career for disgraceful reasons. His modern defenders tend to explain that as the result of factional conflicts in the government, but that interpretation is inapplicable in many cases. To give a few examples, in 1599 Heo was appointed as an auditor (*dosa*) to the northwestern province of Hwanghae, a position of junior fifth rank. Within months, there were reports that he had installed prostitutes in the government office, that he went about with an entourage of thugs and petty criminals, and that both he and his concubine granted official favors under corrupt circumstances. The ridicule and criticisms he incurred from his behavior became so widespread in the province that King Seonjo was obliged to dismiss him at the end of the year.[28] In 1608, he was dismissed again from his position of city magistrate (*moksa*—senior third rank) of Gongju after a government inspector, overseeing the conduct of administrators in Chungcheon Province, reported Heo's official behavior as frivolous and dissolute.[29] And in 1610, there was the already mentioned incident in which he was accused of favoritism as a judge in the civil examination. Heo was not only dismissed from his post but arrested by the Office of the Deliberation of Forbidden Affairs, flogged, and exiled from the capital. He complained in his writings that he was a scapegoat who was singled out for punishment.[30] It does appear that the incident was a case of widespread corruption involving a number of other officials, including Yi Icheom, who managed to avoid punishment because they simply had better connections in the government. Yet Heo never claimed that he was innocent of the charge. There were a number of other occasions in which an appointment he received had to be revoked because of protests from officials that he was unsuited for the position, given past reports of incompetence and misbehavior.

Anecdotes found in the *Sillok* records also provide examples of Heo's scandalizing, dissolute, and unprincipled conduct. In 1594, upon the death of his mother, he had to leave the capital and go to his hometown of Gangneung. During the mourning period he was supposed to live simply by the gravesite and avoid social company, but it became known that he often enjoyed himself with prostitutes. And, in 1602, when Heo was a section chief (*jeongnang*—senior fifth rank) at the ministry of military affairs, he became involved in a minor controversy over the proper punishment of a prisoner accused of treason.[31] When Sim Huisu, the second minister (*panbusa*—junior first rank) at the Military Affairs Commission (*jung-chubu*), expressed an opinion, Heo responded by saying, "Old man, what you are saying is wrong. Old man should leave now and get some rest." Considering that Sim was senior to Heo by twenty-five years and outranked him by three grades, this was a shockingly disrespectful thing to say. Friends of Sim managed to calm the enraged official and dissuade him from pursuing official action against Heo, but others who were present at the meeting were so upset that they reported the incident to the king, requesting that he dismiss Heo from his position. The monarch promised to investigate the matter, but, luckily for Heo this time, it did not result in further action.

Given the negative view of his character held by just about every Joseon commentator, combined with his history of repeated dismissals from official posts, it may seem a wonder that he had any kind of career in government service at all. There were two reasons that he was able to return to officialdom repeatedly despite his dismal record. The first was his reputation as an able diplomat, and the second was the protection of powerful people in the court. In 1597, in the face of a new wave of Japanese invasion, Joseon sent a diplomatic mission to Ming China to request additional military aid. As one of the envoys, Heo Gyun was thought to have excelled in his task, impressing Chinese officials with his vast knowledge and profound appreciation of Chinese literature. Some came to respect Heo's erudition to the extent of asking him to put together collections of Korean poetry for them (he included the verses of his beloved late sister Nanseolheon, so that they would become known in China). Even after Heo was dismissed from various posts for disgraceful reasons, he was brought back during visits by Chinese diplomats. King Gwanghae also sent him to China as an envoy on two occasions.

Also, as the son of a revered leader of the Eastern faction of the court, Heo had powerful patrons who intervened to save his career despite repeated missteps and the negative reputation he was accruing. One of his most important protectors was his significantly older half-brother Heo Seong, a lauded figure who served as the headmaster (*daesaseong*) of the National Confucian Academy and the censor-general (*daesagan*) of the Office of the Censor General (*saganwon*) before heading the ministries of rites, military affairs, and personnel. He was also connected to the royal family as the father-in-law to Lord Uichang, one of King Seonjo's sons by a concubine. When Heo Seong died in 1612, Heo Gyun lost his most powerful protector in the government, which necessitated that he latch onto another person of influence. And that takes us to the final phase of Heo's life and his involvement in court politics.

The secret report accusing Heo Gyun of treason was written by an official by the name of Gi Jungyeok, who submitted it at the end of 1617. Like Yi Sik, Gi had been a student of Heo's but felt compelled to move against his former teacher in order to save his father, the former chief state councilor (*yeong uijeong*) Gi Jaheon, who had been dismissed from his position and exiled because of Heo Gyun's actions. There are good reasons to be skeptical of many parts of Gi's desperate accusations, but they do provide a general picture of what led to Heo's spectacular rise and sudden fall in the last year of his life.

According to Gi Jungyeok, Heo found himself in a dire situation in 1613. His name had been mentioned during the interrogation of the criminals in the incident known as the Arrest of Seven Secondary Sons. Although his involvement in their actions was dismissed without further investigation, Heo felt insecure from the lack of a powerful patron who would protect him if things went awry, as his half-brother had passed away in the previous year. He consequently offered his services to Yi Icheom, his friend from their days of studying together at the National Confucian Academy. Yi had risen to become the most powerful official in the court, the leader of the Greater Northern faction that had supported King Gwanghae's ascendance to the throne. Not all of Gi's multiple accusations against Heo are plausible, but the historical context of the time needs to be explicated in order to understand the role Heo played in the political events of 1617 and 1618.

As mentioned in the previous chapter, Gwanghae became king in 1608 under controversial circumstances. As the son of King Seonjo's concubine, he had an older brother who had a claim to the throne, and there was also the son of the former king's queen, a two-year-old boy, Grand Lord Yeongchang. The Great Northern faction, headed by Yi Icheom, in order to solidify their power, set about eliminating all the major players they deemed to be threats, even though the king himself was reluctant to support some of their bloody actions. In 1609, they prosecuted and executed the king's older brother, Lord Imhae, with the accusation that he planned to usurp the throne. Four years later, Yi Icheom coerced some of the seven secondary sons into making false confessions about another conspiracy, implicating Queen Dowager Inmok, her father, Kim Jenam, and other powerful officials who opposed the Greater Northern faction. Kim Jenam was tried and executed; the eight-year-old Grand Lord Yeongchang was deprived of his title, exiled, and killed off a year later; and all the major enemies of Yi Icheom and his group were purged from the court. That only left the queen dowager to dispose of. At the end of 1616, after she was placed at West Palace under house arrest, discussions began in the court of whether she, as the daughter of a traitor, should be deprived of her royal title and prosecuted. This issue, dealing with someone everyone knew to be an innocent but politically inconvenient woman, proved to be highly controversial. Many officials, even some of the Greater Northern faction, could not bring themselves to support it, angering Yi Icheom with their recalcitrance.

In early 1617, a soldier by the name of Kim Yunhwang, on guard at West Palace, reported that while patrolling the grounds he had found an arrow with an attached note. The writing, addressed to the queen dowager, was brought to the king. It spoke of how the current ruler was a bastard who had stolen the throne by murdering his own father (there were scurrilous rumors to that effect) as well as his older brother. It also assured her of an imminent uprising led by a royal relative and advised her to make use of officials with the family names of Yu, Bak, and Gi.[32] The last name seemed to be a reference to Chief State Councilor Gi Jaheon, since he was the highest-ranking official who opposed the prosecution of the queen dowager. Gi offered the king his resignation, but the monarch refused, finding the whole arrow-and-note incident dubious. Later, however, Gwanghae succumbed to pressure from Yi Icheom's group and dismissed Gi from his post and exiled him.

It was at this point that Gi Jaheon's son, Gi Jungyeok, submitted the secret report accusing Heo Gyun of treason. One of the charges leveled against Heo was that he had written the note attached to the arrow and that he had done so at the behest of Yi Icheom, who fabricated it to use against the queen dowager. It turned out that the wife of the soldier Kim Yunhwang was a servant girl in Heo's household, so he had acted under

Heo's instructions to carry the arrow into the palace grounds and tell his superiors that he found it there, pretending that someone had shot it over the wall. According to Gi Jungyeok, Heo had done all this to please Yi Icheom and that these acts were merely the first step in his ultimate plan to take control of the state himself, a long-standing ambition of his. Gi claimed that when he and Heo had been on amicable terms, his teacher had told him that he had always harbored the desire to become the most powerful man in the kingdom through an intimate connection to the throne. He had first plotted to achieve this by urging King Seonjo to name Lord Uichang as his heir. Lord Uichang, a favored son by a different concubine than the mother of King Gwanghae, had married the daughter of Heo Gyun's older brother Heo Seong and so was his nephew-in-law (the prince would be exiled as a result of this testimony but would survive his half-brother's reign). When this stratagem had failed with the naming of Gwanghae as the crown prince, Heo Gyun had planned to support Grand Lord Yeongchang and become close to his mother so that if the boy became king, Heo would rise as the queen mother's chief advisor. This too had failed with the ascendance of Gwanghae to the throne, so Heo had finally conceived a scheme to insinuate himself as a henchman of Yi Icheom.

Despite the seriousness of the charges and repeated petitions to the king to investigate the matter, Heo Gyun was not called upon to answer them for eight months. In all probability, he was being protected by Yi Icheom, who was using the arrow-and-note incident to persuade the king to finally deprive the queen dowager of her title. Gi's accusation that Heo had masterminded the whole thing at the behest of Yi could have undermined the entire effort. In the eighth month of 1618, however, Heo was placed under arrest. In the course of the interrogations that followed, Heo was not questioned, but many of his friends and servants—even his concubine—were. They collectively affirmed Gi's accusations, offering additional information on how exactly Heo was planning to take control of the state.

It was alleged that Heo was gathering a band of armed men who were awaiting his command just outside the capital. After the service he had rendered Yi Icheom in helping depose the queen dowager, he planned to ask the king for permission to take soldiers into West Palace and "commit an act" (that is, probably, killing the queen dowager).[33] Once he received the monarch's approval, Heo would lead his men into the royal residence and take the king prisoner before forcing him to abdicate. There was also testimony that he had instructed his collaborators to spread rumors throughout the capital that the Jurchens were invading the country from the west, having already crossed the Amrok River (the Yalu), and that the people of Yugu (the Ryuku Islands—today's Okinawa) were coming from the sea, having already hidden themselves on a nearby island. A public notice that announced the invasions was put up on the Great South Gate of the city. With the memory of the Japanese war of 1592–1598 still fresh in the minds of many, it caused a panic, and people began to flee the city in droves. Heo Gyun was accused of waiting for the situation to turn into chaos before putting his coup d'état into action.

On the final day of the trial, which occurred on the twenty-fourth day of the eighth month of 1618, Heo Gyun finally spoke out, "I have something to say," but he was not allowed to defend himself.[34] With the king's approval, he and his accused co-conspirators were taken to the execution ground on the west side of the city, where they were ordered to put their names on an official document that detailed their crimes. Heo Gyun refused to do so, throwing away the brush handed to him, but he was manhandled into signing. He and the others were then executed before officials who served as witnesses to the punishment.

To summarize, there were three related accusations leveled against Heo Gyun by Gi Jungyeok: first, that he was involved in the crimes of the seven secondary sons; second, that he had fabricated the arrow and note found at West Palace, at the behest of Yi Icheom; and third, that he planned to take over the state by creating chaos in the capital, bringing his soldiers in and dethroning the king. Given Gi's motive of trying to save his father and the complex political situation of the time, is it possible to determine if Heo was actually guilty of any, some, or all of the crimes? One can make some reasonable guesses based on historical evidence.

The first accusation is unlikely, given that he was friendly with only two of the seven secondary sons (Sim Uyeong and Seo Yanggap), and Gi Jungyeok never offered any real evidence of Heo's involvement in their acts. In his report, Gi engaged in establishing guilt by association by describing how close Heo had been to Sim and Seo, to the extent of giving them nicknames and exchanging poems with them. That accusation was really about questioning his character by pointing out that he consorted with people who turned out to be heinous criminals. It was to this accusation that Yi Sik later added the role played by the Chinese novel *Water Margin* in corrupting their natures.

The second accusation, however, is not only plausible but probably true. Gi Jungyeok was right in pointing out that Heo became an active member of the Greater Northern faction after the death of his half-brother in 1612 and the Arrest of Seven Secondary Sons incident of 1613–1614. It makes perfect sense that he would try to insinuate himself into Yi

Icheom's favor as a trustworthy partisan in the debate over the fate of the queen dowager by providing what appeared to be a smoking gun, or rather a fallen arrow, evidence of the danger she posed to the king. Following the incident, Heo became one of the most vociferous advocates of the queen dowager's ouster. At the end of 1617, Heo received the highest position he would attain in the government, sixth state councilor (*jwachamchan*—senior second rank), probably as a reward for the service he had rendered to Yi. Gi Jungyeok's secret report was submitted two weeks after the appointment. As previously mentioned, the fact that it took eight months for the matter to be taken up in the court was, in all likelihood, thanks to Yi's protection of Heo. Then things took a sudden and fatal turn for Heo as he was arrested and then executed after a very quick trial. What precipitated Heo's change of fortune? There is a simple explanation for his downfall.

One of the ways Yi Icheom had solidified his position as the most powerful official in the royal court was by marrying his granddaughter to the crown prince. She failed, however, to produce a child, which necessitated that a concubine be chosen for the royal heir. In the middle of 1618, it became apparent that the leading candidate for the position was Heo Gyun's daughter. The situation turned Yi's loyal ally Heo into a political threat, so Yi began to plot his demise. After months of advising the king to ignore the accusations against Heo, Yi now urged him to open up an investigation because sufficient evidence of his treasonous plans had come to light. The *Sillok* records show that just after Heo was placed under arrest, Yi sent a servant to him with a message to have patience. Yi assured him that he would get through the trial unscathed and that his daughter was about to be confirmed as the concubine to the crown prince, so he had nothing to worry about.[35] In the meantime, Yi was busy making certain that the trial would be a quick one and that Heo would be executed at its conclusion. He was anxious for this to happen because he feared that if Heo realized what was going on, he might reveal "all the foul deeds that they had committed together" and expose him to danger. This is most likely a reference to the arrow and note, which Heo might confess to having fabricated at the behest of Yi. The king himself expressed surprise at the urgency with which Yi and other officials were calling for the execution of Heo and his co-conspirators without giving Heo a chance to defend himself. The monarch worried about the propriety of such a quick trial but was ultimately pressured into ordering their deaths. Heo realized only then that he had been tricked into silence, but when he tried to say something, he was not given the chance. The important thing to understand here is that Heo Gyun, at the end of his life, was a political opportunist who worked to dishonor and possibly cause the death of an innocent woman (Queen Dowager Inmok) in order to solidify his position in the dominant faction at the court. And it was his overreaching attempt to become the father-in-law to the crown prince, and thereby possibly the grandfather of the future king, that caused his downfall.

On the third accusation, the question of whether he was actually planning a coup d'état so he could take control over the state is improbable. It was likely an exaggerated charge, one commonly used to bring down people in power. In fact, Yi Icheom and his followers used similar allegations to get rid of the king's older brother, Lord Imhae, the queen dowager's father, and a number of others they deemed to be threats. It is somewhat ironic that Heo fabricated evidence to be used in such an accusation against the queen dowager only to become subjected to the charge himself. It is also possible that he did receive permission from the king to take armed men into West Palace and kill the queen dowager.[36] But the accusation that followed, that he was planning to dethrone the king, is probably a scurrilous one that originated with Yi Icheom. It would have been ludicrous for Heo to imagine that he could have single-handedly carried out a coup d'état with a group of armed henchmen and without the cooperation of a royal relative. When a successful coup did occur in 1623, engineered by the Western faction that overthrew King Gwanghae and brought Lord Neungyang (King Injo, r. 1623–1649) to the throne, it was a well-coordinated affair involving multiple officials in important positions and commanders of major military units.

As for the testimonies of Heo's treason, including by those accused of being co-conspirators, it must be pointed out that often the true purpose of an official interrogation in politically motivated cases like this was the extraction of confession rather than the determination of truth. Torture was routinely used to achieve this, which often resulted in confused and inconsistent testimony. A good illustration of this is from the time Heo Gyun's name came up during the Arrest of Seven Secondary Sons. Yi Icheom and his allies used the theft-and-murder case as an opportunity to attack the queen dowager and her father by forcing the criminals and their associates to tell false stories of a conspiracy against the king. In the course of the interrogations, which was overseen by the king himself, a prisoner by the name of Kim Eungbyeok, a merchant whose aunt was a servant at the royal palace, pointed to Heo Gyun and his half-brother Heo Seong as two among several people whom he frequently saw in the company of Kim Jenam. The king asked the prisoner why the Heo brothers would be meeting with Kim Jenam, since they were in the opposing Eastern faction. The prisoner replied, "How could I know who was an

Easterner and who a Westerner? I cannot stand the pain [of torture] any-more, so I said it hoping for a quick death."[37] On that occasion, the idea of Heo's involvement was dismissed without further comment. So the testi-monies affirming Heo's treason can easily be explained as false confes-sions extracted by torture or desperate bids for survival by those who knew that Heo was already doomed and sought mercy through compli-ance with the authorities.

The fall of Heo Gyun is sufficiently explained by his becoming a threat to his protector Yi Icheom after Heo's daughter became the likely future concubine to the crown prince. Many modern scholars, however, persist in their belief that Heo was a would-be revolutionary. They base the idea not only on their reading of *The Story of Hong Gildong* as a narrative mani-festo of his egalitarian ideas but also through a comparison of the text to Heo's other writings, particularly to his political essays and five biograph-ical sketches. As discussed in the previous chapter, in short treatises like "Essay on Discarded Talent" (*Yujaeron*) and "Essay on the Heroic Person" (*Hominron*), Heo expressed his belief that people of merit and talent should be allowed to serve in the government regardless of their background, that people in power should fear nothing more than the common people's wrath in the face of corruption and incompetence, and that there may come a time when heroic men will rise up and lead commoners to redress the wrongs perpetrated on the weak and the poor by the powerful and the wealthy.[38] Scholars have pointed to these and similar writings by Heo as the expression of his radical political ideas, which also inspired him to write the subversive work *The Story of Hong Gildong.*[39]

The glaring problem with this argument is that when one reads those works in the context of Confucian political thought since the time of the first philosophers Kongzi (Confucius) and Mengzi (Mencius), the ideas in Heo's essays that many modern scholars interpret as revolutionary reveal themselves to be rather commonplace. Far from being radical, subversive, or novel notions, they can be described as nothing more than Confucian clichés. Such ideas as the importance of recognizing people's merits re-gardless of their background and the need for the powerful to think con-stantly of the welfare of the common people were central philosophical tenets that just about every political writer was obligated to give lip ser-vice to. If one were to regard the ideas in Heo's writings as subversive, then one would have to come to the absurd conclusion that just about ev-ery Confucian intellectual from China, Joseon, and elsewhere was a po-litical radical when they were merely reiterating the ideas of Kongzi and Mengzi. It is only through the distorted view of Heo Gyun as a would-be revolutionary that the contents of his political essays appear radical.

Heo Gyun also wrote five biographical sketches of extraordinary people he had personally known or heard of, and these have also been misread as narratives of individuals who were treated unfairly by Joseon society. Kichung Kim asserts that the most striking similarity between *The Story of Hong Gildong* and the five sketches is that they are stories of people "each of whom is somewhat of a misfit and nonconformist, an outcast who is given little recognition by the world despite his innate gifts."[40] Similarly, Jae-Yung So claims that because "of their low stations in life they are unable to rise in the world from behind the barriers of society even though they possess superior talents. In this wide world there is no place to give them accommodation because of the impregnable thick social wall."[41] In one modern edition of Heo's selected writings, the section on the character sketches bears the title "Stories of the Lives of Five People Who Could Not Realize Their Will."[42] When one reads them with fresh eyes, however, such descriptions appear problematic.

When one compares the sketches (all of them written in literary Chinese) to *The Story of Hong Gildong,* it becomes immediately apparent that they differ greatly in content as well as style. The five lives are concise biographies of only a few pages, and they feature no extended narrative of action-oriented adventure. And none of them seem to be about the frustrated ambitions of social outcasts. The one that may seem to fit that characterization best is "The Story of the Scholar Songok" (*Songoksanin jeon*), an appreciative portrait of Heo's teacher Yi Dal (1539–1612; Songok was his literary name), a renowned poet who was a secondary son of a *yangban* and a courtesan. Heo does say that Yi's poetry "is treasured, but he has been discarded and not made use of," meaning that because of his background he could never utilize his considerable intellect and talents in government service.[43] But the majority of the piece is on his achievements as a literary figure, the characteristics of his personality, and the view of people who knew him. It is a stretch to say that Heo wrote it to expose the plight of talented *seoja* men because that issue is mentioned only briefly.

Another story, "The Story of Eom the *Cheosa*" (*Eom cheosa jeon*—*cheosa* denotes a scholar who passed the civil examinations but does not hold a government position), contradicts the notion that the character sketches are about frustrated outcasts. Eom Chungjeong, the subject of the piece, is a man of impoverished *yangban* background who dedicates himself to looking after his widowed mother. As a scholar of great intellect, he easily passes the civil examinations but does not enter into government service. When his beloved mother dies, he takes great care to conduct all the proper funeral rites. At the end of the mourning period, he is urged by friends to begin his official career, but he refuses, saying that he only took the examinations for the sake of his mother. Instead, he moves into a mountain and lives simply and happily without a thought to the pursuit of ambition or wealth. He is twice offered positions at the capital but turns them down. He dies at the age of seventy-eight, a beloved figure to his neighbors and students. The piece ends with a lament by a scholar that Eom's talents could not shine in government service, but the story makes it clear that he lived a happy and peaceful life without needing worldly success. In other words, Eom could very well have pursued a career as an official if he wanted to, but he chose personal contentment instead. This is the very opposite of a story of a man of frustrated ambitions.

The protagonists of the three remaining stories, "The Story of Scholar Jang" (*Jangsanin jeon*), "The Story of Master Jang" (*Jangsaeng jeon*), and "The Story of Namgung the Teacher" (*Namgung seonsaeng jeon*), are all individuals who led extraordinary lives. Jang Hanung is a doctor of wondrous powers who can heal any illness, raise people from the dead, summon supernatural spirits, and order tigers to do his bidding. He is killed by Japanese soldiers during the war, but his spirit lingers in the world to visit a good friend. He finally goes to Geumgang Mountain to live as an immortal spirit.[44] Master Jang is an itinerant entertainer of extraordinary beauty and talents who can move anyone with his singing and mimic the sound of any animal. With the money he earns from his performances, he spends enough to live modestly but gives the rest away to the poor. When a servant girl he has been teaching to play the lute comes to him in distress because her precious hairpin has been stolen, he takes her to the lair of the thieves, who return the object to her out of their respect for Jang. One day, he is found dead on a bridge, but, like Jang Hanung, he appears later to a friend and tells him, "I did not really die. I am actually on my way to the East Sea in search of an island." He instructs his friend on how to stay alive during the upcoming Japanese invasion. He then leaves, never to be seen in Joseon again.[45] And finally, Namgung Du is a man of *yangban* background whose family fell out of status because his grandfather and father did not take the civil examinations and worked as provincial clerks. But Namgung is more ambitious, and he successfully passes the tests and moves to the capital to take up a government position. But then he catches his concubine with another man and ends up murdering them both. After his wife breaks him out of prison, which results in her and their daughter dying in captivity, Namgung becomes a fugitive. Like Jang Hanung, he makes a bid to become an immortal spirit when he meets a powerful Daoist master, but he ultimately fails to transform himself despite the fact that he is shown visions of the supernatural world by his teacher. He returns to the world only to find that so much time has passed that his former house is gone and his fields changed ownership three or four times. When Heo Gyun meets Namgung Du, he is impressed by his appearance, as he looks like a man in his forties though he is actually in his eighties. After Namgung relates his life story, Heo considers that the study of Daoism is neglected in Joseon despite the fact that it can offer much wisdom and many wonders.[46]

While it is true that none of those people led the lives of respectable *yangban*, it is impossible to interpret their stories as social criticism in any significant way. Scholars who have uncritically accepted Heo Gyun's authorship of *The Story of Hong Gildong* have imposed Heo's supposedly radical political views on the sketches. In the process, they have also exaggerated what only amount to superficial similarities between them and *The Story of Hong Gildong*. For those unfamiliar with classic East Asian literature, such plot elements in the sketches like Jang Hanung's ability to summon supernatural spirits to do his bidding, the appearance of a den of thieves in the story of Master Jang, Jang's departure from Joseon to a faraway island, and Jang Hanung's transcendence as an immortal spirit may be reminiscent of similar episodes in *The Story of Hong Gildong*. In actuality, they are age-old motifs and clichés in the imaginative writings of East Asia, in the manner of the recurring themes in Western literature of the hero knight of medieval romances ending his adventures by becoming a monk, or an explorer in early modern fiction discovering a utopian community on a remote island, or a Faustian character making an unwise deal with the devil. Modern scholars, however, have pointed to the common elements in the sketches and *The Story of Hong Gildong* as evidence of Heo's authorship of the latter. What they ignore is that the short pieces composed in literary Chinese and the significantly longer work in *hangeul* are of such different styles and formats that the idea that they are the works of a single author is implausible.

As previously mentioned, it is possible that Heo Gyun wrote another such character sketch about the bandit Hong Gildong, which has become lost. He may have even destroyed it himself after he was accused of treason, fearing that the story of an outlaw could be used against him. If he did write such a piece, it would have been written in literary Chinese and much shorter than *The Story of Hong Gildong*. But it is just as possible that Yi Sik wrote down a scurrilous rumor of how the treasonous statesman had once written a story glorifying a criminal.

Much of the misinterpretation of *The Story of Hong Gildong*'s significance is based on the idea of Heo Gyun's authorship and on the view of Heo as a radical revolutionary. To point out two essential facts yet again— there is not a single definitive record of anyone having actually read or even seen a work entitled *The Story of Hong Gildong* until the second half of the nineteenth century, and no one considered Heo Gyun a revolutionary of radical egalitarian ideology until Kim Taejun described him as such in the twentieth century. During the Joseon dynasty, Heo had a generally negative reputation as an unprincipled and dissolute official of low morals who met his end either by actually planning a treasonous act or by becoming a hapless victim of court machinations. Admiration for him was reserved only for his literary erudition.

Given the specious nature of the attribution of *The Story of Hong Gildong* to Heo Gyun, not to mention the view of Heo as a radical political figure, the question of how such ideas became so firmly established in modern Korean scholarship must be explored. For that purpose, we go to the 1930s and examine the circumstances under which Kim Taejun affirmed them in his pioneering work *History of Joseon Fiction*.

KIM TAEJUN AND *HISTORY OF JOSEON FICTION*

One of the seminal events in modern Korean history began on March 1, 1919. All across the peninsula hundreds of thousands of people came out to protest Japanese colonial rule, with public declarations of independence accompanied by shouts of *manse* (literally "ten thousand years," an expression meaning "long live," as in "long live the Korean nation" and "long live Korean independence") that reverberated throughout the country. Now familiar to every Korean as the March First Movement, the event demonstrated that the people, far from demoralized and docile to the authorities, could be mobilized for mass action. The initial suppression of the peaceful demonstrations was brutal, resulting in numerous atrocities that brought the critical attention of the international press. The subsequently appointed governor-general, Saitō Makoto, sought to assuage local discontent by softening the iron-fisted image of the government. Through a new policy that was called "Cultural Rule," the colonial government reformed the legal system, made the salary scale for Korean civil servants fairer, demonstrated tolerance for native cultural and market practices, built modern schools, and issued permits for native-language journals and magazines.[47]

The central importance of the March First Movement to the Korean struggle for independence cannot be denied, but nationalist activists were faced with a serious dilemma in its aftermath because the event had failed to bring about freedom from foreign rule. In fact, afterward, the overtly lighter touch with which the colonial government conducted its policies—which was accompanied by a significant expansion of the police force and the network of native informers—dampened people's enthusiasm for confrontation with the authorities. As a result, two general positions emerged on how to carry on the fight for Korean independence: a moderate one, which advocated the concentration of effort on the educational, economic, and spiritual improvement of the masses in preparation for future independence, and a radical one, which called for direct and violent action. Because the moderates were willing to defer independence until Koreans were ready to become able citizens of a modern nation, they generally worked within the laws of the colonial government and sometimes cooperated with the authorities to create opportunities for the betterment of the people. The Japanese, in turn, allowed moderate nationalists a great deal of leeway in their activities and public expression of their ideas, using their tolerance as evidence of the liberalism of the new policies. It also allowed the government to concentrate its resources on stamping out the activities of the more dangerous radical nationalists, who came to regard the moderates as either dupes of the colonial authorities or outright collaborators.

For the radical nationalists, the newly introduced ideology of communism became a major source of inspiration. After the news of the Bolshevik Revolution reached Korea, Marxist-Leninist ideas filtered into the peninsula in the early 1920s, mainly through Korean students in Japan who had contact with local communists. There were also nationalists operating in Russia and China who became converts to the ideology.[48] Many of them were drawn to communism not just for its call for revolution but also for its program of radically remaking a nation into an egalitarian society. Achieving independence from Japan would be only the first step, as the bourgeois state would then have to be dismantled and replaced with a socialist one. There was also the further attraction of the possibility of receiving military and financial support from the Soviet Comintern.

Despite the Japanese colonial government's close scrutiny of radical nationalists in Korea, various leftist groups managed to form a united Korean Communist Party in 1925, founded by Kim Yaksu, Kim Jaebong, Jo Bongam, Bak Heonyeong, and others. Four years later, however, a roundup by the police devastated the organization, forcing those of its leadership who managed to escape arrest to flee abroad. It was in China and Russia that Korean communists were better able to organize and engage in resistance activities against the Japanese military, though they failed to form a united front because of factionalism.

Kim Taejun was born in 1905, in the town of Unsan in the northern province of Pyeongan.[49] He attended the Japanese-founded Keijō Imperial University (Keijō being the Japanese name for Joseon's capital city,

Gyeongseong), where he studied Korean and Chinese literature and became a committed nationalist as well as a convert to communism. In 1930, when he was twenty-six and still a student at the university, he began publishing a series of articles on Joseon-dynasty fiction in the newspaper *Donga ilbo*. As mentioned in the previous chapter, the work is an overtly nationalistic one, with the central purpose of preserving the richness and dignity of traditional writing at a time when Korean identity was in severe crisis. But Kim was writing not only against Japanese cultural imperialism but also the old feudal order of Joseon.

From the beginning of Korean nationalism in the 1880s, one of the central agendas of the movement was modernization, which entailed a radical transformation of the country through the dismantling of the traditional social, political, and cultural system.[50] The attempt to enact such changes by progressive politicians during the period of the Gabo Reforms (1894–1896, "Gabo" signifying the Blue Horse Year of 1894) ended in failure, leading eventually to colonization in 1910. Radical nationalists like Kim Taejun laid the blame for the currently subjugated and backward state of Korea squarely on the monarchs and the *yangban* of the old dynasty. The Joseon elite had failed to strengthen the country through modernization because of their corruption, intolerance, and conservatism, leaving the nation vulnerable to domination by a foreign power. The nationalists saw two aspects of the traditional order as particularly responsible for the country's downfall: the *yangban* literati's fanatical adherence to Confucianism, which made them incapable of adopting modern ideas, and their devotion to Chinese authority and culture (*sadae*, "serving the great"—a central tenet of Joseon-dynasty ideology), which stunted the growth of an authentic native culture.

For a literary scholar like Kim Taejun, writing at a time when modern fiction was fast becoming an important means of preserving and enlarging Korean culture, literature, and language, the history of Joseon fiction provided a meaningful narrative. Yet even as Kim sought to bolster Korean pride in native culture by discussing notable works of literature from the past, he felt compelled to criticize severely both the rulers and the culture of the fallen dynasty. In the introduction to *History of Joseon Fiction*, Kim rails against the notion that Joseon did not produce any real work of fiction.[51] He admits, however, that despite all the great literary achievements of the period, it did not produce a writer on the level of Dante, Shakespeare, or Goethe or works that can rival the great classic novels of China, though he believes that writings like *The Story of Hong Gildong*, *The Story of Chunhyang*, and *The Story of Heungbu* should be given their due.[52] He blames the lack of a world-class fiction writer on the traditional order's persecution of those who produced writings that deviated from strict conformity with Confucian ideology. As a result, written narratives of the time tended to be passive, provincial, moralistic, and narrow minded, emphasizing the values of "feudalistic fealty, loyalty, and honor."[53] Kim expands on the point by taking up a theme commonly found in nationalist writings about the past: the search for the historical moment when the country went down the wrong path, preventing it from becoming a powerful nation in the modern period.

Nationalist intellectuals working in a variety of fields at the time subscribed to the general narrative of a unique native culture in Korea that became distorted and degraded by foreign influences, resulting in the weakening of the national spirit and the ultimate loss of its autonomy. In an insightful study of Korean archaeology and prehistory, Hyung Il Pai has shown that it was Japanese scholars and imperial authorities who initially explained the backward and stagnant nature of the Korean state and culture in terms of the country's subservience to China from the Unified Silla period (668–935) to the end of the Joseon dynasty.[54] That idea was used to justify the ostensible imperial mission to civilize and modernize the inferior natives. Korean nationalist intellectuals like Kim Taejun and historians like Choe Namseon and Sin Chaeho wrote in opposition to the imperial agenda, but they uncritically accepted the explanatory narrative of the decline of Korean culture as the consequence of political and cultural subservience to foreign powers. As a result, they took an antagonistic attitude toward Confucianism and Buddhism, which they regarded as foreign pollutants that had eclipsed the native shamanistic tradition.[55] The hope for the future of the Korean people lay in retrieving the uniqueness of their original culture.

For Kim Taejun, the time of the greatest cultural potential for Koreans was all the way back in the time of the Three Kingdoms (ca. 57 BCE–668 CE), which he considers to be comparable to the European Renaissance and the Spring and Autumn period of China (770–476 BCE). At that time, the people of the peninsula had laid the foundation of a vibrant culture, one that never had the opportunity to blossom because of the "poisonous" intrusion of foreign ideologies from China (Confucianism) and India (Buddhism). The age of the Three Kingdoms came to an end in 688, when the southeastern state of Silla defeated its rivals to the west and north with the help of Tang China. From this period on, according to Kim, as successive Korean dynasties paid fealty to China and sought to emulate the Chinese in all things, the stranglehold of Confucianism and Buddhism prevented the rise of an authentic Korean culture. He sees King Sejong's invention of the phonetic script that better represents the everyday language of the people as a major attempt to rectify the situation, and he discerns a protodemocratic impulse for self-expression on the part of the common people in the proliferation of prose fiction from the reign of King Sukjong (1674–1720) to that of Jeongjo (1776–1800). Kim bitterly criticizes the Confucian officials of the Joseon dynasty for stunting the growth of such forms of writing. He asserts, however, that there were certain works that resisted and sought to subvert the stultifying status quo. And for Kim, the greatest example of that was *The Story of Hong Gildong*.

Kim's subchapter on *The Story of Hong Gildong* overtly features leftist ideas as he makes use of Korean translations of Marxist concepts. He begins the section with a brief summary of the work's plot before referring to Yi Sik's attribution of the writing to Heo Gyun. In the biographical sketch of Heo that follows, Kim writes that he must first provide a brief historical context of his life and works, though it "pains him greatly" to do so.[56] In the most overblown descriptive passage in the writing, he characterizes Joseon society during Heo's time period:

> Following the Japanese Invasion of the Imjin year [1592], as the state of the nation deteriorated like the crumbling of a brick house, an angel wearing the mask of peace sat upon the king's seat. But from behind the throne came the snorting of an evil spirit, which reverberated from one government office to the next. It was the laughter of a vampire that was enjoying itself at will, which provided the singing chorus to the scene of the decline of central authority. The bickering of the factions at the court, the *yangban*'s monopoly of political power, the myriad exploitations and abuses suffered by lowborn people forced to lead purposeless lives, and the empty rituals and meaningless formalities of society! In the midst of all that, there was rampant laziness and pleasure-seeking among some, while the vast majority of simple people found their lives falling into ruin! What wise man would not regard that with pity? It was in that troubled and tumultuous time that the Heo family, one of the most illustrious lines of the Joseon dynasty . . . saw the birth of Heo Gyun, the third son of Heo Yeop.[57]

Kim depicts Heo Gyun as a first-rate writer who, despite coming from a noble family, understood the thoroughly corrupt and tyrannical nature of *yangban* rule and dedicated himself to creating a better society for the common people. As a reformist turned revolutionary, a friend of oppressed commoners and people of secondary-offspring status, he joined the Greater Northern faction solely for the purpose of gaining the power he needed to enact a social revolution. Kim describes Heo as "a passionate defender of justice," "a trouble-maker who could not countenance the indignation he felt in the face of wrongdoing," and "a noble champion of profound idealism who sought to realize his ideas no matter what the cost."[58] As for the negative reputation he earned as the result of consorting with prostitutes and other dissolute behavior, Kim asserts that they were Heo's attempts to break away from the "false consciousness" (*heowihan uisik*) and meaningless moral principles of his society.[59] All that he wrote as a controversial writer and did as a maligned statesman was for the purpose of arousing the people's consciousness toward the creation of a "revolutionary movement" (*hyeokmyeong undong*). His closeness to lower-class people, for which he was criticized, was part of his effort to

> gain the perspective of commoners so that he could become the leader of the people in their conflict against the aristocrats, the wealthy, and the self-entitled *yangban*, who were also the enemies of Heo Gyun in his effort to work for the benefit of the masses [*daejung ongho*] and to achieve a social revolution [*sahwoe hyeokmyeong*].[60]

Kim Taejun believes that Heo Gyun was indeed involved in the conspiracy of the seven secondary sons as well as the coup d'état he was accused of planning, all for the purpose of leading a revolution that would radically alter Joseon society into a classless egalitarian state. Based on this view, Kim interprets *The Story of Hong Gildong* as a kind of autobiography of Heo Gyun's ideal version of himself as well as a narrative manifesto of his political ideals. Kim sees three prominent themes in the story.

> 1. Call for the overthrow of the social hierarchy, especially the prejudicial policies toward people of secondary offspring status. 2. Contempt for the landed gentry and the aristocracy, in the taking of illegitimately acquired wealth of provincial officials for the purpose of aiding the impoverished. 3. [Hong Gildong's] entrance into the Chinese island nation of Yul to become its king.[61]

Kim asserts that the first two themes are taken from the actions and motivations of Heo's life. His final assessment of the work is laudatory.

> Written by the hand of someone as erudite as Heo Gyun, *The Story of Hong Gildong* is the first Joseon fiction that is worthy of the name. . . . The depiction of the character of Hong Gildong, who rose up in rebellion against myriad tyrannies and prejudices of the *yangban* regime, is consistent and complete; and the story's status as the Joseon dynasty forerunner of the modern serialized novel makes it a work of authoritative importance.[62]

It must be reiterated that Kim Taejun, in the 1930s, was the very first writer to depict Heo Gyun and *The Story of Hong Gildong* in such a way, namely,

Heo as a would-be political revolutionary who sought to gain power in order to remake Joseon into a classless society and the novel as an expression of his protosocialist ideas.

Benedict Anderson, in a chapter on "Memory and Forgetting" added to the 1991 edition of his classic work on nationalism *Imagined Communities*, describes how in the rhetoric of revolutionaries seeking to establish a modern nation-state there is an emphasis on the novelty of their endeavor, of an attempt to create something unprecedented that constitutes a sharp break with the past.[63] Paradoxically, however, once such a nation is established, its spokesmen turn to history in an effort to establish a precedent or a movement toward the modern state even in far antiquity. The creation of the nation is then no longer described as the result of a rupture from the past but rather as an "awakening from sleep" of the national spirit that had always been there.[64] Anderson points out, for instance, that in the American Declaration of Independence there is no mention of such historical markers as Christopher Columbus, Roanoke, and the pilgrims, which subsequently became important symbols of American national identity.[65]

Korean nationalists like Kim Taejun were engaged in the same contradictory task. As they struggled for Korean independence and the subsequent creation of a modern nation-state, they felt obliged to denigrate the old feudal order of the Joseon dynasty. But they were also seeking evidence in that very past of the sleeping spirit of the Korean nation and national consciousness. History was something that had to be overcome for the people to gain their freedom and dignity, but it was also the place where they looked for crucial inspiration for contemporary struggles.

For Kim, *The Story of Hong Gildong* and the life of its putative author represented that very spirit, which was seeking to realize itself in the repressive environment of Joseon society. He consequently interpreted the work as a subversive one that criticized the feudalistic-aristocratic hierarchy and culture of the dynasty. He affirmed the authorship of Heo Gyun and turned him into a protosocialist revolutionary in order to demonstrate the existence of a native tradition of resistance. And the antiauthoritarian actions of the fictional outlaw and the revolutionary ideals of his creator provided Kim with models for fighting against the tyrannical powers of his day.

There is an interesting dissonance in Kim's ideological reading of *The Story of Hong Gildong* in that he thought he had found in Heo Gyun a writer of the first order, the closest Korean rival to Dante, Shakespeare, and Goethe. Yet as a socialist, Kim abhorred the entirety of the *yangban* class that Heo came from, which had exploited the common people and stunted the growth of an authentic native culture for so many centuries. His solution was to invent the idea of Heo as an elite intellectual who became awakened to the social and economic inequities of his time and envisioned a society without class or exploitation. One might speculate that the persistence of this idea in modern scholarship may be reflective of an intellectual elitism that would prefer to regard the beloved classic of Korean fiction as the work of a learned *yangban* rather than of an anonymous commercial writer of lower social status and educational level. (Perhaps such elitism informs the skeptics of Shakespeare's authorship as well.) This is ironic, considering that the contrary notion of the work as a popular fiction written by and for commoners would have fit better into Kim's leftist ideology, one that would have made the wholly invented notion of Heo Gyun as a radical writer unnecessary.

Given Kim Taejun's political agenda in writing *History of Joseon Fiction* and his laudatory interpretation of *The Story of Hong Gildong*, Lee Yoon Suk has recently made a startlingly ironic discovery about the attribution of the work to Heo Gyun.[66] It turns out that Kim Taejun was not the first modern scholar to associate Heo with the *hangeul* work. The claim already had been made in 1927 by Kim's professor at Keijō Imperial University, Takahashi Toru (1878–1967), a Japanese scholar of Joseon literature. Takahashi was familiar with Yi Sik's claim that Heo Gyun had written a work called *The Story of Hong Gildong*, so he assumed that the extant writing of that title was that work. It is interesting, however, that Takahashi found it implausible that it was originally composed in *hangeul*, since *yangban* writers eschewed the phonetic script. He concludes, "The currently existing *The Story of Hong Gildong* is in *eonmun* [vulgar script]. It is an absolute certainty that Heo Gyun wrote the original work in literary Chinese. No evidence has surfaced that would allow us to determine when that original work became lost."[67] It should be reiterated here that Kim Taejun never claimed that *The Story of Hong Gildong* was the first work of fiction originally written in *hangeul*. The assertion was made by Yi Myeongseon in his 1948 work *History of Joseon Literature* (*Joseon munhaksa*),[68] possibly based on a misreading of Kim Taejun's description of the writing as "the first Joseon work that is worthy of being described as *soseol*."[69] But Kim did uncritically accept the highly problematic attribution made by his Japanese teacher and deployed it for his own nationalist and leftist purposes.

In 1939, the year Kim Taejun published a new edition of his work on Joseon prose fiction, he joined the underground organization Gyeongseong Com (communist) Group, headed by Bak Heonyeong, one of the founders of the Korean Communist Party. Three years later, Kim was arrested, along with most of its members, after it was infiltrated by the Japanese police. In 1944, he fled to Yenan, China, where leftist nationalists were gathering to organize military action against the imperial army. When the war ended, Kim returned to the divided country, to the capital of what was to become South Korea. He began teaching Korean literature at Gyeongseong University (formerly Keijō Imperial University). He also joined the newly formed South Korean Worker's Party, the new communist organization founded by Bak Heonyeong and others, and became the head of its cultural division. In 1946, he was dismissed from his university position because he had joined the protest against consolidating Gyeongseong University and a number of other institutions in the capital into Seoul National University (there were concerns over the loss of autonomy for many of the institutions and over the fact that an American military officer was to head the new university). In early 1949, following the previous year's serious mutiny of a regiment of the South Korean army in the cities of Yeosu and Suncheon, which was joined by communist partisans, Kim was caught up in the general roundup of prominent leftists in the country. In November of that year, like his hero Heo Gyun, Kim Taejun was executed under the charge of treason.

In this chapter I have endeavored to demonstrate that most of what is commonly believed in modern Korea about the origin and significance of *The Story of Hong Gildong* are really myths based on highly problematic historical assumptions. The notion that Heo Gyun wrote the work originates from his ex-student Yi Sik's mention of Heo's authorship of a writing that Yi apparently had not read or possibly even seen. Yi's assertion was repeated a number of times by other writers over the following centuries, but there is not a single record of anyone demonstrating familiarity with the work's content. It is only in the second half of the nineteenth century that we can ascertain that a *hangeul* fiction entitled *The Story of Hong Gildong* became a popular work. In the twentieth century, Kim Taejun popularized the notion of Heo Gyun's authorship, but he had received that idea from his Japanese professor at Keijō Imperial University, Takahashi Toru, who was the first modern scholar to associate the extant work with Heo based on an uncritical reading of Yi Sik. Kim also drew a wholly imagined picture of Heo as a revolutionary thinker of radical egalitarian ideology who wrote the story as a political manifesto of his protosocialist views. Because Kim's *History of Joseon Fiction* became an essential work of classic Korean fiction, his claims about *The Story of Hong Gildong*'s authorship, the character of its writer, and the subversive nature of its content became widespread and firmly established in modern scholarship.

The specious nature of the historical evidence for such claims raises two essential questions about the nature of the work. First, if Heo Gyun was not the author of the extant *The Story of Hong Gildong,* could the actual period of the work's production be determined? And second, if the view of the story as a subversive one written by a radical political thinker is a misinterpretation, what is the true significance of the narrative? I address those questions in the next chapter, with a further consideration of Kim's interpretation of the work's radical nature, followed by an examination of the historical development of Joseon prose fiction in the eighteenth and nineteenth centuries and a comparison of the writing to other classic works of similar nature.

CHAPTER THREE

The Imagined Hong Gildong
at the Twilight of a Dynasty

Analyzing a literary work by fitting it into one of the binary categories of "subversive" or "conservative" is usually unproductive. Such an approach tends to be an exercise in simplification, since a text of any complexity eludes such stark characterization. And a scholar's predisposition to reading it as one supportive of the status quo or critical of it often determines the judgment of which elements of the writing are seen as central and which insignificant. An additional problem is that notions of conservative and subversive are meaningful only within specific contexts, as what is disruptive of the dominant paradigm at one time and in one sector of a society can turn into a tool of conservatism in another, and vice versa. The feminist theorist Judith Butler has pointed out that the judgments of whether an idea is subversive or conservative cannot be made out of context, and

> they cannot be made in ways that endure through time ("contexts" are themselves posited unities that undergo temporal change and expose their essential disunity). Just as metaphors lose their metaphoricity as they congeal through time into concepts, so subversive performances always run the risk of becoming deadening clichés through their repetition and, most importantly, through their repetition within commodity culture where "subversion" carries market value. The effort to name the criterion for subversiveness will always fail, and it ought to.[1]

A careful analysis of *The Story of Hong Gildong* must avoid such simplistic categorization. But before the work can be examined in a nuanced manner, Kim Taejun's subversive reading has to be addressed, since the enormous influence of his work has led most scholars to follow his perspective. It is still the mainstream view in Korea that *The Story of Hong Gildong* was written by a seventeenth-century radical revolutionary to criticize the Joseon-dynasty order, from its rule by the corrupt *yangban* to its policy on secondary offspring. To give one example from a standard work of Korean history, Ki-baik Lee, in his *A New History of Korea*, characterizes *The Story of Hong Gildong* as "a work of social criticism that scathingly attacked the inequities of Yi society with its discriminatory treatment of illegitimate offspring and its differences based on wealth."[2] Because such a perspective has become an idée fixe in modern views of the work, it is necessary to examine its assumptions in detail.

THE STORY OF HONG GILDONG, A SUBVERSIVE WORK?

Interpreters of *The Story of Hong Gildong* point to a number of plot elements as critiques of Joseon society. The most obvious is Hong Gildong's repeated complaints that despite his considerable talents and noble pedigree, he is barred from pursuing a career in the civil or military service because he is a secondary son. I have already pointed out in chapter 1 that the controversy over the status of the *seoja* has a long history, with periodic attempts at reform, culminating in King Yeongjo's removal of all barriers to civil examinations and government service for secondary sons in 1772.[3] Hong Gildong's lamentations are no doubt eloquent and moving expressions of a *seoja*'s frustrations, but the work's depiction of his condition should not be interpreted simplistically as subversive, since the issue of illegitimate children was openly discussed throughout the dynasty's history. So its appearance in the story would not have been particularly shocking to Joseon readers.

The aspect of *The Story of Hong Gildong* that would have been more scandalous was the heroic portrayal of an outlaw. In the traditional Confucian view, a ruler can lose legitimacy (Heaven's Mandate) through misrule, but there are prescriptions for conducting a proper protest by concerned officials as well as for changing the leadership of the country. What is not allowed is for the common people to violate the laws of the land willfully, resulting in disharmony in the relationship between the ruler and his subjects. Once Hong Gildong becomes the leader of bandits, he names his group Hwalbindang ("group dedicated to aiding the impoverished") and targets places where food and treasures are hoarded, such as Haein Temple and the provincial administrative center of Hamgyeong. He also steals gift treasures (*bongsong*) that are sent by regional officials to the capital city as bribes. And he disguises himself as a government inspector to punish corrupt officials. Such activities are no doubt criminal, but there is nothing in the text that supports the view of the hero and his creator as radical revolutionaries. Hong, far from seeking to subvert the social order of the country, is motivated by the desire to participate in it as a legitimate official. He does not steal tax money or the property of the common people. And he makes his aspirations clear when he faces the king, and the monarch is eventually persuaded to grant him the position of minister of military affairs, which brings Hong's career as an outlaw to an end. In other words, once his dream of attaining an official position has been realized, he supports the status quo by leaving the country with his band, sparing the king the embarrassment of having an ex-outlaw as his minister. In fact, this interesting deviation from the standard narrative of the noble robber described by Eric Hobsbawm, that the surviving hero ultimately returns to the community of origin, leads us to the next aspect of what many interpreters have commonly claimed to be a major subversive element of *The Story of Hong Gildong.*

Kim Taejun, in his summary of *The Story of Hong Gildong,* describes the last third of the narrative in just one sentence—"Gildong leaves his country afterward and, on his way to Namgyeong, slays the monsters of Mangdang Mountain, and becomes the king of Yul Island where he creates an ideal nation."[4] That characterization of the final phase of Hong's adventures has been repeated many times, often with the use of the term "utopia" in English-language works to describe the state that the hero creates. To give some examples, W. E. Skillend relates how at the end of *The Story of Hong Gildong* the hero "leaves Korea to become king of his own Eutopia"[5]; in *A Bibliographical Guide to Traditional Korean Sources,* edited by Tai-jin Kim, the plot summary of *The Story of Hong Gildong* ends with Hong leaving "the country, entering the Land of Yulcho [sic], which he builds into a utopia"[6]; the entry on "Hong-Giltong-Jŏn" in Keith Pratt and Richard Rutt's *Korea: A Historical and Cultural Dictionary* describes how Hong "eventually becomes king of a utopian state"[7]; and Peter H. Lee, in his *A History of Korean Literature,* characterizes Hong's island as "a utopia of contemporary popular imagination."[8] A few recent writers have gone further in detailing aspects of Hong's ideal country. For Kim Yong-bock, Yuldo is a "paradise, which is characterized by the absence of social division and contradictions between the yangban class and the common people"[9]; similarly, Sang Yaek Lee depicts the place as a "symbolic country, a utopia free from hierarchy and oppression"[10]; Ian Haight and T'ae-yŏng Hŏ claim that the laws of Hong Gildong's realm allow "more opportunity for women, those who are not of noble class, and the poor"[11]; and Kyung Moon Hwang describes how "Hong and his followers [settle] into a kind of socialist utopia without hierarchies and discrimination."[12]

Given the assumption of *The Story of Hong Gildong* as a work of radical ideology, it would make sense that the story ends with the hero's establishment of an egalitarian utopia. The depiction of an ideal state radically different from Joseon in its lack of hierarchy and oppression would serve as a powerful critique of the kingdom's political and social system. It has to be pointed out, however, that there is no textual evidence that supports any such descriptions of the society Hong Gildong builds on Yul Island. In addition, the use of the term "utopia" is problematic. Ever since Thomas More coined the word in the sixteenth century, from Greek root words meaning "no place," utopia has come to signify not just an optimally functioning society but one that has achieved such a state through a novel and imaginative arrangement of its community different from ones that exist in the world.

Because of the influence of Kim Taejun's interpretation of the work, people who have never read *The Story of Hong Gildong* might expect some description of the egalitarian system that Hong supposedly establishes on Yul Island. They might be surprised to find out that there is no such thing in the text, as it features only a few sparse descriptions of the happy state of its people. In the *pilsa* 89 version, it is described how after Hong Gildong defeats the original king of Yul and ascends the throne, he "ruled with such benevolence that his subjects drummed their full stomachs and sang happy ballads. 'A time of peace and prosperity has come, like in the days of Yo and Sun.'"[13] The last two are references to Yao and Shun, two semimythical rulers of ancient China who were regarded as ideal monarchs.[14] Later on, after the episode involving the death of Hong's mother, it is related that "Through the benevolent rule of the king, the country was at peace and saw rich harvests, the people feeling secure with their households well-stocked. No inauspicious incident disturbed the country." In the *gyeongpan* 30 version, by the third year of Hong's reign over Yul Island "the country was at peace and there was no ill occurrence anywhere, so the place was secure and the people lived in comfort,"[15] and "an age of great peace came upon the land when the songs of children could be heard on the great roads and old men sang happy ballads, a time comparable to those of Yo and Sun."[16] And after Hong disappears, "Harvest was plentiful year after year so the people happily sang ballads of the countryside," and his descendants "ruled the land in great peace."[17] These passages are the entirety of the descriptions of the state of Yul Island under Hong's rule. In actuality, they are nothing more than depictions of people's contentment under the reign of a good and able monarch, not of a novel system of governance for which the word "utopia" would be appropriate. In other words, various interpreters' ideas that the story tells of a utopian state with a radically different political and social system from Joseon, one devoid of hierarchy or caste, is the product of their imagination and the imposition of their political desires upon the story with no actual textual evidence to support it. The origin of that view can be traced back, once again, to Kim Taejun's writings, which were influenced by Western and, more specifically, communist ideology's aspiration for the establishment of an egalitarian state.

Those who want to hold onto a radical reading of *The Story of Hong Gildong* may insist that Yul Island as a utopia is implied rather than explicit and that one must read between the lines to discern the revolutionary agenda of the work. Such an insistence on "implication" is more indicative of an idée fixe on the part of an interpreter than it is of what is actually present in the work's subtext, especially in view of overt evidence that contradicts such a reading. What Hong Gildong establishes on Yul Island is a kingdom with himself as an absolute monarch, and references to the titles he grants his officials indicate that he essentially replicates the Joseon political system in his realm. In the *pilsa* 89 version, furthermore, he also adopts the one-legitimate-wife-per-man policy, making his wife Bek the queen but taking Jeong and Jo as his concubines.[18] The secondary sons by the concubines are given the ranks of *gun* (a noble title for a prince) and *bek* (the highest rank of nobility) and sent out to live on Jae Island, which evidently becomes a subordinate territory to Yul Island. In the *gyeongpan* 30 version, he does take two wives, who are both given the title of queen (*wangbi*), but there is no mention of whether this reflects a general allowance of polygamy or if it is a royal privilege. It is also mentioned that he has three additional children by palace ladies (*gungin*).[19]

The notion that the story implicitly points to an egalitarian ideology is made even more implausible when considered in view of the work as a narrative manifesto of Heo Gyun's radical politics. If that were the case, why is there not even a hint of an innovative social, political, or legal policy enacted on Yul Island that would represent such ideas? Why hide them so deeply within the description of what appears to be a standard hereditary monarchy (Hong's son by his queen succeeds him upon his abdication) that they are completely invisible? That makes the work a poor political manifesto, especially given that it is impossible to detect any kind of radical notion in the conclusion of the work. Even in the case of the secondary-offspring issue that is featured so prominently in the first part of the story, Hong the king seems to have forgotten completely the frustrations of his early life as the son of a lowborn concubine. If the essential purpose of writing *The Story of Hong Gildong* was to protest Joseon policy toward the *seoja*, why is there no mention of Hong allowing people of his background to pursue social advancement without legal impediments on Yul Island?

In an interesting parallel, Jamie K. Taylor has pointed to a similar problem in the characterization of outlaw communities in medieval English literature in utopian and egalitarian terms.[20] In the fourteenth-century narrative *Fouke le Fitz Waryn*, for instance, a nobleman of royal blood is exiled from court and becomes the leader of forest-dwelling bandits.[21] But rather than creating a new kind of society among them, "he heads a community that maintains similar hierarchical social and governmental structures."[22] In fact, Fouke, just like Hong, confers ranks among his followers and distributes booty based on the system, which belies "the fantasy of a horizontally affiliated, purely egalitarian society that challenges the entrenched hierarchies of royal systems of power."[23]

I want to state clearly at this point that the problematic nature of the subversive reading of the work does not necessarily lead to the view of the story as being conservative. Hong's moving lamentations in the first part of the narrative are indeed powerful calls for the reader to consider the plight of secondary offspring in Joseon society. Also, the heroic portrayal of an outlaw questions the legitimacy of legal authority that is incompetent or corrupt. Stephen Knight has made a similar point in his analyses of the many Robin Hood texts, different elements of which could be used to support interpretations that range from "quasi-revolutionary left to highly conservative right."[24] In response to more conservative readings of the fifteenth-century work *A Gest of Robin Hood*, however, Knight points out that the story does advocate "massive theft from the church, civil insurrection against and murder of a properly appointed sheriff, breach of legitimate agreement with the king; and it imagines that all these things can lead to a lengthy and happy life."[25]

The point of this chapter so far has been to show that analyzing the work on the basis of its subversive or conservative nature is unproductive, simplistic, and distorting. There are many elements of the narrative that could be used to argue one way or the other, depending on which are emphasized at the expense of others. A holistic view of the work's significance that goes beyond such narrow binary distinctions must begin with an attempt to place it in proper historical context.

THE DEVELOPMENT OF COMMERCIAL FICTION IN THE LATE JOSEON DYNASTY

Because of the influence of Kim Taejun's *History of Joseon Fiction*, contemporary scholars have had to grapple with numerous inaccuracies, simplifications, and unsupported assertions in the work. One important issue of contention has been over Kim's narrative of the development of popular fiction in the Joseon dynasty. He asserts that there was a flowering of *hangeul* fiction written for popular consumption after the Japanese invasion of 1592–1598 and through the Manchu invasions of 1627 and 1636.[26] He accounts for the development of the common people's discontent toward the *yangban* class responsible for the disasters of the era and for their desire for a vernacular literature that would allow them to express themselves in a more natural language than the highly stylized prose of *yangban* literature. This idea has been featured in most historical surveys of classic Korean literature. For instance, Kim's words have been repeated almost verbatim in English by Kim Hŭnggyu and Peter H. Lee in their essay on Joseon fiction in *hangeul*—"after the Japanese and Manchu invasions . . . a great number of commoners, the main consumers of vernacular fiction, demanded a literary form corresponding to contemporary reality."[27] Among the works of fiction produced for the people (*minjung*) in the seventeenth and eighteenth centuries, Kim Taejun points to the genre of the "martial narrative" (*gundam*), which tells stories of heroic men who engage in combat.[28] He notes the influence of Chinese military romances[29] such as *Three Kingdoms* and *Water Margin*, which Joseon writers imitated in telling stories inspired by the country's experience of war.

Recently literary scholars have questioned this idea because of the glaring problem of the complete lack of any historical evidence for a flowering of popular *hangeul* fiction in the seventeenth century. The notion also invites skepticism given the low rate of literacy among the common people at the time and the absence of a commercial system for the publication and distribution of texts for general consumption. In a recent article assessing scholarly attempts to identify the first work of prose fiction written in *hangeul*, Lee Pok-kyu has pointed out that the task is a practically impossible one because no original manuscript, only copies or printed texts, of Joseon fiction has survived. There is also precious little evidence on the circumstances of composition.[30] Scholars who have discounted *The Story of Hong Gildong* as the first *hangeul* fiction have put forward other candidates for the distinction, such as Kim Siseup's late fifteenth-century *New Tales from Golden Turtle Mountain* (*Geumo sinhwa*) and Chae Su's early sixteenth-century *The Story of Seol Gongchan* (*Seol*

Gongchang jeon). Their research, however, has led to no conclusive result. In all probability, *hangeul* versions of those early writings were translations of the original compositions in literary Chinese, as the *yangban* persistently resisted using King Sejong's script for literary writing. Lee Pok-kyu asserts that a few works may have been written originally in *hangeul* in the late seventeenth century, possibly the 1690s work *Record of Lady Sa's Journey to the South (Sassi namjeong nok)*.[31]

The difficulties posed by both the paucity and the uncertain nature of historical evidence make it impossible to determine the proper place of *The Story of Hong Gildong* in the history of Joseon fiction through external evidence alone. A more fruitful approach would be a comparative analysis of the work in the context of the general development of Joseon fiction. To make such an exploration possible, it is essential to establish an evidence-based history of the rise of popular fiction in the dynasty.

As previously mentioned, the *yangban* literati did not regard prose fiction as a respectable genre, as reflected in the literal meaning of the word *soseol* (lesser narrative). Kim Taejun has pointed out that this attitude resulted in Joseon's failure to produce a body of fiction that rivals the dynasty's illustrious tradition of poetic, philosophical, and historical writings. The situation also explains the general characteristics of fiction written by *yangban* writers before the advent of popular works in the late eighteenth century, which can be described in the following terms:

Writing Format: Lee Pok-kyu has pointed to precious few works of fiction from the late seventeenth century that may have been composed originally in the phonetic script, but the preponderance of historical evidence points to the fact that almost all literary texts were composed in literary Chinese. Some of them were subsequently translated into the phonetic script for the readership of aristocratic women and men of secondary and commoner status.

Background: Most full-length stories take place in China with Chinese characters, in imitation of the classic Chinese novels.

Plot: There were many types of stories that were categorized as *soseol*, including records of old legends, incidental anecdotes, character sketches, and Buddhist dream narratives, but the genre that was particularly popular in the seventeenth century was the family drama, which takes place within a single household, involving tensions among the wives and concubines of a scholar-official. A nefarious wife or concubine typically conspires against another who is depicted as the moral exemplar of patience and steadfast fidelity. The fortunes of the household are tied to those of an official in government service, his rise, fall, and return to power determining the fate of the women and their children. A typical example is

Record of Demonstrating Goodness and Stirring of Virtue (*Changseon gamui rok*), a work of uncertain authorship that has been attributed to either Jo Seonggi (1638–1689) or Kim Dosu (?–1742). It takes place in Ming-dynasty China and involves the conflicts among the three household women of a retired official and their children.

Theme: *Yangban* fiction tends to be moralistic and allegorical, illustrating an ethical principle or philosophical concept. The stories are built around the theme of such traditional virtues as filial piety, spousal fidelity, loyalty to the monarch, and service to the country. *Record of Lady Sa's Journey South* narrates the trials and tribulations of the faithful and uncomplaining wife of a Ming-dynasty official who is ousted from her household through the connivance of a concubine. After her husband recovers from his own fall from power, Lady Sa is rewarded for her fidelity when she is reunited with him. The novel *Nine Cloud Dream* demonstrates the Buddhist idea of the transience of human life through a complicated plot involving a Chinese monk named Seongjin who is reincarnated and enjoys the successful career of a government official, only to find out that his entire life has been a dream.

In contrast to such works written by the *yangban* for *yangban* readership, Kim Taejun saw the rise of a new kind of *soseol* in the seventeenth century in the form of prose fiction for a popular audience. Recent scholarship on Joseon popular fiction has produced a much more plausible and well-supported narrative of the proliferation of popular fiction at a significantly later period, providing vital clues on the place of *The Story of Hong Gildong* in it.

Ian Watt, in his classic study of the rise of the realist novel in eighteenth-century England, analyzes the phenomenon in the context of the expansion of the middle class, the rise of literacy, and the subsequent development of a book trade that catered to the new readership.[32] Interestingly, a comparable development on a more modest scale occurred in Joseon in the second half of the same century. The 1700s was a time of remarkable peace, prosperity, and innovation in the dynasty's history, overseen by three extraordinarily capable monarchs—Sukjeong (r. 1674–1720), and then, after the brief and inconsequential rule of Gyeongjong, Yeongjo (r. 1724–1776) and Jeongjo (r. 1776–1800). Through their effective and benevolent leadership, the rulers kept factionalism in the court under control, enacted economic reforms that favored the common people, introduced innovative agricultural techniques that significantly improved production, and encouraged cultural and intellectual activities through personal patronage.[33] The kings were able to concentrate fully on domestic issues because East Asia in general was at peace, with the northern people who plagued Joseon's border under the firm control of Qing China and the Tokugawa Shogunate of Japan in an isolationist mode. The situation resulted in the expansion of wealth and opportunities for secondary- and commoner-status people. An important consequence of this development was the expansion of the *yangban* class through upward social mobility.

The determination of the number of people in each of the four social statuses in any given period is a difficult task, but historians have estimated that at the foundation of the Joseon dynasty the *yangban* consisted of about 5 percent of the population. Its number increased incrementally in the following two centuries, but that becomes hard to affirm in the mid-period of the dynasty because most of the population registers were destroyed during the Japanese invasion of 1592–1598. JaHyun Kim Haboush has shown that by the late seventeenth century the percentage of the *yangban* was somewhere between 9 and 16 percent.[34] Only half a century later, the number jumped to 30 percent, almost a third of the population.

Under the favorable economic conditions of the eighteenth century, many newly wealthy people of secondary and commoner background legally purchased certain *yangban* privileges, a practice that had been around since the late sixteenth century as a measure to bring in extra revenue to the government. Others bribed local officials to fabricate lineage records that allowed them or their sons to take the civil examinations.[35]

Such expansion of wealth and opportunities resulted in a marked rise of literacy. Increasing numbers of people not only gained the economic wherewithal to provide themselves and their sons with books, writing implements, and tutors but also the leisure time to enjoy entertaining literature. And just as middle-class people of eighteenth-century England found the realist novel to their taste, the upwardly mobile of Joseon also exhibited a penchant for a new kind of narrative that was distinct from the heavily moralistic works by *yangban* writers. For those who did not have the resources and the time to master literary Chinese, they could easily learn the phonetic script, which consequently became the writing of literary entertainment for secondary- and commoner-status people.

The scarcity of historical sources on Joseon popular culture prior to the second half of the nineteenth century makes the subject a difficult one to explore, and scholars of nationalistic bent have tended to exaggerate the extent and significance of "people's culture" in the premodern era. There is, however, ample evidence that points to the establishment of sufficient general readership in the last decades of the eighteenth century, which led to writers producing works of fiction for popular consumption, which in turn gave rise to a market system for producing and disseminating such texts.[36] Records from that period indicate that works of fiction that were written for profit were initially handwritten with brush on paper. After a few copies of a text were made, a dealer lent them out to readers for a fee. If it proved to be popular, additional copies were made to keep up with demand. Owners of printing presses did not solicit original material but took handwritten works that were already successful and made print versions of them to be lent out or sold. If a particular work continued to be popular over an extended period of time, producers of both handwritten and printed texts put out abbreviated versions to save money in the cost of production (shorter texts required fewer sheets of paper). So the long-term success of a work like *The Story of Hong Gildong* can be gauged by the existence of many variant manuscripts of different lengths, of which thirty-four have survived. Such market practices are the reason scholars have pointed to the longest extant handwritten version, the *pilsa* Kim Donguk 89, as the oldest one that is either a copy of the original work or closest to it. (See appendix for details on the extant manuscripts of *The Story of Hong Gildong*.)

Lee Yoon Suk has discovered three significant lists of such commercial fiction that enjoyed popularity in the late eighteenth to the mid–nineteenth centuries. They can be found in the Japanese *Shōsho Kibun* (Notes of interpreters), a record of information provided by foreign emissaries compiled by Oda Ikugoro in 1794; in the collected writings of the poet Jo Sunam (1762–1849); and in the notes to Hong Huibok's *A Singular Tale of Marvel* (*Jaeil giyeon*), a translation completed sometime between 1835 and 1848 of the Chinese novel *Flowers in the Mirror* (*Jing huayuan*) by the Qing-dynasty writer Li Ruzhen.[37] Together they name no fewer than twenty-seven works that were known at the time. Lee notes that *The Story of Hong Gildong* does not appear in any of the lists, which points to the possibility that it was not available until the second half of the nineteenth century.

To reiterate some points made in the last chapter, a number of Joseon writers from the seventeenth century onward made references to a work entitled *The Story of Hong Gildong* written by Heo Gyun, but all of them were essentially quoting Yi Sik's original assertion, and none of them provided any evidence that Yi or anyone else had actually read or even seen the writing. The very first independent testimony of the existence of a popular fiction of the title does not appear until 1876, in the introduction to an edition of the martial narrative (*gundam*) *Record of the Black Dragon Year*,[38] in which the following description is found: "There are tales of old times that are widely known from town to town, about people like So Daeseong, Jo Ung, Hong Gildong, and Jeon Uchi. Each of those books was written in the *eonmun* script [vulgar script, i.e., *hangeul*] and narrates the life story of a single character."[39]

While it is possible that *The Story of Hong Gildong* was written at an earlier time but did not become popular until the mid–nineteenth century, there is no evidence of anyone being familiar with its content before 1876. It must also be remembered that with only a few exceptions, all surviving manuscripts of Joseon prose fiction are from the nineteenth or early twentieth century, even of writings that are known to have been composed significantly earlier. In the case of *The Story of Hong Gildong,* among the thirty-four extant manuscripts, only fourteen handwritten manuscripts and one printed text indicate the date of publication, and the earliest one that does (the Yi Gawon 21) comes from the year 1893, though the *gyeongpan* 30 can definitively be dated to 1892 or slightly earlier.[40]

Kim Taejun asserts that the era of Joseon popular fiction began in the early 1600s, pointing to *The Story of Hong Gildong* as a prime example. In fact, the two assertions about the beginning of popular fiction and the traditional dating of *The Story of Hong Gildong* are used to support each other in a circular manner (dating the work to the early seventeenth century based on the notion of the rise of popular fiction at the time, then using the work as evidence of the rise of popular fiction in the early seventeenth century). As pointed out before, a sufficient readership and a market for popular fiction developed only in the late eighteenth century. There were many types of such writings produced in this period, including romances like *The Story of Chunhyang* (*Chunhyang jeon*); family narratives like *Record of Three Generations of the Yu Family* (*Yussi samdae rok*) and *Record of Three Generations of the Jo Family* (*Jossi samdae rok*); literary renderings of folktales like *The Story of Heungbu* (*Heungbu jeon*), *The Story of Sim Cheong* (*Sim Cheong jeon*), and *The Story of the Rabbit* (*Tokki jeon*); and martial narratives like *Record of the Black Dragon Year.* A genre related to the last is the heroic narrative, featuring a single protagonist of extraordinary talent and power who engages in a series of conflicts with various antagonists. Examples of such works are *The Story of Jo Ung* (*Jo Ung jeon*), *The Story of So Daesong* (*So Daeseong jeon*), *The Story of Yu Chungryeol* (*Yu Chungryeol jeon*), and *The Story of Jeon Uchi* (*Jeon Uchi jeon*). Some general characteristics of the genre of heroic narrative are as follows:

Writing Format: Because such commercial works were all written by anonymous writers and surviving manuscripts date from the nineteenth and early twentieth centuries, it is difficult in many cases to affirm definitively whether they were composed in literary Chinese or the phonetic script. While almost all *yangban* prose fiction was in literary Chinese, there is good evidence that a significant amount of the new type of fiction was originally written in *hangeul*, indicating that they were produced for the readership of commoners.

Background: Like traditional *yangban* fiction, many of these new works take place in China, with Chinese characters—for example, *The Story of Jo Ung* during the Song dynasty and *The Story of So Daeseong* and *The Story of Yu Chungryeol* during the Ming. But many also take place in Korea. This is related to martial narratives set in the time of actual wars in the country, like *Record of the Black Dragon Year* (the Japanese invasion of 1592–1598), *The Story of Lady Bak* (*Bakssi jeon*—the Manchu invasions of 1627 and 1636), and *Record of the White Sheep Year* (*Sinmi rok*—the Hong Gyeongnae Rebellion of 1812).

Plot: The genre narrates the adventures of a heroic individual with martial prowess and/or magical powers. They feature detailed scenes of combat, of the hero fighting by himself against various enemies and/or leading an army in a full-scale battle.

Theme: Traditional moral principles of Confucianism such as loyalty to the monarch, filial piety, and spousal fidelity are featured in the works, but in contrast to traditional *yangban* fiction, the demonstration of such virtues is secondary to the unfolding of exciting actions at the foreground of the narratives. The heroes are indeed moral exemplars who defend the country, right wrongs, and remain faithful through adversity, but they draw admiration primarily through the display of extraordinary talent and power, especially in situations of physical conflict. In other words, they are heroic in martial prowess first and moral character second. Some of them even contravene traditional morals and propriety, as when the sorcerer Jeon Uchi (from *The Story of Jeon Uchi*), in a manner reminiscent of Hong Gildong, tricks a Goryeo-dynasty king into giving him a pillar of gold and then, when his subterfuge is discovered, uses his magical powers to elude various attempts by the authorities to capture him.[41] The motif of challenging corrupt and abusive people in power provides the stories with a critical attitude toward the social and political status quo that secondary- and commoner-status people would have identified with.

Given that such popular fictions from the late eighteenth and nineteenth centuries were written anonymously, not one individual has been identified as the author of any particular work. As already mentioned, such writers were in all probability from secondary or commoner backgrounds who wrote for profit rather than to display their literary abilities. It is not beyond the realm of possibility that the author of a work like *The Story of Hong Gildong* was a lapsed *yangban* who had to resort to writing for money. But it is highly unlikely that a nobleman of good standing would have engaged in producing narratives in a genre that he would have regarded as lowly both for its literary quality and its commercial nature. This is all the more the case given the probability that *The Story of Hong Gildong* was originally composed in *hangeul*, which the *yangban* only used for study guides and private correspondences. As previously pointed out, every tradition of *hangeul* fiction written by a *yangban* writer, including Heo Gyun's purported authorship of *The Story of Hong Gildong* and the notion that Kim Manjung wrote *Nine Cloud Dream* and *Lady Sa's Journey South* in the phonetic script for his mother, is based on flimsy or implausible evidence. While one cannot say for certain that no *yangban* writer ever wrote original prose fiction in what he would have called the vulgar script, there really is no definitive evidence of such a practice until the end of the Joseon dynasty. Furthermore, if one examines prose tales written by the *yangban* in literary Chinese, they read very differently from the late commercial fiction. One such writer whose fictions have been compared to *The Story of Hong Gildong* is Bak Jiwon (1737–1805), a reformist philosopher of the *sirhak* (practical learning) school.[42] While his satirical tales, especially *The Story of Scholar Heo* (*Heo saeng jeon*), share some common themes with *The Story of Hong Gildong* in the appearance of bandits and the critique of corrupt officials, they are all significantly shorter and overtly moralistic.[43] In fact, they closely resemble Heo Gyun's five extant biographical sketches, that is, as part of the genre of the didactic tale written in the satirical or allegorical mode. Neither Heo nor Bak, nor any other *yangban* writer for that matter, is known to have produced the kind of extended and descriptive narrative of heroic adventures written primarily for the purpose of popular entertainment. All historical evidence points to the fact that such works were written, produced, commercialized, and consumed in the milieu of literate secondary- and commoner-status people.[44]

For those unfamiliar with traditional East Asian literature, the numerous references in *The Story of Hong Gildong* to Chinese history, philosophy, and literature may give the impression that the writer was a highly educated person. But most of the allusions, such as the idyllic state of affairs under the rule of the ancient monarchs Yao and Shun, the literary prowess of the poets Li Tai Bai and Du Mu, and the assassination attempt on the king of Qin by Jing Ke, were so well known that you did not have to be a particularly learned intellectual to be familiar with them. Comparable examples would be a Western writer's use of Helen of Troy as the symbol of supreme feminine beauty or Alexander the Great as the archetype of a military genius. Familiarity with these figures would indicate some education but not necessarily a high level.

Recently, Jang Hyo-hyon has presented a new argument for the extant *The Story of Hong Gildong* being substantially the work of Heo Gyun, but with additions and revisions that were made in the following centuries that explain certain anachronisms in it.[45] Jang's assertions are worth analyzing in detail as an example of persistent attempts by contemporary scholars to preserve the traditional attribution. The central evidence for his theory is a fascinating legend about Hong Gildong that is related in a mid-eighteenth-century work.

The scholar Hong Manjung (1643–1725) produced a work entitled *Extraordinary Events of Haedong* (*Haedong ijeok*—"Haedong" being an ancient name for Korea), a collection of biographical sketches of extraordinary people from both legend and history. In the following generation, Hwang Yunseok (1729–1791) added sixty-three new sketches to Hong's thirty-eight in the new edition of the work, *Enlarged Edition of Extraordinary Events of Haedong* (*Jeungbo Haedong ijeok*). In one of Hwang's additions, Hong Gildong makes an appearance.

> I have once heard that in the mid-period of the Joseon dynasty there lived a person by the name of Hong Gildong who was an illegitimate younger half-brother of High Minister Hong Ildong, who lived in Achagok of Jangseong County. He was confident in his talent and vigor which made him magnanimous in spirit, but due to his status as a secondary son the laws of the land prevented him from pursuing distinction through the attainment of a government position. So he suddenly ran away one morning. At a future time, an emissary returning from Ming China said that an envoy from a country across the sea came to Beijing, bearing a letter from the king of that country whose family name was Gong. The *gong* had the ideogram *su* beneath it, so what kind of a character was this? One might suspect that perhaps this was a subtle mixing up of the character "Hong" by Gildong.[46]

The last sentences can be explained only by showing the Chinese characters that were used. The name Hong is represented by the ideogram 洪, which is a combination of the character *gong*—共 (together) and the radical of the character *su*—水 (water) on its side. In this legend, the foreign king's name is Gong, which is written in an unusual way, with *su* placed below *gong* instead of on the side, like so—

to form a unique ideogram. It is, in fact, such a strange character that it arouses the speculation that Hong Gildong created it to mask his true name. The legend goes on:

Gildong then suddenly appeared, coming alone on a horse to see Ildong and to congratulate him on his birthday. He stayed with him for a few days, but when it came time for him to leave, he wept and said, "Once I go, I will never be able to return," before he quickly departed. Given the overall grandness of his character and the restlessness of his actions, he must have resolved never to live beneath the power of another, so he ran away to some foreign place where he made himself king.

The passage concludes, "Some people have said that the story made up by Heo Gyun cannot be trusted, so how could this tale be believed?"[47]

Jang Hyo-hyon, in his analyses of this legend, points to three elements that relate it to *The Story of Hong Gildong*: First, the discrimination that Hong Gildong experiences as a secondary child motivates him to run away. Second, Hong Gildong becomes the king of a foreign country. Third, Hong Gildong returns home for a visit.[48] Based on these similarities, Jang concludes not only that *The Story of Hong Gildong* was written significantly earlier than the mid–nineteenth century but also that Heo Gyun wrote the original version, which was altered and supplemented over the following centuries. In other words, the extant work is substantially the work of Heo Gyun, and all anachronistic elements in it (including the mention of Jang Gilsan, a historical outlaw who lived decades after Heo Gyun's death) can be explained as later corruptions and additions. But a close examination of the legend in *Enlarged Edition of Extraordinary Events of Haedong* makes the argument problematic on several levels.

Despite the three points of similarity between the legend and the fictional work, there is the glaring problem, briefly acknowledged by Jang,[49] of the complete absence of any mention of Hong Gildong's activities as an outlaw. According to Yi Sik, Heo Gyun wrote *The Story of Hong Gildong* in imitation of the Chinese bandit epic *Water Margin*. But in this legend Hong leaves home and disappears completely without committing any crime, until he makes his royalty known at the imperial court of Ming China (not the royal court of Joseon, as related in *The Story of Hong Gildong*).

One fascinating element of the legend is that Hong Gildong is identified as the illegitimate half-brother of Hong Ildong (in different versions of *The Story of Hong Gildong*, the name of the brother is Ilhyeong, Inhyeong, Inhyeon, or Gilheyon) of Jangseong County, who was a real-life figure, a government minister who died in 1464. Hong Ildong's father was Hong Sangjik, who was also a high minister whose death is referred to in the *Sillok* record of 1428, in which it is noted that his widow has completed her mourning period, which puts the year of his death at 1426 at the latest.[50] This presents a major problem for those attempting to link the secondary son of the legend, the historical bandit, and the fictional character of *The Story of Hong Gildong*. If Heo Gyun did write the work with the historical outlaw in mind, and if that outlaw was the illegitimate half-brother of Hong Ildong, then he could not have been born after 1426. This means that when Hong Gildong was captured in 1500, the youngest age he could have been was seventy-four. The very idea of a bandit leader in his seventies running around committing crimes in fifteenth-century Joseon is so absurd that it suggests an alternate explanation. If the legend of the secondary son by the name of Hong Gildong who ran away from home has any basis in history, the illegitimate son of High Minister Hong Sangjik was in all probability a different person altogether from the bandit leader captured in 1500. One piece of evidence for this is the fact that their homophonic names were written in varying Chinese characters. The name of the bandit leader who appears in the *Sillok* is written as 洪吉同, with the third character of *dong* written with the ideogram for "same," while the secondary son in *Enlarged Edition of Extraordinary Events of Haedong* is identified as 洪吉童, with the last ideogram for "child." These alternate characters show up in different versions of *The Story of Hong Gildong*. The majority of the manuscripts write the name as 洪吉童, but two, including the *pilsa* 89, write it as 洪吉同, and one, the recently discovered *wanpan* 34, writes it idiosyncratically as 洪吉東 (the last character meaning "east"). One reasonable speculation that can be made is that the plot of *The Story of Hong Gildong* is a conflation of two distinct legends, one about the illegitimate son of a high minister who ran away eventually to become the king of a foreign country and the other about a bandit leader who committed his crimes sometimes in the guise of a government official. In other words, the fictional Hong Gildong could very well have been inspired by stories of two different people with the same-sounding name. It is also possible that the true (nineteenth-century) writer of *The Story of Hong Gildong* got the plot elements directly from *Enlarged Edition of Extraordinary Events of Haedong* and combined them with separate tales of the heroic bandit, giving the outlaw the background of a secondary son from the household of a high minister.

It is unclear how the legend supports Jang Hyo-hyon's view that *The Story of Hong Gildong* is substantially the work of Heo Gyun. A close reading of the passage in *Enlarged Edition of Extraordinary Events of Haedong* reveals that there is a great deal of uncertainty in the relationship between the legend and Heo's supposed authorship. The opening of Hwang Yunseok's account makes it clear that he is relating a story he once heard, not something he read as Heo Gyun's writing. And the wording of Hwang's point that "Some people have said that the story made up by Heo cannot be trusted" makes it impossible to tell if people thought that there was something about Heo Gyun's writing on Hong Gildong that made it suspect or if they thought it could not be believed because of the untrustworthiness of Heo himself. It is probably the latter, given the negative depiction of Heo Gyun's character in Yi Sik's writing. This complicates the question of the exact relationship between the legend and Heo Gyun.

What is apparent is that Hwang Yunseok, like every Joseon writer after Yi Sik who repeated his claim that Heo authored a work entitled *The Story of Hong Gildong*, had neither read nor seen the work himself. The story is presented as an orally transmitted one. By bringing up Heo Gyun, Hwang implies that the legend has its basis in a work Heo is reputed to have written. As mentioned in the last chapter, it is possible that Heo did write a work about Hong Gildong, which has become lost. If Hwang's legend comes from Heo's lost story, its content must have differed significantly from the existing *The Story of Hong Gildong*, since it does not involve the protagonist's role as an outlaw. But if Heo's work was only about a secondary son who runs away and becomes the king of a foreign country, that contradicts Yi Sik's claim that Heo wrote *The Story of Hong Gildong* in imitation of *Water Margin*, which is all about heroic outlaws. It is apparent that such confusions are the result of a wholly unnecessary and ultimately futile attempt to establish a viable historical link among the disparate elements of the legend of Hong Sangjik's secondary son, whose existence cannot be proven, the historical bandit Hong Gildong, about whom little is known, Heo Gyun's writing on Hong Gildong, which may or may not have existed, and the extant work *The Story of Hong Gildong*. In all likelihood, the legend in *Enlarged Edition of Extraordinary Events of Haedong* is a traditional tale about the illustrious Hong family of Jangseong County that is unrelated to the bandit who was captured in 1500, which Hwang unthinkingly associated with Yi Sik's claim that Heo Gyun had authored a story about the outlaw Hong Gildong.

Those who want to hold onto the notion of Hwang Yunseok's account of the legend as historical evidence of Heo Gyun's authorship might accuse me of minimizing the significance of the three plot elements that it shares with *The Story of Hong Gildong*, namely, Hong's frustration as a secondary child, his rise to the kingship of a foreign country, and his subsequent visit home. Even if one were to set aside the essential differences between the two narratives, it is inadvisable to draw a connection between the two texts solely on the basis of superficial similarities in plot.

To illustrate this point, I ask the reader to indulge me in an extended hypothetical scenario. Suppose that the play *Doctor Faustus* by the Elizabethan playwright Christopher Marlowe (1564–1593, a contemporary of Heo Gyun) became lost in the early seventeenth century and that the knowledge that it once existed was preserved in a single contemporary record that provides a brief description of its plot—"Marlowe wrote a play about the alchemist Faustus, who sells his soul to the devil Mephostophilis for knowledge and ends up being damned for it." Suppose, then, that in the late nineteenth century a discovery is made of a play in German called *Faust* written by an unknown author (let us say that for some reason Goethe never mentioned the work to anyone and abandoned the manuscript somewhere without writing his name on it). If the fact that Marlowe wrote a play about Faustus was well known among literary scholars through repetition by numerous writers in the course of the seventeenth, eighteenth, and nineteenth centuries, an inept scholar might jump to the conclusion that the newly found work was a German translation of the English play, pointing to the similarities of character names and plot.

Even if the Hong Gildong legend in *Enlarged Edition of Extraordinary Events of Haedong* is derived from a work by Heo Gyun about a runaway secondary son, for which there is no evidence, that does not necessarily lead to the conclusion that the extant *The Story of Hong Gildong* is substantially the work of Heo. One could not possibly consider Goethe's *Faust* to be a German translation or corruption of Marlowe's *Doctor Faustus*, because the two are completely original works of differing styles, themes, and literary contexts. In other words, general similarities in plot and characters cannot be regarded as sufficient evidence for identifying one work with another.

In the hypothetical *Faustus-Faust* situation, for a scholar who is skeptical of the idea that the work is a German rendering of the Marlowe play and suspects that it originated in the nineteenth century, there would be a number of ways to make the case. The notion of translation could be attacked by pointing to rhymes and wordplays that work only in German, indicating that it was originally composed in that language. Also, the play's literary style and philosophical ideas could be shown to be those of a significantly later period than the Elizabethan era. But the most effective way to argue that it is a nineteenth-century work would be to place it in comparative context of other such writings from the time, to demonstrate that while it differs significantly from English drama of the sixteenth century, to the extent of making that dating implausible, it has a great deal in common with German plays of the later period. The same approach could be taken with *The Story of Hong Gildong* in the effort to establish its true historical place.

THE STORY OF HONG GILDONG AS A POPULAR HEROIC NARRATIVE

If Yi Sik had never claimed that Heo Gyun wrote a story entitled *The Story of Hong Gildong*, and if Takahashi Toru and Kim Taejun had not associated Heo with the extant work of that title, scholars attempting to determine the origin of the work would have begun by making comparisons with other narratives of its type. Working free of the idée fixe that it was composed in the seventeenth century by a *yangban* writer, they would have easily identified it as a prime example of the popular heroic martial narratives that began to appear in the late eighteenth century. As previously mentioned, the very first evidence of the work's existence, independent of any reference to Yi Sik's attribution of its authorship to Heo Gyun, did not appear until 1876. Given the demonstrable popularity of the work in the late nineteenth and early twentieth centuries, attested to by the production of so many variant manuscripts of the tale in both handwritten and printed versions, it is reasonable to suppose that the ur-text was written sometime in the middle of the nineteenth century by an anonymous writer of secondary or commoner status who composed it for popular consumption and profit. It is possible that it was written a few decades earlier, but any attempt to place its origin prior to the mid–nineteenth century takes the scholarship into the realm of pure speculation, given the total lack of evidence.

The implausibility of Heo Gyun's authorship of *The Story of Hong Gildong* is not just about the fact that no work of that type was produced in Joseon until the late eighteenth century. The most convincing evidence of the writing being a product of the nineteenth century lies in its close resemblance to other heroic and martial narratives that appeared at the time, in all the aspects of writing format, background, plot, and theme. To give a few among numerous examples, the stories begin with the birth of the hero, which is heralded by a dream vision that visits one of the parents, foretelling the coming of a great personage. This is followed by a description of the birth and the extraordinary talents of the child. In *Record of the Black Dragon Year*, the future mother of Choe Ilgyeong (the fictional hero of the work who acts as a wise and steadfast advisor to the Joseon king throughout the Japanese invasion) has a vision in which Guan Yu (a central character of the Chinese epic *The Three Kingdoms* and a deity associated with war) informs her that the Heavenly Emperor himself is sending down his own child to be born as her son. The description that follows of the young Choe closely resembles that of the young Hong Gildong:

> And indeed she became pregnant from that month on, and after the tenth month gave birth to a precious boy. His appearance was extraordinary and his stature handsome, so [his father] named him Ilgyeong and loved him unceasingly. By the time Ilgyeong was three or four years old, his manners were ten times better than those of an ordinary person. At seven he could comprehend the *Four Books* and the *Three Summaries* and was well versed in the works of various schools of philosophy. He knew astrology, geomancy, and the rise and fall of dynasties from times past—indeed, there was nothing he did not know.[51]

Compare that with similar passages in the *pilsa* 89 version of *The Story of Hong Gildong*:

> And so time passed, through ten lunar months, until . . . Chunseom gave birth to a precious boy whose face was the color of white snow and whose presence was as grand as the autumn moon. He was born with the appearance of a great hero. The minister was delighted and granted him the name of Gildong.
>
> As the boy grew up, he exhibited magnificence in both the strength of his body and the astuteness of his intellect. He only needed to hear one thing to understand ten things, and learning ten things allowed him to master a hundred. He never forgot a single thing he heard or saw just once.[52]

Later on, Hong Gildong also masters the *Four Books* (classics of Confucian philosophy) and the *Three Summaries* (classics of military strategy) and becomes adept at astrology and geomancy. At this point, their life stories diverge, Choe passing the civil examinations and attaining government positions, Hong barred from that course because he is a secondary child.

A similar motif is found in *The Story of Yu Chungryeol*, which tells the story of a Chinese official of the Ming dynasty who is exiled from the imperial court due to court machinations but eventually leads an army to save the empire from foreign invaders. Before his birth, his mother is visited by a heavenly spirit riding a blue dragon who announces the coming of a great child. Indeed, she "became pregnant from that month on, and after the tenth month gave birth to a precious boy."[53] By the time he is seven years old, he displayed "superior strength and extraordinary intelligence," to the extent of exceeding the talents of the historian Sima Qian and the calligrapher Wang Xizhi and rivaling the military theorists Sunzi and Wuzi in cleverness and courage. He also "mastered the arts of astrology and geomancy as well as the *Six Teachings* and the *Three Summaries*, and lacked nothing in his proficiency at horse riding and archery."[54]

The narrative of the sorcerer Jeon Uchi, *The Story of Jeon Uchi*, set in the Goryeo dynasty, also begins with a dream his pregnant mother has of the coming of an extraordinary child, a heavenly spirit who must live as a human for a transgression he committed in the supernatural world. When Uchi is born, he turns out to be such an intelligent child that "he could understand ten things from hearing one."[55] After he outwits a fox woman and gains magical powers by swallowing her soul, he becomes a master of astrology and geomancy, and his writing skills rival that of Li Tai Bai and his calligraphy that of Wang Xizhi.[56] Jeon Uchi is eligible to take the civil examinations because he is the son of an aristocrat, but he is too impatient to go the respectable route of a government official. Instead, he appears before the king in the guise of a heavenly spirit and demands a pillar of gold from the monarch. After Jeon receives the treasure and sells off a part of it to support his widowed mother, his trickery is discovered by officials, who report it to the king, resulting in the ordering of his arrest. As with Hong Gildong, Jeon pretends to surrender to soldiers but then escapes from them using magic, which infuriates the king. After a few deeds of helping impoverished and unjustly persecuted people, Jeon suddenly appears before the monarch to beg forgiveness for his transgressions. The king, fearing that Jeon will use his magic again, decides not to punish him, instead granting him a government position, so he will cause no more trouble. This is reminiscent of Hong Gildong promising to stop his outlaw activities if he is made the minister of military affairs. In an ensuing episode that is interesting for its similarities as well as differences from *The Story of Hong Gildong*, a bandit leader named Yeon Jun causes a great deal of disturbance in the provinces, prompting the king to ask who among his officials will step forward and handle the crisis.[57] Just as Yi Heop, the commander of the Police Bureau, volunteers to capture Hong Gildong, Jeon Uchi takes on the task. The ensuing conflict between Jeon and Yeon Jun plays out in a similar manner as parts of *The Story of Hong Gildong*, except in this case the hero uses his magical powers to capture the bandits, including creating an illusory doppelgänger to confuse the enemy. Jeon and Yeon ultimately fight a duel, described in terms that resemble the fight between Hong Gildong and the king of Yul Island. When Yeon and his outlaws are defeated, however, Jeon forgives their crimes and allows them to go home after they swear to become peasants and loyal subjects of the king. Although Jeon is lauded for his achievement, he eventually loses the trust of his monarch after his enemies falsely accuse him of treason. Jeon eludes capture again and leaves the capital in disgust before playing another Hong Gildong–like magic trick of making 360 people look exactly like him, leading to the arrest of all of them and utter confusion at court. At the end of the story, he meets a sage who is even more knowledgeable and powerful than himself and, like Hong Gildong again, retires with him on a mountain to live as an immortal spirit. Kim Taejun found *The Story of Jeon Uchi* so similar to *The Story of Hong Gildong* that he speculated that they were written by the same author (that is, Heo Gyun).[58]

In addition to such similarities in plot, theme, and narrative structure, there are many specific images and descriptive conventions that the authors of the stories borrowed freely from one another. In *Record of the Black Dragon Year*, the Chinese general Yi Yeosong (Korean for Li Rusong, 1564–1598, loosely based on the historical general who led the Ming army into Joseon to fight the Japanese) decides to deplete the geomantic power of Joseon by destroying the vital centers of its mountains. In the midst of the effort, he is lured deep into a mountain by an old man on an ox and meets a boy dressed in a blue robe, which is how Hong Gildong appears to lure Yi Heup to his lair. Yi Yeosong gets into an argument and then a physical confrontation with the boy, who appears to him in a magical manner—"The boy in the blue robe rode a crane and danced with jasper flowers on his head. In his hand was a jade flute which he played as he sat in a decorous manner."[59] In *The Story of Hong Gildong*, when the assassin Teukje comes to murder him, Hong appears to him playing a jade flute, and in the *wanpan* version he is also riding a white crane. Many descriptions of war, in works including *Record of the Black Dragon Year*, *The Story of Yu Chungryeol*, *The Story of Jo Ung*, and *The Story of So Daeseong*, also bear close resemblance to the battle for Yul Island in *The Story of Hong Gildong*.

When *The Story of Hong Gildong* is compared with the heroic and martial narratives that began to appear in the late eighteenth century, becoming popular in the nineteenth, it is striking how naturally the work fits in among them. Once a scholar's perspective is freed from the traditional idée fixe that it was written by a *yangban* writer in the seventeenth century, placing its true origin close to the first mention of the work in 1876 becomes plausible. With the proper historical place of *The Story of Hong Gildong* established in the mid–nineteenth century, we can delve further into the text itself to gain a deeper understanding of its content. I will do so first by examining the heroic status of Hong Gildong and then by engaging in a comparative analysis with the archetypal image of the noble robber described by Eric Hobsbawm.

THE HEROIC STATUS OF HONG GILDONG

For Kim Taejun, Hong Gildong's heroic nature came from his embodiment of the radical ideology of revolution and egalitarianism that his creator, Heo Gyun, endowed in him. Kim, consequently, depicts Hong as a moral exemplar in his struggle against the corrupt and iniquitous status quo on behalf of the common people. Given the implausible nature of such a political reading of the story, can we still speak of Hong Gildong as a heroic character? In modern culture, the concept of a hero is defined by righteousness of actions, even if they are committed in defiance of laws and legal authorities. When *The Story of Hong Gildong* is approached with a fresh perspective, one free of Kim's ideological reading and the influence of the internationally known figure of Robin Hood, the issue of Hong's heroic nature turns out to be rather complicated.

There is no doubt that Hong Gildong is portrayed as a moral figure who is out to help the common people and punish the corrupt. In the *pilsa* 89 version, after Hong successfully leads the raid on Haein Temple, he tells his followers:

> We will go forth across the eight provinces of Joseon and seize wealth that was ill-gotten, but we will also help the impoverished and the oppressed by giving them goods. . . . We will go after the powerful who obtained their riches by squeezing the common people and take away their unjustly gained possessions.[60]

In the *gyeongpan* 30 version, it is described how Hong led his men

> across the eight provinces of Joseon Kingdom. In every town he came to, if he found out that the local magistrate had ill-gotten gains, he robbed him of his wealth, and if he found people suffering in dire poverty with no one to turn to, he gave them aid. And he made certain that his men did not violate the common people or touch even the slightest amount of property belonging to the country.[61]

It is clear, however, that like the other protagonists of the genre of martial narrative, Hong Gildong's heroic nature comes primarily from his extraordinary powers, ambitions, and successes. In other words, his status as a moral exemplar is secondary to the predominant portrait of a powerful magician, warrior, and leader who is able to steal from well-guarded places, elude capture by soldiers, and defeat an army in battle. In many modern revisions of his story, discussed in the next three chapters, Hong is moved to act by the plight of the common people, whose poverty and oppression are unaddressed by indifferent and rapacious authorities. In *The Story of Hong Gildong*, it is apparent that he is motivated primarily by personal frustration at not being able to pursue a respectable career in the government. The acts of social good that he commits mimic the work of a responsible official, as when he goes about in the guise of a government inspector to punish corrupt magistrates and send reports of his deeds to the king. In other words, Hong's deepest desire is to demonstrate his talents by working within the established social and political system. As he is prevented from doing so because of his social status, he resorts to play-acting the righteous official he could have been. This is evidenced by his ultimate price for ending his criminal activities, namely, a royal appointment to a ministerial position, not the addressing of a social problem that is causing misery to the common people, not even the kingdom's discriminatory policy on secondary offspring. In fact, once Hong receives recognition from the king, he seems to forget his frustration as a *seoja* completely. Instead of using his newly acquired official power to effect any kind of social or political reform in the country, he supports the status quo by removing himself and his band of outlaws from the kingdom. And when he establishes his own realm, he replicates the Joseon political and social system, including all the trappings of a traditional monarchy.

Such aspects of the plot make it problematic to read *The Story of Hong Gildong* as a work of radical politics. As previously discussed, this is not to say that the story is devoid of real criticisms of Joseon society. But *The Story of Hong Gildong* was written for popular consumption at a time when there was sufficient readership to make such a venture potentially profitable for the writer, printer, and distributor. As such, its primary purpose was to entertain. There is no doubt that it features elements of traditional values, and it also depicts social conditions that readers of secondary and commoner status would have found moving, infuriating, and inspirational. But any political and social perspectives, subversive or conservative, that a scholar may legitimately discern in the work have to be understood as plot devices and triggers of emotional identification that are used to keep the reader engaged. Hong Gildong does act in a beneficial way for the common people, but he is presented as a hero primarily for his demonstration of marvelous powers, through which he is able to overcome the circumstances of his early life and achieve great things.

Many modern interpreters, however, have held onto Kim Taejun's notion of Hong Gildong as a moral exemplar, characterizing him as a champion of the oppressed and the impoverished. This has led some of them to alter the text or add new passages in modern retellings of the story, to provide moral justifications for some of Hong Gildong's actions. The most egregious cases of such distortions can be found in recent English-language versions. For instance, the first act that Hong commits after he becomes a bandit leader is the raid on the Buddhist temple of Haein. In both the *pilsa* and the *gyeongpan* versions, no rationale is given for attacking the place other than the fact that it has much treasures to steal. It was targeted for the same reason that the American outlaw Willie Sutton, apocryphally, gave for robbing banks: "Because that's where the money is." It is after the successful raid that Hong declares that they will not go after the property of the common people or the government's legitimately collected tax money and goods. In the *wanpan* version, when Hong justifies the plundering of Haein Temple to the king, he delivers a rant against the practitioners of Buddhism.

> Buddhism is a pack of lies for the monks to fool the world with, to delude the common people, to take away their grain without doing any farming themselves, to wear clothes made by them without doing any weaving themselves, to damage the hair and skin they inherited from their parents and go about like the barbarians of the north, to abandon their king and their fathers to steal tax money. So are they not guilty of the greatest crime of all?[62]

This provides a moral justification of a sort, but later revisionists have tended to emphasize the corruption of the monks without having Hong express such animosity toward Buddhism itself. In Horace Newton Allen's loose English rendering of the story (1889), the temple is described as one that was "well patronized by officials, who made it a place of retirement for pleasure and debauch, and in return the lazy, licentious priests were allowed to collect tribute from the poor people about, till they had become rich and powerful."[63] Two recent English-language children's books on Hong Gildong feature similar distortions. In the bilingual *Brave Hong Kil-dong* by Kim Youg-kol (1990), Hong Gildong wonders how the temple can be so rich and accuses the monks, "I don't think you got them honestly."[64] Anne Sibley O'Brien makes up a new scene in which some commoners come to Hong for help because "It is the monks of Hae In Temple. Every month they demand tribute. They have taken nearly everything we have. If we give more we will have nothing left for the winter."[65] In fact, almost every modern retelling of the story features two scenes that do not appear in the original text at all, one of the people supplicating Hong Gildong for relief from oppression and poverty and the other of Hong and his band distributing their loot to the people. Such additions in modern works bolster the morality of Hong's actions but depart from the significance of the original text. In addition, one can discern the modern influence of the Robin Hood story in the scenes of taking from the rich to give to the poor.

But the episode in *The Story of Hong Gildong* that poses the greatest problem for the characterization of Hong Gildong as a moral exemplar is the one on Yul Island. In many summaries and retellings, the circumstances under which he leads an army to the place is either erased or distorted. What is apparent in the text itself is that after Hong successfully settles his bandits and their families on Jae Island, he launches an unprovoked invasion of Yul for the purpose of conquest and personal glory. In the discussion with his generals, it is made clear that they are going to start the war not out of moral imperative or practical need but because it will provide them with the opportunity to demonstrate their military prowess and masculine strength. The *wanpan* version of the story overtly states that Hong planned the invasion out of a desire to become a king, as he declares to his generals, "Why should this be the only island we rule over?"[66] In the *pilsa* 89 version, one of his generals agrees to the course by replying, "How can a true man find contentment in growing old while leading a leisurely and mediocre life?"[67]

The lack of any moral dimension to the enterprise is further evidenced by the fact that in both the *pilsa* and the *wanpan* versions Yul Island is portrayed as a peaceful and prosperous country with competent and benevolent rulers. It is also emphasized that the place is an independent state not subordinate to any foreign power, a criticism of Joseon's tributary relationship to China. *Pilsa*: "There was an island country near Jae, and its name was Yul. Its land stretched out for tens of thousands of *ri*, its provinces managed by no less than twelve governors. It did not pay fealty to a greater country and its rulers governed with benevolence from one generation to another, so the country was wealthy and its people lived in peace."[68] *Gyeongpan*: "There was an island country called Yul, a place of thousands of *ri* which featured sloping hills that formed a vast natural fortress protecting a highly fertile land. Gildong had always kept the place in mind as he harbored a desire to become a king."[69] *Wanpan*: "There was a country nearby, an island country called Yul. It never submitted itself to the rule of China, and the tens of generations of its rulers became well known for their virtues, through which the land was at peace and the people lived in plenty."[70] There is only one version of *The Story of Hong Gildong* that deviates from such descriptions.

In a three-volume handwritten text that was found in Japan, at the Tōyō bunko library in Tokyo, it is written that "Because the king of Yul Island lacked virtue, he neglected his administrative duties and indulged himself with liquor and women, resulting in his people falling into dire poverty."[71] This is a rather late text of 1901 and contains many new additions, especially in the descriptions of battle on Yul Island. Since such a negative portrayal of the condition on Yul Island cannot be found in any other text, it appears to be an attempt by a later writer to provide a moral justification for the invasion, albeit a rather feeble one. Even in this version, addressing the plight of the island's people is not presented as Hong's motivation for launching his attack.

Kim Taejun, in his summary of the plot, does not mention the invasion at all, concluding only that Hong Gildong creates an ideal country on Yul Island. Every modern commentator I mentioned earlier in this chapter who, inappropriately, described Hong's realm as a "utopia" also neglects to reveal the circumstances under which he comes to rule over the island. In Horace Newton Allen's rendering, it is mentioned in one line—"Other outlying islands were united under Kil Tong's rule, and no desire or ambition remained ungratified."[72] Zŏng In-sŏb, in his 1952 *Folk Tales from Korea*, invents a new justification for the invasion that is not found in any versions of *The Story of Hong Gildong*: "When [Hong's] period of mourning was over he turned his attention to the problem presented by the neighboring kingdom of Yug-Do [*sic*]. It was a wealthy and powerful country, and presented a serious threat to the people of his island."[73] The bilingual children's book *Brave Hong Kil-dong* ends with the statement that "Kildong then gathered his band of men and led them across the ocean to a small island. He founded a new nation there which he named Land of Laws [one of the meanings of the Chinese character *yul*, 律, is 'law,' though in the original story Hong does not name the island]. He worked hard for justice and lived happily ever after."[74] Anne Sibley O'Brien concludes *The Legend of Hong Kil Dong* with the invented utopian description of Hong's island realm, with no mention of the war: "It is said that KIL DONG and his men sailed to an island where they made a just society with KIL DONG as its ruler, a society in which men advanced by skill and virtue, not by parentage."[75] A recent Korean retelling by Jeon Jongmok in an illustrated book for juvenile readership repeats the passage from the Tōyō bunko version: "South of Jae Island, there was a country of Yul Island which was wide and wealthy. After a long period of peace, however, the king of Yul Island began to indulge in extravagance and ceased looking after his country."[76]

The unprovoked invasion of Yul Island poses a problem for those who would interpret Hong Gildong's heroic nature as that of a moral exemplar. That does not mean that it would be wrong to regard Hong Gildong as a heroic figure at all. There is no question that he fits in perfectly among the protagonists of the genre of heroic and martial fiction, but primarily on the basis of his talents, ambitions, and triumphs. The purpose of the description of the war on Yul Island is obviously to demonstrate Hong's prowess as a military commander.

It is important to understand the heroic nature of Hong Gildong as he appears in the work, apart from the way he has been interpreted by modern scholars with a political agenda, such as Kim Taejun, or by reading Hong Gildong under the influence of Robin Hood. That is not to say, however, that considering his story in archetypal terms would necessarily result in distortions and simplifications. In fact, analyzing the work in view of cross-cultural narratives of the noble robber, as articulated by Eric Hobsbawm, could yield significant insights into the work, as long as careful attention is paid to ways in which it both shares in universal themes and departs from them.

HONG GILDONG AS A NOBLE ROBBER

Ever since Eric Hobsbawm pioneered the study of "social banditry" with his 1959 work *Primitive Rebels* and his 1969 *Bandits*, his ideas have come under some criticism variously on the questions of the subversive or conservative nature of premodern outlawry, of the discrepancies between the actions of legendary outlaws and the behavior of actual bandits, and of how actually widespread the phenomenon of social banditry was.[77] In response, Hobsbawm elaborated on the complex relationship between various historical bandits and the political structures they operated under and clarified the distinction between the legends of outlaws and the historical reality of banditry.[78] Despite the critical nature of many works on historical and legendary outlaws that have appeared since the publication of Hobsbawm's works, his ideas have continued to provide useful insights into the phenomenon.[79]

Among the different types of social bandits described by Hobsbawm, the one that can be applied to Hong Gildong is the "noble robber." In the following use of the nine-point characterization of the figure from the book *Bandits*, it is not my purpose to try to fit the Korean literary figure into the mold or to assert that Hobsbawm's ideas provide the best way of understanding *The Story of Hong Gildong*. I utilize his list for a general descriptive purpose rather than as a set of absolute qualifications a figure must meet in order to be considered a righteous outlaw. In fact, the characteristics that do not apply to Hong Gildong are just as important in drawing out significant themes of the narrative. This comparative exercise seeks to demonstrate the ways in which *The Story of Hong Gildong* is simultaneously a quintessential work of popular fiction from nineteenth-century Joseon and a narrative that partakes in the international tradition of the noble robber.

In Hobsbawm's *Bandits*, the figure of the noble robber is given the following characteristics:

> First, the noble-robber begins his career of outlawry not by crime, but as the victim of injustice, or through being persecuted by the authorities for some act which they, but not the custom of his people, consider as criminal.
>
> Second, he "rights wrongs."
>
> Third, he "takes from the rich to give to the poor."
>
> Fourth, he "never kills but in self-defence or just revenge."
>
> Fifth, if he survives, he returns to his people as an honourable citizen and member of the community. Indeed, he never actually leaves the community.
>
> Sixth, he is admired, helped and supported by his people.
>
> Seventh, he dies invariably and only through treason, since no decent member of the community would help the authorities against him.
>
> Eighth, he is—at least in theory—invisible and invulnerable.
>
> Ninth, he is not the enemy of the king or the emperor, who is the fount of justice, but only of the local gentry, clergy or other oppressors.[80]

Let us examine *The Story of Hong Gildong* in terms of each point.

1. *The noble-robber begins his career of outlawry not by crime, but as the victim of injustice, or through being persecuted by the authorities for some act which they, but not the custom of his people, consider as criminal.* This characteristic seems to fit Hong Gildong's story very well, since the hero regards himself as a victim of both injustice and persecution at the beginning of the narrative. He feels that it is unjust that despite his considerable talents he is not allowed to pursue his ambitions in government service. The situation is in contradiction to the traditional Confucian principle of meritocracy, which makes Hong's discontent legitimate rather than seditious. He also becomes the target of a nefarious conspiracy by his father's senior concubine, who hires an assassin to murder him. Once Hong kills the assassin as well as the conspiring shaman and physiognomist, he has no choice but to leave home, as he will surely be arrested and bring shame upon the household for committing what are, in his view, acts of self-defense. One could question, however, whether this narrative fits exactly into what Hobsbawm had in mind.

Usually the injustice and persecution the hero is subjected to have a larger social significance, in the sense that he is the victim of a wrong that is suffered by the common people of his milieu, typically through the abuse of power on the part of local authorities. So the people not only identify with the plight and frustration of the protagonist but also approve of his acts of defiance, which, in their view, are not criminal in nature. One can very well make the case that the discriminatory law against secondary offspring is the larger social wrong that is oppressing Hong. The point can be stretched further to regard the law as representative of all statutes of discrimination against people of secondary, commoner, and lowborn status, which the work is criticizing through the story of a frustrated *seoja*. A close reading of the story makes this interpretation problematic.

The first part of the narrative takes place entirely within the Hong household, as the hero is not even allowed to leave the family compound. There is, consequently, no real representation of the common people as a whole—no group of villagers or townspeople who suffer what the hero suffers, who cheer his acts of resistance, and who later receive help from him and, in return, help him evade the authorities. One could argue that individual members of the Hong family represent sections of the populace, for instance Hong's mother, Chunseom, as the representative of lowborn slaves, but it is difficult to draw much meaning out of such a generalization. What is clear is that Hong Gildong's frustrations are essentially individual in nature, in the sense that his lamentations are always couched in terms of how he, as one talented person, is not allowed to pursue his ambitions. There is no doubt that the moving portrayal of Hong's condition stands as a critique of discriminatory laws toward people of lower status, but the point should not be exaggerated as the central theme of the story when in the rest of the narrative Hong hardly mentions it beyond the repeated declaration that it was his personal frustration that sent him on the course to outlawry. It has to be reiterated yet again that when he becomes the king of his own realm, there is no mention of a policy he institutes that forbids status discrimination.

While the first characteristic of the noble robber fits the case of Hong Gildong, it must be noted that unlike most stories of righteous outlaws, Hong's does not begin in a larger social setting that depicts a conflict between oppressive authority figures and the common people. The first part unfolds like a traditional Joseon family drama dealing with the tensions and conflicts among the members of the household.

2. *He rights wrongs.* Most of Hong Gildong's actions as a bandit leader involve stealing goods from places where they are hoarded, for the purpose of enriching his band and demonstrating his skills as a leader and a strategist. In a conversation with the king, he justifies the taking of gift treasures (*bongsong*) by claiming that they were being sent to "officials

who were conducting their duties in an incompetent manner, and who were squeezing the common people by taking unjust amounts of their goods."[81] One could argue that stealing the treasures from those officials is an act of punishing them for their wrongdoing, but that is not claimed as the main reason for the theft. While Hong makes a clear distinction between legitimate targets of theft (hoarded wealth and goods belonging to corrupt officials) and illegitimate ones (legally collected tax money and goods and the property of the common people), it is not the explicitly moral reason of righting wrongs that is presented as the prime motivation for his band's activities.

The clearest case of Hong acting as a dispenser of justice occurs when he pretends to be a government inspector:

> He also toured the eight provinces, and if he came across a corrupt official, he appeared in the guise of a government inspector and executed the unjust before sending a letter to the king, which read as follows.
> "Your subject Hong Gildong makes a hundred obeisances to Your Majesty. I report that during my tour of the eight provinces, whenever I came across a corrupt official who acted with injustice, who stole the property of the common people, and who lacked benevolence, I have executed him for his crimes." (*Pilsa* 89)[82]
> He also dressed himself up as a government inspector to arrest and summarily execute corrupt and oppressive provincial magistrates. He even went so far as to send reports of his deeds to the king. (*Gyeongpan* 30)[83]

It is significant that he goes to the trouble of mimicking the routine of an actual government inspector who makes rounds of the provinces, metes out punishment to the corrupt, and sends reports of his actions to the king. Hong is certainly committing a serious crime by pretending to be an official, as apparently did the historical outlaw Hong Gildong, but it reveals his desire to be in government service.

3. *He takes from the rich to give to the poor.* As previously pointed out, almost every modern retelling of the story of Hong Gildong features scenes of oppressed and impoverished people seeking the help of Hong and of the redistribution of goods taken from the rich and the corrupt. Despite the fact that Hong gives his outlaws the lofty name of Hwalbindang, there is no such scene in the work. It would be reasonable to speculate that the modern additions are the result of the influence of Robin Hood, the most famous of all noble robbers. Interestingly, the charitable act is a later addition in the Robin Hood tradition as well.

Stephen Knight has shown that the name of the English outlaw first appeared in fourteenth-century writings, but it is only in works from the sixteenth century and after that feature scenes in which he gives away his loot to the people, for instance in the Scottish chronicler John Major's claim that he "would allow no woman to suffer injustice, nor would he spoil the poor, but rather enriched them from the plunder taken from abbots,"[84] and in the ballad *The Noble Fisherman, or, Robin Hood's Preferment*, in which the hero says, "with this gold, for the opprest / An habitation I will build / Where they shall live in peace and rest."[85] In works written prior to 1500, he is a wily trickster who resists authority, not a champion of the poor and the oppressed. If Robin Hood is the exemplary archetypal figure of the noble robber, Hong Gildong should not be disqualified as one because of the absence of the iconic scene of wealth redistribution in his story.

4. *He never kills but in self-defense or just revenge.* This is generally true of Hong Gildong during his time as a bandit leader, as his initial killings of Teukjae, the shaman, and the physiognomist are clearly acts of self-defense and just revenge. One could even justify his execution of corrupt officials as righteous punishment for their abuse of authority. The situation changes drastically, however, when Hong leaves Joseon with his bandits and takes on the role of a military commander. I have already discussed the unprovoked invasion of Yul Island, which results in the death of its king and crown prince, not to mention all the soldiers who perish in the war. Modern readers might also be disturbed by an earlier episode in which he commits what amounts to genocide on the creatures known as the *uldong*. Hong considers them to be evil creatures who do not count as human beings, but the way in which Hong murders the king of the *uldong* through trickery and then proceeds to exterminate all the rest seems rather excessive, even though it is done in order to rescue kidnapped women. It is as if once he leaves Joseon, he stops being a noble robber proper and so is no longer beholden to the rule of justifiable homicide in the lands of monsters and foreigners.

5. *If he survives, he returns to his people as an honorable citizen and member of the community. Indeed, he never actually leaves the community.* Narratives of noble robbers often end with the hero obtaining a pardon from the ultimate authority of the land and returning to his people. He is redeemed from his criminal status and recognized as having been a loyal subject all along. In *A Gest of Robin Hood*, the outlaw is forgiven by the king and even enters into his service but eventually returns to the forest to live with his old companions,[86] and in *Water Margin* the former bandits not only submit themselves to the Chinese emperor but also fight for him as a military unit against foreign invaders.

This point may be *The Story of Hong Gildong*'s most glaring departure from the archetypal narrative of the noble robber, since Hong leaves his home country to settle down in a foreign land. That is true in the literal sense, but it is also possible to interpret the story to allow its conclusion to fit the noble-robber pattern. Because the first part of the narrative takes place entirely within the Hong family compound, there is no larger community of people that provides the social context for the protagonist's transformation into an outlaw. One could assert, then, that since Hong Gildong did not start out with a community in the first place, he cannot return to it.

It could also be argued, however, that Hong is actually part of two communities, that of his extended family and of the elite scholarly class of Joseon. But he occupies a liminal place in both because he cannot participate fully in either. Given his status as a *seoja*, he is a son who cannot even address his father as Father, and he is an educated son of a nobleman who is barred from government service. In the Confucian worldview, there is a close association between the power and authority of the father and the king (that is, the father of all his subjects), so Hong makes an identical lament to both figures about his frustrations as a *seoja*. Unable to obtain what he feels to be his rightful place in the two communities, he leaves both and enters into the mountain lair of bandits and their families, and this becomes his newly adopted community. When he is pardoned by the king and granted the position of minister of military affairs, he is relieved of his lifelong frustration and halts his criminal activities. Despite his recognition as a full member of Joseon's ruling class, however, he must repay the king for his favor by sparing him the embarrassment of having an ex-outlaw for a high-ranking official. So even as he is reintegrated into that community, he has to depart from it. But he compensates for that by creating his own kingdom that replicates the community he had to leave behind.

When Minister Hong is on his deathbed, he tells his older son, "if Gildong should return, then lay aside the practice of separating legitimate children from the illegitimate, and act without discrimination toward him as if he were born of the same mother as you."[87] So after his death, the older son allows Hong Gildong to make the funeral arrangements, including the choice of burial site, and participate fully in the rites, which a secondary son could not usually do in Joseon. This represents Hong's reintegration into the community of his extended family as well.

In this ingenious variation on the theme of the noble robber's ultimate return to his people, Hong becomes fully recognized as a son as well as a ruler, all the while maintaining his place in the adopted community of former bandits and their families. As he then takes the leading role in the funerals of his father, stepmother, and mother, who are buried in his realm, the first community of his extended family is brought both symbolically and physically into the new community of his kingdom, which closes the circle of his former alienation and renegade status. And once the process of the hero's reintegration into the various communities is complete, his story comes to an end.

6. *He is admired, helped, and supported by his people.* In relation to the previous point, this characteristic fits *The Story of Hong Gildong* if the term "his people" is restricted to his community of bandits. While he is constantly praised and regarded with awe by his men, there is no scene of him being admired or supported by the general populace of Joseon. In fact, the only sentence in which regular commoners make an appearance at all is in the description of how the captured Gildong was sent to the capital—"As stories of Gildong's powers were well known, people from every town came out to see him as he was transported through the roads."[88] There is no mention of whether they approved of his actions, and there is no scene of the people helping him in his activities.

7. *He dies invariably and only through treason, since no decent member of the community would help the authorities against him.* This characteristic is not applicable, since Hong Gilding does not die at the hand of another but enjoys a long life before being transformed into an immortal spirit.

8. *He is, at least in theory, invisible and invulnerable.* There is certainly no character in the story who can best him in contests of physical strength, hand-to-hand combat, military strategy, or magical power. True to the tradition, his ability to elude those attempting to entrap him is a skill that is emphasized in the story. The ballad *Robin Hood and Guy of Gisborne* bears an interesting resemblance to the episode involving Yi Heup, the commander of the Police Bureau.[89] In both cases, the hero befriends an antagonist who is out to capture the outlaw, they engage in a friendly competition that the hero wins, and finally the hero reveals his identity as the very outlaw the other is seeking. Hong Gildong shows Yi Heup mercy, but Robin Hood kills Guy.

9. *He is not the enemy of the king or the emperor, who is the fount of justice, but only of the local gentry, clergy, or other oppressors.* This characteristic applies well to *The Story of Hong Gildong*, but it has to be noted that while in *A Gest of Robin Hood* the hero submits himself to the king as soon as the monarch reveals his identity, Hong Gildong initially has a somewhat antagonistic relationship with his sovereign, and he plays a series of infuriating tricks on him. Hong yearns for paternal approval from the king, but the narrative makes it clear that while the monarch may indeed be the

fount of justice, Hong has to push him into making what is, from his perspective, the right decision. Hong repeatedly declares his undying loyalty to the king and points out that it is not his purpose to destabilize the realm, since what he always wanted was to demonstrate his capabilities within the established order. The monarch is neither an absolute nor a perfect authority. Hong has to teach him how to be a wiser and more benevolent ruler. Resorting to illegal acts for the purpose of educating the king is not a legitimate course in the Confucian view, of course, but it is a central tenet of the philosophy that a loyal subject has the duty to correct and encourage his ruler into making proper moral decisions.

To summarize, *The Story of Hong Gildong* is not only one of the best prose narratives produced during the Joseon dynasty, but it is also the finest example of popular fiction that began to appear in the late eighteenth century, in the context of the expansion of the common people's wealth, social mobility, and literacy. Such conditions led to the creation of an audience and a market system for writing, copying, lending, printing, and distributing sensational plot-driven stories composed by anonymous writers of secondary and commoner status for popular consumption. As a product of the late period of the dynasty, the work differs significantly from the moralistic fiction produced in previous eras by *yangban* writers, in that it is primarily a work of entertainment featuring a fast-paced plot that alternates between scenes of high emotion and exciting action. All available evidence points to the fact that it was originally composed in *hangeul* to accommodate the increasing number of common people who could read the phonetic script.

There are many elements in the story that could be used for both subversive and conservative readings of the work. The moving portrayal of the hero's frustration as a secondary son, his role as the leader of outlaws, and his challenges to authority figures from local officials to the king can all be read as critiques of the status quo. But one must also consider the fact that Hong Gildong's aspirations are always couched in the traditional terms of desiring to work as a government official. As an intrepid and invincible leader of loyal bandits, he never seriously tries to change the society he lives in, and he ultimately submits to his monarch once he is granted an official position. He, furthermore, replicates the traditional monarchical state in his own realm. Whatever kind of political interpretation can be made of the work, its central purpose is not ideological advocacy.

Among all the works of Joseon prose fiction, one aspect of the work that makes it unique is that it is the only one featuring a protagonist who is a secondary son of a nobleman. It is interesting that the work that rivals *The Story of Hong Gildong* in its popularity and importance to Korean culture is *The Story of Chunhyang*, which is the only work that features a protagonist who is a secondary daughter of a nobleman. That narrative choice was probably made to arouse emotions born of the frustrations and aspirations of secondary- and commoner-status people at the twilight era of the dynasty.

In direct contrast to the eighteenth century's social stability, economic expansion, and able leadership of monarchs, Joseon in the following century was faced with one crisis after another, and these ultimately led to its downfall. The government was effectively controlled by the families of queens to a series of boy kings. Their incompetence and rapacious behavior caused great economic hardship among the common people and left the country vulnerable to incursions by foreign powers. A number of serious rebellions broke out, starting with the Hong Gyeongnae Rebellion of 1812, led by disgruntled elites of the northern province of Pyeongan, and ending with the Donghak Rebellions of 1894, which played a major role in the destruction of the dynasty, with both Chinese and Japanese armies marching into the country under the pretext of helping the kingdom put down the disturbance. With the outbreak of the first Sino-Japanese War and the retreat of China's presence in Joseon, there was a moment of hope in the reforms of the Blue Horse Year of Gabo (1894), when the traditional status system was dismantled, slavery abolished, the civil examination system based on the Confucian classics done away with, and government service made open to all. Only two years later, however, some of the reformist statesmen were killed by an angry mob, and the Japanese assassination of Queen Min sent King Gojong fleeing to the Russian embassy for protection. Less than ten years after that, at the end of the period of the wishfully named Great Empire of Korea, the country became a protectorate of Japan, then lost its sovereignty altogether in 1910. It was in those tumultuous decades that the story of an invincible hero from a secondary-son background became a popular work.

As a sign of the times, there are interesting parallels in the themes of *The Story of Hong Gildong* and the ideology of the last great rebellion of the century. In the 1860s, a scholar by the name of Choe Jeu from a lapsed *yangban* family created a new syncretic religion called Donghak (eastern learning), which combined elements of Confucianism, Buddhism, Daoism, and shamanism along with reformist political ideas that criticized the corrupt nobility for failing in their duty to take care of the common people.[90] Despite the fact that the name of the movement denoted its opposition to *seohak* ("western learning," that is, Catholicism) and to the political and cultural influence of foreign powers in general, Choe adopted the monotheism of Christianity by transforming the abstract Confucian notion of Heaven into a personal deity. In 1864, Choe was executed for disseminating subversive ideas, but his religion survived, catching on especially among the people of the provinces of Jeolla and Chungcheong as their living conditions deteriorated through economic mismanagement by the central government and the corrupt behavior of local elites and officials. It all culminated in the great Donghak Rebellion of 1894, in which massive peasant armies attacked noblemen, confiscated their property, defeated government forces, took over the city of Jeonju, and marched on the capital. They were finally defeated and dispersed in November after the Chinese and the Japanese intervened with military force.

In the decades after Korea's liberation from Japan in 1945, historians tended to interpret the event in nationalistic and protodemocratic terms as a genuine people's movement that was reacting to both the inequities of the Joseon order as well as the increasing encroachment of foreigners. But Young Ick Lew has pointed to conservative aspects of both the leadership and the political program of the rebellion.[91] There is no doubt that both the original ideology of Donghak and the goals of the 1894 movement were subversive in nature. They were critical of the *yangban* leadership of the kingdom, and it was the explicit purpose of Jeon Bongjun, the commander of the rebel army, to take over the capital and bring about a change in the country's leadership. Despite the originality of the new religion, however, many of its principles were expressed in traditional Confucian terms of loyalty to the country; righteousness in personal, social, and political action; and the duty of power holders to work ceaselessly and benevolently for the well-being of the people. The slogans of the rebels expressed their commitment to eliminating the powerful and the noble without harming the common people or destroying their property.[92] But other radical political programs that have been associated with Donghak, including the abolition of slavery and the hierarchy of social status, the prohibition of class and regional discrimination, and the redistribution of wealth through land grants and comprehensive tax reform, were mostly imagined by later colonial-era nationalists who imposed their ideals on the past movement. The Donghak leader Jeon Bongjun was a *yangban* of the Confucian mold who probably masterminded the rebellion with other disgruntled noblemen rather than assuming leadership after a spontaneous peasant uprising, as he claimed in his trial. Lew presents evidence that rather than establish a representative state, Jeon planned to reinstate the conservative Lord Daewon, King Gojong's father, who had ruled as regent but was then out of power, once the capital was taken. The leadership of the movement, furthermore, opposed the modernizing Gabo reforms, which they associated with Japanese influence. So despite the fact that the adherents of Donghak resorted to open rebellion, much of their ideology was based on traditional notions and did not look forward to a radically novel system of government and society. It rather looked back to the old Confucian ideal of a harmonious state ruled by a moral and benevolent ruler who would keep the nobility in check, punish the corrupt, defend the country against outsiders, and take good care of the common people.

The Story of Hong Gildong is a literary work of the period that also looks forward and backward at the same time. Like the Donghak rebels, the hero finds his station in life impossible to endure, so he becomes an outlaw. And even as he steals from and fights against the authorities, he makes a commitment to leave the common people and their property alone, targeting only the corrupt and the greedy. Once he gets a chance to rule over his own country, as the Donghak leaders aspired to, he replicates the traditional order of the monarchical state in its ideal form. The people of his kingdom rejoice by saying, "A time of peace and prosperity has come, like in the days of Yo and Sun," referencing the mythical Chinese rulers Yao and Shun. In the Donghak manifesto that is attributed to Jeong Bongjun, Yao and Shun are also evoked. The document asserts that King Gojong has the potential to become as great as the ancient rulers, if he could only overcome the influence of corrupt and conniving ministers in his court.[93] So the Donghak rebels were not claiming that the traditional system of monarchy had to be destroyed. The ills of the country came from the fact that the king was surrounded by unrighteous officials and that it was the duty of his loyal subjects to deliver him from their clutches so that he could rule as an enlightened and benevolent sovereign. The common theme in *The Story of Hong Gildong* and Donghak ideology is this combination of the subversive call to action in fighting against the inequities of the established order and the conservative adherence to Confucian principles and the traditional ideal of a harmonious state ruled by a righteous monarch.

There is no evidence that links the Donghak movement with *The Story of Hong Gildong*, which was being read avidly at the time of the rebellion, though some have made much of the fact that there was an actual outlaw group calling itself Hwalbindang that appeared in 1900. Scholars have assumed that they were inspired by the fictional work in adopting the name for themselves and have further asserted they were former Donghak rebels who stole only from the rich and the powerful and distributed their booty to the poor, finally joining the *uibyeong* (righteous army) anti-

Japanese resistance movement in 1904.[94] There is, however, very little reliable historical evidence that can affirm any of those claims. The noble characterization of their actions invites skepticism, considering that similar descriptions of the Donghak rebels were largely imagined decades later. Since the concept of *hwalbin* (saving the poor) was a commonplace notion at the time, it is possible, actually probable, that the Hwalbindang of 1900–1904 was just an ordinary group of bandits who adopted a lofty-sounding name for themselves and who were later mythologized by nationalists in the same manner as the Donghak rebels, who were depicted as revolutionaries of egalitarian and protosocialist principles. But a reasonable case could be made that the similarities in the themes of the literary work *The Story of Hong Gildong* and the ideology of Donghak may have originated from the same set of concerns and aspirations of the age. In a time of great frustration and uncertainty for the people, Hong Gildong was the perfect hero of the age, one who fought against the corrupt and the unjust of Joseon society. When he gains his own realm, he recreates the traditional monarchical order at its best, as it was meant to be in the vision of the oldest and wisest philosophers. In such a way, he points to a way of overcoming the crises of the present by moving forward but also backward to an ideal that had been articulated in the antique past.

As popular as the story of Hong Gildong was in the period of its first reception, when the Joseon dynasty went into decline, the time of the hero's greatest fame was yet to come. Like the trick Hong performs of turning a group of straw men into versions of himself, it was in the modern period that he appears again and again in different guises in fiction, film, television, and comic books, becoming ever more multiple and diverse in the Korean imagination.

PART II

THE MANY AFTERLIVES OF HONG GILDONG

CHAPTER FOUR

The Colonial Period, 1921–1936

In my last year as a graduate student, I attended an academic conference on the Jewish legend of the golem, an artificial being made by learned rabbis who replicated God's method of creating the first man.[1] In a discussion on the appearance of the fantastic creature in contemporary literature, the novelist Thane Rosenbaum asserted that it is such a powerful figure for Jewish American writers because it is the closest thing that Jews have to a superhero of their own. But Rosenbaum also pointed out that the golem is a problematic superhero because, despite old tales of how it protected Jews from pogroms, it failed to save them from the great calamities of the modern era. That is also an apt description of how the figure of Hong Gildong has functioned in the modern Korean imagination, as he was deployed by countless writers, filmmakers, artists, and polemicists to speak of the state of the country.

In the course of the twentieth century, the people of the peninsula went through the tumultuous events of colonization; the imposed division of the country into the Stalinist state of the North and the right-wing dictatorship of the South; the devastating war of 1950–1953; the rapid modernization and industrialization of the South in the 1970s and 1980s that became known as the "economic miracle on the Han River"; the solidification of totalitarianism in the North with a dynastic system of succession; the long and painful but ultimately triumphant struggle for democracy in the South; the economic devastation of the North in the 1990s that resulted in a horrific famine; the spectacular success of the South as an international exporter not only of manufactured goods but of cultural products, in the phenomenon dubbed *hallyu* ("Korean wave");

and the current stasis of the two nations, which have become such radically different states since their founding in 1948. And all throughout that history, the Joseon-dynasty hero appeared in the north and the south, the east and the west, in many different guises. In times of national crisis, Hong Gildong the invincible warrior was put forward as the symbol of the indomitable spirit of the Korean people in the face of powerful enemies. Hong Gildong the righteous outlaw also represented resistance to authority, in the common people's struggles against oppressors, whether they are corrupt officials, the rapacious rich, or a tyrannical government. In other imaginative works, his figure was used critically to lament the loss of the traditional values the literary character embodied as well as to depict contemporary rebels as poor imitators of the great hero. Hong Gildong was also used to represent idealized Korean manhood.

In these new manifestations of Hong Gildong, the nature of the character and his story was altered in varying degrees for various literary and ideological purposes. Consequently, many retellings of the outlaw's narrative exhibit only a casual interest in understanding the original writing. It suited the interests of both North Korean communism and South Korean nationalism to accept Kim Taejun's interpretation of *The Story of Hong Gildong* as a work of subversion and resistance to Joseon feudalism. In the North, Hong became a protosocialist revolutionary, as Kim depicted him, one who also served as a model for the nation's continuing defiance of foreign powers. In the South, the hero became a fighter for the dignity and the empowerment of the common people, in the context of the nation's rise to economic and cultural prominence on the world stage. Takahashi Toru and Kim Taejun's attribution of *The Story of Hong Gildong* to a sixteenth-century figure also served the nationalist desire to discern in the remote past signs of the dormant spirit of the people that was destined to awake with the onset of modernity and independence.

While revisionists freely altered the plot and reinterpreted the significance of the hero's adventures, the one story element that was never changed was the hero's status as a secondary son. As mentioned in the previous chapter, one unique aspect of *The Story of Hong Gildong* is that it is the only known work of classic fiction that features a *seoja* son as its hero (*The Story of Chunhyang* featuring the only secondary daughter). Hong's lament that he cannot pursue his ambitions in a legitimate way or address his father as Father and his older brother as Brother has been depicted so many times in modern versions of the story that every modern Korean is overly familiar with it. The theme is an effective device with which to arouse readers' emotions in sympathy for the character. It also serves to echo their own frustrations at whatever social discrimination they are subject to, a crucial factor in the elevation of the secondary-son character as a national superhero.

For the people of the peninsula, much of modern Korean history has been experienced as a series of humiliations from colonization, forced division, and domestic oppression. As a result, one central agenda in the political rhetoric of both North and South Korea has been the recovery of national dignity and respect, often through massive displays of newly acquired power in the realms of the military, economy, and culture. From the attempt by imperial Japan to convince Koreans that they were inferior relatives who had to be civilized through colonial tutelage, the liberated but divided nations felt like the bastard children of foreign powers that had set their destinies in motion without consulting them on their own desires for the future. As a result, the theme of being disrespected, unappreciated, and underrated by callous and unwise authority figures blind to the significant talents and emotional needs of the protagonist, so well depicted in the first part of *The Story of Hong Gildong*, has a profound resonance in the Korean psyche. In other words, through the agonizing twists of history, the Joseon-dynasty story of a secondary son seeking to overcome the disadvantages of his background and the oppression of his society in order to prove his true worth as a man, a leader, and a ruler has become the story of modern Korea itself.

It is not the purpose of this chapter and the next two to provide a comprehensive account of every new version of Hong Gildong's story, a task that would require an entire book of its own. I have endeavored, however, to survey and analyze the most significant manifestations of the righteous outlaw, to demonstrate the great variety and richness of the eternal hero's many afterlives.

HONG GILDONG FROM A JAPANESE PERSPECTIVE

E. Taylor Atkins has written a revealing work on the Japanese interest in Koreana during the colonial period, showing how historians, archaeologists, and anthropologists conducted researches into Korean culture, many of them motivated by a genuine desire to understand the people.[2] Japanese scholars operated from the general belief that the people of Japan and Korea originated from the same stock but took radically different paths, resulting in the progressive development of one and the backward stagnation of the other. The narrative justified the imperial mission as one of civilizing the primitive relatives of the peninsula.[3]

Hosoi Hajime (1886–1934), a journalist, author, and publisher, was a quintessential figure in the Japanese effort to elucidate the nature of

Korean culture in the service of the empire.[4] An ardent pan-Asianist and imperial apologist, Hosoi first came to Korea in 1907 to participate in the creation of the first colonial administration. Although he was expelled in 1911 for espousing socialist beliefs, he returned seven years later and witnessed the mass protests of the March First Movement of 1919. He laid the blame for the event on the faulty colonial policy of demonstrating "no sign of love (*jinai*), chivalry (*kyōyū*), but only menace (*ihaku*)" toward the Korean people[5] and became convinced of the urgent need to understand them better for the imperial enterprise to succeed. As Serk-Bae Suh has shown, Hosoi thought that the best way to comprehend them was to examine their literature, which embodied their essential national characteristics.[6] Upon his return to Japan, he founded Jiyū tōkyūsha (Free Research Company) in 1920, which published Japanese translations of classic Korean works of history and literature. The press released *Ko Kichido den* (1921), the first Japanese-language version of *The Story of Hong Gildong*, rendered by a scholar named Shiraishi Shigeru.[7] The translation was an abridged version of the three-volume handwritten text at the Tōyō bunko library in Tokyo, and it did not identify an author, since it was published six years before Takahashi Toru attributed the work to Heo Gyun. It also features a startling change in identifying Hong Gildong's realm on Yul Island as Ryukyu, the island chain that Japan formally annexed in 1879 and turned into the prefecture of Okinawa. This alteration was probably made to create a sense of familiarity for Japanese readers. But the change is also interesting from a historical perspective, since it has the hero invade the very islands that the Japanese empire had taken over only a few decades before the publication of the translation. The assimilation of Okinawans into the Japanese state was well under way at this time, and the imperial authorities hoped to replicate the process in Korea.

Hosoi's short but revealing introduction to the translation is an important artifact in the study of *The Story of Hong Gildong* in the modern era.[8] In the description of what he regards as the prime characteristics of the work, Hosoi displays a mixture of patronizing sympathy for the Korean people and contempt for their backward culture and incompetent leaders. He begins by mentioning the figure of Gang Gidong (1884–1911), a military officer who became a leader of the Righteous Army (*uibyeong*) resistance movement against the Japanese after the imperial takeover. He was ultimately arrested and executed by the Japanese authorities, which, in postliberation Korea, made him into a renowned martyr in the struggle for independence.

Hosoi, however, describes Gang Gidong as nothing more than a leader of bandits and an instigator of riots. During the colonial period, the Japanese tended to characterize all Korean acts of resistance and rebellion as banditry, including that of the Donghak Rebellion of 1894. Hosoi makes the further claim that Gang was an avid reader of *The Story of Hong Gildong*, which made him want to become "a second Gildong."[9] This is reminiscent of Yi Sik claiming that reading *Water Margin* inspired Heo Gyun and his friends to become criminals. Hosoi then provides a derogatory reading of the work, discerning in it the many shortcomings of Korean culture. He employs the standard narrative of how the corruption and conservatism of the Joseon dynasty made the country stagnant and its people "the most pitiful in the world." With the collapse of the old order, there was a promise of change and renewal in the form of the "light of modern rational government in the eastern sky" (that is, Japan). Unfortunately, Koreans became subjected to a new oppressor, "the new tyrannical power of pillagers who forced the people into blind submission under the motto of independence." In other words, once the common people became free of the yoke of the old Confucian order, they immediately found themselves beset by ruthless and conniving bandits who stole from them under the false pretext of fighting the Japanese for the sake of their freedom. He characterizes those lascivious criminals as "packs of minor Hong Gildongs."[10] The situation is the result of the Korean people's lack of capacity for flexible thought, which makes them liable to follow any false dogma imposed on them. Hosoi concludes with a general assessment of *The Story of Hong Gildong*:

> Hong Gildong is a sly, cunning rascal who is full of plots and tricks. He only knows how to take but does not know how to give. Japanese legends and folk tales are full of tales of justice and chivalry, blood and tears, but the story of Gildong lacks any concern for the betterment of the world or love of the common people, as he does nothing but lead his subordinates on misadventures. That is the central point that the reader should keep in mind while reading this book.[11]

This interpretation stands in striking contrast to Kim Taejun's view of the work, which was published nine years later.

As shown in the last chapter, Korean nationalists like Kim Taejun accepted the Japanese explanation of Korea's subjugated state as a consequence of the backward and stagnant nature of Joseon culture—its corrupt feudalism, fanatic adherence to Confucianism, and slavish devotion to all things Chinese. So Kim, in fact, agreed with Hosoi that *The Story of Hong Gildong* depicts the inequities of traditional society that needed to be overthrown for the country to progress into modernity. From that point, however, they departed radically in their readings, Hosoi viewing the deeds of the outlaw protagonist as further negative symptoms of that society, as the depredations of a wily and immoral criminal, and Kim seeing them as acts of righteous resistance and subversion against the status quo. Kim exaggerated Hong Gildong's role as a champion of the common people in his effort to portray him as a social revolutionary, while Hosoi built his own image of him as a devious, selfish, and opportunistic criminal, specifically mentioning the absence of wealth redistribution in the story. Hosoi deliberately ignored the themes of Hong's punishment of corrupt officials, reflecting the hero's thwarted desire to become an upright government official; his commitment to stealing only hoarded and ill-gotten wealth while leaving alone the property of the common people; and his benevolence as an able ruler of his own realm. What Hosoi found in the work was evidence for the standard Japanese perception of Joseon, of a country ruled by incompetent and abusive rulers over a submissive people who blindly obey every authority figure, even bandits claiming to be freedom fighters but who are in fact nothing but unscrupulous thieves and murderers. The work that featured an egotistical protagonist and depicted the sorry condition of the common people illustrated for the Japanese critic why Korean culture was so resistant to the civilizing efforts of a superior nation. For the imperial assimilation of the colonial subjects to succeed, the people had to be educated out of their primitive ways. And criminals like Gang Gidong, who sought to emulate Hong Gildong by fighting against the government and pillaging his own people in the name of independence, had to be eradicated.

So Hosoi Hajime, a Japanese imperial advocate, and Kim Taejun, a Korean leftist nationalist, despite being in agreement that the legacy of the Joseon dynasty was something that the Korean people had to overcome, reached diametrically opposed conclusions about the significance of *The Story of Hong Gildong*. This demonstrates that the work had already become an important text, one with which people were pondering the nature of Korean identity. Such ideological readings by scholars like Hosoi and Kim, however, were not the only ways the story was being reimagined during the colonial era. Given the established popularity of the exciting tale of the heroic outlaw, it was natural that it would be retold through that most modern of media, cinema.

LIMITS OF RESISTANCE: HONG GILDONG IN EARLY KOREAN CINEMA

Motion pictures were first introduced into Korea at the turn of the century, possibly in 1897 and 1898 but more definitely in 1903, when they were used to advertise cigarettes and electric streetcars.[12] Theaters specifically for the showing of films were built from 1906 onward, quickly becoming popular venues for mass entertainment in the capital city. The first original works that were produced in Korea were "kino dramas" (or "kine-o-ramas"), which combined projected images on the screen and live acting on the stage.[13] The earliest example of such a work was *Righteous Revenge* (*Uirijeok gutu*), directed by Kim Dosan, first performed in 1919 to great success. The first silent feature film, *The Vow under the Moon* (*Wolha ui maengseo*), directed by Yun Baeknam, was shown in 1923; the movie that could be described as the first Korean blockbuster, the legendary director Na Ungyu's *Arirang*, opened in 1926; and the first "talkie," *The Story of Chunhyang* (*Chunhyang jeon*), by Lee Myeongu, was released in 1935. Brian Yecies and Ae-Gyung Shim have identified 1926 to 1937 as "the first golden age of cinema in Korea" when 115 movies were produced, including twelve talkies.[14] This was part of the flowering of cultural expression in Korea under the "Cultural Rule" of the colonial government, which adopted a looser censorship policy after the March First Movement of 1919. Yecies and Shim also make the important point that many of the films were actually Korean-Japanese co-productions, made with Japanese crewmembers and financing.[15] Korean directors and cinematographers had to continue learning the latest in the art and technology of filmmaking from their Japanese colleagues, and they often had to seek funding from Japanese sources, as local resources were poor. The rise of film as a major medium of mass entertainment in Korea was curtailed in 1937 when the Second Sino-Japanese War began and newly imposed censorship laws turned cinema into a tool of wartime propaganda.[16]

A detailed study of colonial-era films is difficult to conduct because only a few works have survived, most of them in incomplete and/or damaged form. Even the most important movies, such as *Arirang* and *The Story of Chunhyang*, have become lost. Film historians, consequently, have had to rely on oral and printed accounts, especially newspaper reports and reviews, for information about these seminal works. This is unfortunately the case for the two *The Story of Hong Gildong* films, the silent version of 1935 and the talkie of 1936. The paucity of contemporary information about both indicates that they were not regarded as particularly significant achievements in the medium. Recent works on colonial-era cinema discuss *Arirang* and *The Story of Chunhyang* in detail but only briefly mention the Hong Gildong movies, if at all.[17] But what can be learned through the examination of a few contemporary sources reveals interesting ways in which the filmmakers retold the story of the heroic outlaw.

In 1972, the Association for the Advancement of Korean Cinema (Hanguk yeonghwa jinheung johap) in South Korea published the book *Collection of Korean Cinema* (*Hanguk yeonghwa chongseo*), a comprehensive listing of every Korean movie made from 1903 to 1970. It references the silent movie *The Story of Hong Gildong* as having been released in 1934, a mistake that unfortunately resulted in the wrong date being given for the movie in a number of future references.[18] The entry provides the following summary of the plot:

> Born as a secondary son of High Minister Hong, Gildong becomes an outlaw in rebellion against the feudal social system. He organizes the Hwalbindang to steal the wealth of corrupt officials, punish them, and help impoverished people. The government tries everything to capture the bandits but it all comes to nothing. Finally, Gildong founds a country on Yul Island and makes himself the king of the realm.[19]

This seems to be a description of the original literary work (with the evident influence of Kim Taejun in the characterization of Hong's rebellion as against the "feudal social system") rather than the movie itself, which the writer was probably unfamiliar with. The film, in fact, was released in 1935, as evidenced by an April 9 article in the newspaper *Donga ilbo*, which announced the completion and imminent release of the movie.[20] The piece also featured a still photograph of Hong Gildong standing before his father, possibly the first-ever visual image of the story (fig. 4.1).

Figure 4.1. Announcement of the upcoming release of the film *The Story of Hong Gildong* in the newspaper *Donga ilbo* (April 9, 1935), with a still photograph of Hong Gildong and his father, Minister Hong.

Two of the most important Korean filmmakers of the time were involved in the project. Yun Baeknam, the writer and director of the first feature film *The Vow under the Moon*, wrote the script, and Yi Pilu, who is credited with being the first Korean cinematographer, shot and edited the work. It was also an example of Korean-Japanese co-production, as the director was Yamasaki Tokihiko, who was credited under the Korean pseudonym of Kim Sobong. Although the film is lost, a sense of its plot and how it departed from its literary source can be discerned from an unusual source.

In 1936, the colonial government sponsored the publication of a journal called *Friend of the Household* (*Gajeong jiu*), aimed primarily at rural women. Its two main purposes were to provide advice on agricultural and residential modernization and to serve as a vehicle for wartime propaganda among the people living in the countryside.[21] The magazine also featured plot summaries of popular films with still photographs. As Theodore Hughes has shown, such summaries, known as "film fiction" (*yeonghwa soseol*), based on scripts with stills or drawn illustrations, ran in serial form in popular periodicals from the 1920s onward.[22] The second issue of *Gajeong jiu* (February 1937) included a nine-page story of "The Story of Hong Gildong," with four images from the 1935 film.[23] The plot description shows that the film departed radically from the original work.

The first part follows the general Hong Gildong narrative, with the differences of Hong neglecting his studies because he does not see the point of it, as he is not allowed to take the civil examinations, and of the assassin Teukjae being a household servant of the shaman who plots with Chorang to kill him. After the familiar lament that he cannot address his father as Father and his older brother as Brother, Hong takes tearful leave of his mother (fig. 4.2).

In the next part, he comes across two bandits and overhears them talking about kidnapping a young woman. According to them, the local magistrate wanted to take possession of the beautiful daughter of an old man named Yi. When Yi refused to surrender her, the magistrate arrested and tortured him to force his consent. The bandits are planning to take the unprotected girl for themselves. Hong, resolved to save the woman and her father, goes to the house of old man Yi and tells the girl to hide.

Hong then uses his magical powers to transform himself into the girl and allows the bandits to take him captive. When he is brought before their chieftain, Hong turns back into himself before admonishing the outlaws, "A true man's duty in life is to give his all in fighting for what is right. So how is it that you have made it your work to murder people and steal their property? It would be an easy thing for me to become

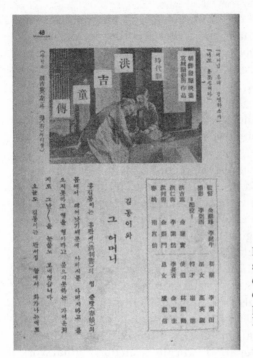

Figure 4.2. The first page of the plot summary of the 1935 film *The Story of Hong Gildong* in the journal *Friend of the Household* (*Gajeong jiu*). The picture shows Hong Gildong taking leave of his mother.

your leader, but first I must correct your ways."[24] And he lectures them on the way of righteousness.

Later on, as Yi is tortured by the magistrate, his daughter appears and begs the official to release him. The pleased magistrate takes the girl into his chamber, but she then reveals herself to be Hong Gildong again. The magistrate throws himself at Hong's mercy, and Hong subsequently releases Yi and takes him back to his house to be reunited with his daughter.

In the last part of the story, Hong's older brother Inhyeong, the governor of Gyeongsang Province, implores him to surrender to the authorities. Hong realizes that he has caused his brother a great deal of trouble, so he allows himself to be captured. As he is being transported to the capital city, he learns that the king has had his mother arrested. The enraged Hong transforms himself into smoke and steals his way to his mother's side in prison. There, he learns that she has been condemned to death by drinking poison. He begs her for forgiveness and drinks the poison to die in her stead. So the story actually ends with the death of Hong Gildong.

The surprising change in the Hong Gildong narrative, from a triumphant tale of a secondary son's rise to power to a tragic story of a righteous man's sacrifice, can be interpreted in the historical context of the colonial era. Narratives centered around masculine dignity and power often feature a test of manhood in the form of a man's imperative to protect the women in his life from harm or, failing that, to avenge them after the harm is done. A mother is often used as a symbol of the larger community, including the nation as a whole, and a young innocent girl as that community's pure soul, both of which are in danger of injury or violation by an outside force or unjust authority. Korean literature and film during the colonial era obsessively featured such themes of endangered manhood, at a time when the second-class citizens of an empire were being bombarded with messages of their racial inferiority and cultural backwardness.

The original *The Story of Hong Gildong* can be read as a narrative of a boy's search for his masculine identity, in a society that has deprived him of his ability to demonstrate his manhood through the legitimate route of taking the civil examinations, entering government service, and achieving renown by performing great deeds for the country. In the course of his adventures as a bandit leader, general of a conquering army, and king of his own realm, his mother is never subjected to danger, and he easily gains the love of three foreign women after he rescues them from monsters. During the colonial era, however, the opportunity for empowerment was much more limited for Hong Gildong. In the film, the central act of righteousness committed by Hong is the protection of an innocent girl, rather than the plundering of hoarded wealth. Her father, representing the old order of the fallen Joseon dynasty, has failed to safeguard the soul of the nation. It is also significant that for Hong to deliver both the innocent woman and her father from danger, he has to take on the guise of a girl, becoming an emasculated object of desire for both the bandits and the corrupt magistrate, before he turns back into a powerful man who successfully overcomes them. But unlike the original Hong Gildong, his ability to resist authority proves to be limited. He allows himself to be captured for the sake of his brother, as in the written work, but when he tries to rescue his mother from mortal danger, he finds that he can do so only by sacrificing himself. Why did the colonial-era film depart so radically from the original work in not allowing Hong to use his magical powers to deliver both his mother and himself to safety? Why does his adventure end tragically in prison instead of triumphantly with the conquest of a kingdom? In the plot description in *Friend of the Household*, the penultimate sentence reads: "And so [Hong] took the poison himself and died in the place of his mother."[25] It is implied that even if he rescued his mother from prison, she would always be in danger, as she has been condemned to death. So the only way that he can make her truly safe is to take on the guise of a woman once again, so his dead body can be taken for that of his mother. The transformation of the hero into a sex-changing rescuer who ultimately has to die for his mother country is indicative of both the crisis of manhood on the part of Korean men as colonial subjects as well as the limited possibility of resistance in the colonial context. As I will show, this theme of the protagonist having to protect or avenge a female character in order to prove his manhood shows up repeatedly in modern versions of the Hong Gildong story. To highlight the significance of the motif in the period, a comparison can be made to a much more significant film of the era—Na Ungyu's 1926 work *Arirang*, the first blockbuster in the history of Korean cinema.

Despite the fact that *Arirang* has also become lost, it has attained legendary status as a nationalist work of anti-Japanese sentiment. Such an interpretation, however, is not readily apparent in its plot. It tells the story of a mentally disturbed young man named Yeongjin, whose beautiful sister Yeonghi is the beloved of his best friend, Hyeongu. O Giho, the household manager of a rich landowner, lusts after Yeonghi and tries to rape her. Hyeongu manages to intervene in time to prevent the violation, but Yeongjin ends up getting involved in the altercation, ultimately murdering O Giho. The sight of the blood he spills makes Yeongjin suddenly lucid, giving him an opportunity to tell the gathered people why he committed the act before he is taken away by policemen. Yecies and Shim have shown that the film's reputation as a subversive work comes from reports of how performing narrators (*byeonsa*) in the movie theaters spun the tale.[26] As an essential part of silent-movie showings, the *byeonsa* often improvised and embellished their verbal descriptions of the plot. There are accounts of how some of them told their audiences that Yeongjin became mentally deranged as a result of being tortured by the Japanese after taking part in the March First Movement protests and that O Giho and his employer were collaborators who became wealthy by helping the Japanese steal the property of the common people. It is impossible to ascertain if the director and actor Na Ungyu (who played Yeongjin) intended the film to be interpreted that way, though a good case for it can be made, considering Na's early history as a nationalist activist.[27] The beautiful Yeonghi, like old man Yi's daughter in *The Story of Hong Gildong*, stands for the soul of the nation that her brother and her lover have to protect in order to prove their manhood. The task is all the more important for Yeongjin, who has been emasculated to the point of madness by the authorities. But the tale also portrays the limits of resistance. The same moment Yeongjin recovers his masculinity by murdering his sister's would-be rapist and regains his sanity, he is taken away by policemen who work for the Japanese. Both *Arirang* and *The Story of Hong Gildong* showed it was possible to resist tyrannical authority, that it was even imperative for a true man to do so, but that the ultimate price had to be paid at the end. Unlike the righteous and invincible outlaw of the bygone era, a happy ending of empowerment through the conquest of a foreign land was not available to the tragic heroes in a time of subjugation.

The difficulty of determining whether a film like *Arirang* was intended by its creators to carry a nationalist message or if that was an interpretive spin added by the *byeonsa* points to the need to avoid simplistic readings of such works. Michael Robinson has pointed out that scholarly analyses of colonial-era culture tend to see things through "the dichotomy of accommodation/resistance to colonial rule."[28] Such a view overlooks the complicated position Korean intellectuals and artists were in at the time, given the often unavoidable necessity of dealing with Japanese authorities and institutions and the fact that there was no consensus among the nationalists on how best to realize their agenda. As Robinson has shown in the cases of newspapers, films, and radio programs, Korean producers had little choice but to cooperate with the authorities to different degrees, but they also found opportunities to resist them as well.

In the case of the 1935 film *The Story of Hong Gildong*, we must remember that it was directed by a Japanese filmmaker and that its plot summary appeared in a government-sponsored journal created specifically for the purpose of disseminating imperial propaganda. So the publishers of *Friend of the Household* apparently saw nothing subversive about the story. Leaving aside the ultimately futile questioning of whether the work is truly resistant or supportive of the status quo, it should be regarded as a representative product of its time and filled with complicated and agonizing questions of Korean identity.

On October 4, 1935, the first Korean talkie, *The Story of Chunhyang*, based on the famous classic romance, opened to great acclaim and financial success, becoming another legendary film that has become lost. It was directed and shot by Yi Myeongu, the younger brother of the pioneering cinematographer Yi Pilu, who had filmed and edited *The Story of Hong Gildong* earlier that year. Yi Pilu was also involved in *The Story of Chunhyang*, responsible for its sound recording. In the following year, the Yi brothers collaborated again in making a talkie version of *The Story of Hong Gildong*, Yi Myeongu once again writing, directing, and shooting and Yi Pilu handling the sound recording. The work premiered on June 10, 1936, and was characterized by the 1972 book *Collection of Korean Films* as a sequel (*hupyeon*), which led to the film being described as such in many reference works. There is, however, no contemporary evidence that it was presented as a continuation of the story from the 1935 work.

Reviews and advertisements referred to the work as *Hong Gildong jeon*, with no indication that it picks up where the plot of the silent movie left off, which would not make any sense anyway, since the hero dies in the earlier film. There is even less available information on the talkie than the silent movie, beyond a few still photographs (fig. 4.3) and a two-sentence plot summary that points to the fact that it departed completely from the original work:

> Yi Gyeongseon, a servant in the household of Yi Geumyong, wants his master's wealth, so he organizes a group of criminals who call themselves the Black Hoods and torments Yi Geumyong. Hong Gildong finds out about the plan, exposes the identity of the Black Hoods, and captures the lot of them.[29]

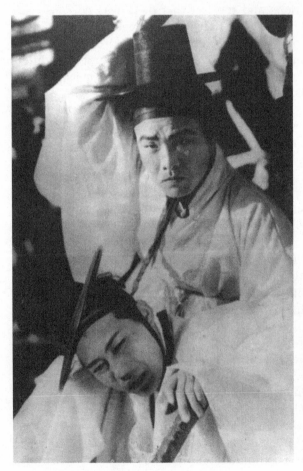

Figure 4.3. Still image from the 1936 talkie *The Story of Hong Gildong*, possibly of Hong Gildong subduing the criminal mastermind Yi Gyeongseon.

In a rather scathing review in the newspaper *Joseon ilbo* that appeared two weeks after the opening, a critic named Kim Gwan complained about the generally poor quality of the film as well as the deficiency of its narration:

> The choice of *The Story of Hong Gildong* as the subject of the film seems to have been made mainly for the purpose of entertainment with apparently not an iota of artistic consideration. Hong Gildong, a superhuman magician, appears out of nowhere, attacks the Black Hoods, and then disappears with no clear explanation of why he saves lives or kills them in the course of combating the mysterious thieves. The film, furthermore, does not deal with the living conditions of downtrodden people at all, so I would like to ask the producer (director) what exactly he was trying to say with the work. The story is all rather obscure. The character Hong Gildong lacks a full personality as all he seems to do is jump around on the screen.[30]

The film was an unsuccessful attempt to make the first talkie action film, with no real connection to the plot of the literary work other than the name and magical abilities of the protagonist. It should also be noted that Hong Gildong is uncharacteristically put on the side of a wealthy man against outlaws, an overt supporter of the status quo with no mention of his background as a secondary son. This surprising "conservative" turn of the Hong Gildong story is interesting in itself, but it is hard to offer any substantial analysis of the work, which has become lost and which few contemporaries have bothered to discuss.

From Hosoi Hajime's contemptuous interpretation of *The Story of Hong Gildong* to the two film versions of the story, the heroic outlaw was already taking on different guises during the colonial period. The history of his many transformations only began at the time, as he would continue to appear in both literary and visual media during the postliberation era of the country that was sundered in half.

CHAPTER FIVE

North and South Korea, 1947–1986

BETWEEN THE NORTH AND THE SOUTH

Bak Taewon's *The Story of Hong Gildong* (1947)

In the 1930s, Bak Taewon (1909–1986) emerged as one of the most important modernist writers in Korea, especially after the publication of his celebrated 1934 novella *One Day in the Life of the Writer Gubo* (*Soseolga Gubossi ui ilil*), which features an early example of the use of the stream-of-consciousness technique in Korean fiction. He was a founding member of the Group of Nine (Guinhwoe), a collective of modernist writers, artists, and filmmakers whose membership changed but was always kept at nine. Their art-for-art's-sake stance has been commonly contrasted to the socially committed agenda of the major group of leftist artists and writers, the Korea Artista Proleta Federatio (KAPF—the original Esperanto name for Korea Artists Proletarian Federation), which was forcibly disbanded by the Japanese authorities in 1935.[1] During the war mobilization period, especially from 1941 onward, Bak occupied himself with producing bowdlerized Korean translations of the classic Chinese novels *Three Kingdoms*, *Water Margin*, and *Journey to the West*.[2]

When the country was liberated in 1945 and Bak returned to writing original fiction, he emerged as a very different kind of writer, having become radicalized as a communist over the previous years. He abandoned the experimental modernist style of the Group of Nine period and became committed to social realism. After the two major leftist writers' organizations that were formed after liberation, the Headquarters for the Construction of Korean Literature (Joseon munhak geonseol bonbu) and the Korea Proletarian Literature Alliance (Joseon proletaria munhak dongmaeng), merged in December 1945 as the Korea Literary Alliance (Joseon munhak dongmaeng), Bak became a central member of the organization.[3] Along with his new political orientation, Bak developed an interest in historical subjects, from the influence of his work on classic Chinese novels.[4] After the outbreak of the Korean War in 1950, Bak joined many leftists in moving to the North, where he became a professor at Pyongyang Literature University. He lost the position in 1956, when he and other intellectuals from the South were proscribed for political reasons, and had to work on a collective farm for the next four years. After he was rehabilitated and returned to writing, he produced the three-volume historical epic *The Peasant War in the Blue Horse Year* (*Gabo nongmin jeonjaeng*), which narrated the Donghak Rebellion of 1894. The first volume was published in 1977 and the final one in 1987, a year after his death.

Before his departure to the north, he published his own version of *The Story of Hong Gildong* in 1947, a representative example of his historical fiction and also the first major literary revision of the classic work as a social-realist novel. Bak sets his story not in the time of King Sejong or Sejo or the fictional Seonjong but during the reign of Yeonsan, when the real-life Hong Gildong lived, though he does not mention the *Sillok* record of the historical outlaw. Since Bak was a committed communist by this time, it is apparent that what attracted him to the original material were the same revolutionary qualities that Kim Taejun discerned in the work. Given the influence of Kim's *History of Joseon Fiction*, it is probable that Bak was familiar with its interpretation of *The Story of Hong Gildong*, though he never mentions Heo Gyun as its author. What is most striking about Bak's version is that it often takes an overtly critical stance toward the original work. He may have been drawn to the story for what he saw as its subversive nature, but he had to rewrite it in order to enhance its political message. In fact, the most interesting aspect of Bak's *The Story of Hong Gildong* is its direct and critical interrogation of the classic work. Pages-long quotations from the original story are included in the novel, which are followed by the author's often denigrating assessments of their lack of realism and historical plausibility.

The raid on Haein Temple is told through the transcription of the entire episode from the *gyeongpan* version of *The Story of Hong Gildong*. The narrator then provides a commentary on the passage:

> The classic text *The Story of Hong Gildong* is interesting simply as a work of fiction, but it has little value as a document of true events.
> As a "story book," *The Story of Hong Gildong*, like most traditional fiction, is filled with fantastic absurdities.

Gildong wields magical powers of metamorphosis and of shrinking distances, he rides a cloud and flies across the sky, he makes identical versions of himself out of straw and sends them out to the eight provinces . . . not to mention the fact that he eventually goes to Yul Island and becomes its king. And the details in the beginning of how he came to leave home are all nonsense based on falsehoods as well.[5]

But then Bak claims that despite the questionable nature of the work as a whole, the description of how Hong Gildong and his men robbed Haein Temple was largely accurate. The only correction he makes is that Hong's men numbered about thirty at the time, instead of hundreds, as in the original story.

Bak repeats this method for the episode on the attack on the administrative center of Hamgyeong Province. He transcribes the entire section from the original *The Story of Hong Gildong* before asserting that the act was not perpetrated by the same group of bandits that stole from Haein Temple.[6] The narrator recounts how Hong took over the leadership of different gangs in the eight provinces before ordering them to attack local targets. Another extensive quotation is employed in describing how Hong Gildong's brother, as the newly appointed governor of Gyeongsan Province, puts up public notices imploring the outlaw to surrender himself.[7] The narrator claims that the event actually occurred, but unlike in the original story, "Gildong did not appear at the administrative center. Nor was there any reason for him to do so."[8] In yet another passage, Yi Heup, the commander of the Police Bureau who has been given the task of capturing Hong by the king, addresses the rumor that Hong is capable of dividing himself into eight Gildongs.[9] He ridicules the idea and speculates that the story arose from Hong's strategy of having different groups of bandits commit acts at the same time in all eight provinces. That made it seem as if Hong was somehow leading his men in all those places at once. Other major changes to the story reflect Bak's effort to turn the story into a realist narrative with a social agenda.

The political aspect of Bak's novel becomes apparent in a number of long passages describing the tyranny and depravities of King Yeonsan and his cronies and the general corruption of the entire *yangban* class. In the beginning of the story, Hong Gildong is frustrated by his lot as a secondary son and utters the familiar lament that he cannot address his father as Father and his older brother as Brother. But that is not the main reason he decides to leave home. In the original work, Hong maintains his respect and love for his father, even when he has to defy him in order to realize his destiny, but in Bak's novel Minister Hong and his legitimate son are portrayed as corrupt and lascivious officials who take advantage of their social position to collect bribes and indulge themselves with pretty servant girls.[10] This results in their household becoming a chaotic place full of petty jealousies and maneuverings, a family utterly devoid of love and loyalty. At the age of seventeen, Hong Gildong cannot countenance the situation any longer and leaves the house in disgust after bidding farewell only to his mother. In other words, Hong's father and half-brother are portrayed as complicit in the corrupt ways of the Joseon feudal system. The hero's growing awareness of his society's inequities is the main reason for his departure, without the plot element of the assassination attempt on his life.

When Hong Gildong's mother realizes she cannot dissuade him from his course, she tells him to go to the town of Seonsan in Gyeongsan Province to find the woman who was his wet nurse. At Seonsan, Hong is welcomed into the woman's household as an honored guest. At this point in the narrative, two original characters are introduced, with detailed background information on both. The first is a middle-aged scholar named Jo, who is referred to as *saengwon*, a title given to someone who has passed the preliminary part of the civil examinations but did not take the final examination. Jo was the son of a powerful official but, like Hong Gildong, became disgusted by his father's corruption in accumulating wealth and power. Jo took the preliminary examination at the urging of his father, but when he passed away, Jo declined to go further. Instead, he set about giving away the enormous wealth he inherited, as he could not bear to possess any of the ill-gotten money and property. Afterward, he moved to the small town of Seonsan, where he worked as a humble teacher. Jo and Hong become friends, and the hero expresses his opinion that given the sorry state of the country under the misrule of the current king, it is no wonder that so many impoverished people are becoming outlaws. Jo agrees and says that he too is considering joining the outlaws.[11]

The other original character in Bak's novel is an unfortunate girl by the name of Eumjeon. She came from an island where her father and brother died at the hands of the Japanese. Her mother remarried an abusive drunk who regularly beat the two of them. When Eumjeon's mother became ill, she advised her daughter to seek out an aunt living in Seonsan. After her death, Eumjeon learned that her stepfather was planning to sell her as a slave, so she ran away to Seonsan, where she was taken in by the aunt. Hong Gildong's pity for her turns into love.

Like old man Yi's daughter in the 1935 film, Eumjeon functions in the story as the pure woman whom Hong Gildong must protect or avenge in order to prove his manhood. That theme is highlighted by the narrator's detailing of King Yeonsan's depravities, including his dispatching of special envoys across the country to pick out pretty girls who are forcibly taken from their families to become palace maidens serving at the pleasure of the king and his cronies. Such an envoy arrives in Seonsan, and Eumjeon is picked to be sent to the capital. When Hong Gildong hears of it, he sets out to confront the envoy's train, but he receives the news that Eumjeon has hanged herself to avoid the humiliation of her fate. This incident convinces Hong that the only way he can fight against injustice is to become a righteous outlaw. Jo *saengwon* agrees to join him as his strategist.

In the ensuing plot, detailing Hong Gildong and Jo *saengwon*'s activities as rebels , Bak rewrites the major episodes of the original *The Story of Hong Gildong* in a realist manner. There are two major elements he adds to the narrative—first, a detailed description of Hong and Jo's strategy in creating a countrywide network of Hwalbindang outlaws, and second, numerous scenes of wealth redistribution. Bak describes bandit groups that were already in existence across the country, some consisting of hundreds of outlaws, others only of a few dozen. Hong and Jo approach one group at a time, starting with the Rabbit Hill Gang of Gyeongsan Province, and assume the leadership of each through the demonstration of Hong's martial skills and Jo's strategic genius. Hong realizes that the Hwalbindang must be active in all eight provinces to punish corrupt officials throughout the kingdom, so he has different groups operate separately in their local areas. This strategy is reminiscent of the organization of activist cells in modern underground revolutionary movements.

Hong Gildong is considered by modern Koreans to be a native Robin Hood who takes from the rich to give to the poor. As shown in previous chapters, in the *pilsa* 89 version, the hero does tell his Hwalbindang men that they will "help the impoverished and the oppressed by giving them goods," and the *gyeongpan* 30 describes how in every town if Hong "found out that the local magistrate had ill-gotten gains, he robbed him of his wealth, and if he found people suffering in dire poverty with no one to turn to, he gave them aid." There is, however, no actual scene of Hong and his men giving away their booty to the common people. Bak Taewon is the first to include such an episode in his version. In an extended comic scene, the people of Seonsan are summoned to the local administrative center to receive money and goods.[12] At first the people are wary because such a thing has never happened before, and some fear it is a ruse on the part of officials to punish them for some reason. When soldiers start handing out bags of money and rice, the people fight among themselves to receive their share. It is revealed later that Hong Gildong and his men had stolen into the place in the middle of the night, imprisoned all the soldiers and officials, and put on their clothes to give away hoarded wealth and goods.

As the Hwalbindang cells repeat the act across the country, they become beloved by the people, who do not regard them as outlaws at all, since they are only returning what was unjustly taken from them by corrupt officials. The king sends out General Yi Heup of the Police Bureau to capture Hong, but Yi is taken prisoner by Hong. In contrast to the episode in the original work, Hong does not humiliate Yi by putting on a show of supernatural beings who threaten to cast him into the underworld. The general is treated with dignity, to the extent of having him sleep in Hong's chamber and allowing him to take part in hunting trips. Yi is so impressed that he ends up joining the Hwalbindang as one of its leaders.[13]

In the last part of the novel, Hong Gildong realizes that no matter how much he tries to help the common people, their suffering will continue as long as the current king remains in power.[14] As he considers how he could dethrone the monarch, the narrative switches to the capital, where a conspiracy by high officials to organize a coup d'état is already under way. As they are finalizing their plans, they receive word from Yi Heup that Hong Gildong is willing to lead the Hwalbindang in support of their venture. The officials consider the offer, some alarmed that word of their plan has somehow leaked and reached the ear of the outlaw leader.

"No! To make use of their support! Are you saying we should act in concert with criminals?"

"But don't you know that the Hwalbindang outlaws are different from other outlaws? That is clear from how they have acted so far . . ."

"That may be so, but criminals are still criminals! Even if we lack enough men for our purpose it is improper to borrow the strength of outlaws. And even if we were to succeed at our tasks with their help, there is no telling what trouble that may bring us afterward."[15]

Bak Jongwon, the historical ringleader of the conspiracy, decides against it, fearing that Hong Gildong may have a secret agenda. The coup proceeds without the help of the Hwalbindang, and King Yeonsan is successfully dethroned.

The novel ends in a disappointingly anticlimactic manner. As the new king makes his way to the royal palace, greeted with shouts of *manse* by the people, a young peasant approaches the procession and shouts, "Your Majesty, do you hear the sound of all your people shouting 'ten thousand years' to you? Your Majesty! Your Majesty must be a good and benevolent king!"[16] Some in the crowd look closely at the peasant and recognize him as none other than Hong Gildong, the leader of the Hwalbindang. "After that no one heard anything of Gildong ever again. And the Hwalbindang disappeared as well, to cause no more trouble in the world."[17]

The rather sudden ending of the novel, in which Hong Gildong and his men play no role in the fall of the wicked monarch, gives the plot a truncated feel.[18] The unsatisfying conclusion reveals a literary as well as ideological problem in Bak Taewon's effort to write a realist version of the classic story. Since Bak was trying to construct his narrative around known facts about the last years of Yeonsan's reign, he could not have Hong and his bandits participate in the king's ouster without violating historical plausibility. Furthermore, despite the subversive radicalism of Bak's Hong Gildong, the Joseon dynasty lasted for almost four centuries after the time of King Yeonsan. If Bak had concluded the novel with Hong creating an egalitarian society in Joseon, that would have disqualified the work as a proper historical novel, and if Bak had Hong achieve his purpose in some foreign island, that would have taken the story into the realm of fantasy, precisely what he criticized about the original work. Also, the fact that he felt compelled to rewrite the story exposes the problem of Kim Taejun's subversive reading of the original work. If *The Story of Hong Gildong* were such a radical work, one infused with Heo Gyun's supposed revolutionary ideology, why was it necessary for a leftist writer like Bak Taewon to rewrite it? It is clear that Bak was drawn to the material for the same reason as Kim, but he apparently found the original work, with its magic, monsters, and adventures in foreign lands, too fantastic and traditional. In his effort to produce a politically committed work that depicts the inequities of the feudal order realistically and in a historically accurate manner, he had to adopt a critical attitude toward the classic work. This points to the problematic nature of the interpretation of the original *The Story of Hong Gildong* as a subversive, antifeudalistic work.

Bak Taewon is best known today in South Korea for his experimental modernist works of the 1930s. This is partly because his later works were banned from publication after his departure to North Korea. They did not become available in the country until 1988, when censorship was lifted with the arrival of democracy. Consequently, the historical novels of Bak's postliberation career have been neglected. His version of *The Story of Hong Gildong* deserves to be better known not only as a major example of such a work but also for the interesting ways in which it attempts to modernize the classic narrative.

HONG GILDONG AS CHILDREN'S HERO

The Illustrated Works of Shin Dong Wu and Shin Dong Heon

In the establishment of Hong Gildong as a major figure in the popular culture of modern Korea, the comic book artist Shin Dong Wu (1936–1994) played the essential role of creating the iconic visual image of the hero. Shin originally came from the town of Hoeryeong in North Hamgyeong Province but moved to Seoul with his mother and three of his six brothers when he was eleven years old.[19] With the outbreak of the Korean War, his family became one of many that were tragically separated across the North and South. After he began his studies as an art student at Seoul National University in 1956, he began to publish cartoons in various journals. He had his first success in 1958, with the comic strip *Swordsman Nassaendori* (*Geomho Nassaendori*), which narrated the adventures of a young warrior in a historical setting. The look of the character was the prototype of the image that Shin would use for Hong Gildong seven years later.

In the course of his long career, Shin emerged as the single most influential comic book artist in South Korea, producing works in a wide variety of genres, including martial adventure that takes place in premodern times, like *Swordsman Nassaendori*; historical drama (for example, a narrative of the 1909 assassination of the Japanese politician Itō Hirobumi by the Korean patriot An Jung-Geun); incidental comedy; science fiction; Westerns; and stories of schoolchildren. His greatest contribution to Korean popular culture came in February 1965, when the first of his comic strips under the title *Hong Gildong, a Hero of Extraordinary Times* (*Punguna Hong Gildong*) appeared in *Sonyeon Joseon ilbo*, a children's journal published by the newspaper *Joseon ilbo*. The series ran for four years in some 1,200 installments and was collected into books starting in 1968.

The importance of Shin Dong Wu's Hong Gildong is that his vision of the character became the defining iconic image in the Korean imagination (figs. 5.1 and 5.2). In the same way that Errol Flynn's Robin Hood, from the 1938 film, became the predominant image of the character, to the extent of being parodied by Mel Brooks in his 1993 comedy *Robin Hood: Men in Tights*, Shin Dong Wu's Hong Gildong is *the* image of the outlaw hero for Koreans. The sturdy boy in a long blue vest and small yellow hat, his sleeves rolled up and a sword hanging from his belt, is as instantly recognizable to Koreans as Superman and Mickey Mouse are to Americans, Tintin is to Belgians and the French, and Tetsuwan Atomu and Doraemon are to the Japanese.

Figure 5.1. Shin Dong Wu's iconic
Hong Gildong.

Figure 5.2. The cover of the first
volume of Shin Dong Wu's collected
comics of *Hong Gildong* (1968). The
newly invented characters of
Chadolbawi and Gopdani are behind
Hong Gildong, along with a flag with
the characters for "Hwalbindang."

The popularity of the image came
not just from the success of the comics and the film but also from its use
in countless print and television advertisements in the late 1960s and
throughout the 70s, which turned it
into a figure of childhood nostalgia
for many Koreans.

The storyline of Shin Dong Wu's
Hong Gildong begins with an abbreviated version of the first part of the
original work, with a physiognomist
(a male one in the comics) visiting
Minister Hong to tell him that his
secondary son Gildong will cause a
disaster to fall upon the family.[20]
Hong Gildong overhears the conversation and volunteers to leave on his
own. That night, the physiognomist,
doing double duty as an assassin,
tries to murder Hong but is bested
by him. He confesses he was put up
to it by Hong's stepmother Chorang,
but Hong immediately leaves the
household without punishing his
attackers.

From that point of the story, Shin
Dong Wu completely departs from
the original work and creates new adventures for his hero. He introduces
original characters, including Chadolbawi ("Sturdy Rock"), an axe-
wielding boy who becomes Hong's
sidekick; Gopdani ("Pretty One"), a
girl who becomes Hong's love interest; Master Baekun ("White Cloud"),
a mysterious old man who teaches
Hong martial arts and magic; and
Lord Eom Gajin, a corrupt and greedy
magistrate who is the villain of the
story. After Hong Gildong meets

Chadolbawi, they become students of Master Baekun, who persuades Hong to become the leader of a band of righteous outlaws. The rest of the story consists of a series of conflicts between Hong and his men versus Eom Gajin and his henchmen and later versus the wrathful Minister of Military Affairs Choe Golhun and his soldiers. Some episodes in the comics have become so famous that many Koreans mistakenly believe them to be from the original work, like Hong Gildong learning magic from an old master, instead of from his own studies, and Master Baekun teaching Hong to fly by having him jump over a corn stalk that grows increasingly higher.[21] Scenes of wealth redistribution are also depicted, including one in which Hong Gildong summons people to take goods out of an administrative center's warehouse, with little Chadolbawi yelling at them to stand in line, which is reminiscent of the comic scene in Bak Taewon's novel.[22]

A striking difference between Shin's narrative and Bak's is that while the latter emphasized the subversive and revolutionary nature of the hero, Shin downplays the criminality of his activities. The cartoon Hong Gildong is portrayed as someone deeply concerned about the propriety of his actions. Even as he punishes the magistrate Eom Gajin, he prevents Chadolbawi from flogging him excessively (Eom caused the death of Chadolbawi's father) because "there are laws in this country, so you must not do as you'd like."[23] When Hong first meets Master Baekun, he expresses reluctance to becoming an outlaw, until the old man explains why that is not necessarily a bad thing.

> Hong Gildong: But . . . I cannot bring myself to do things that would turn me into a robber.
> Master Baekun: Not all robbers are bad people who steal others' property. The robber I am thinking of is a righteous outlaw who is on the side of the oppressed and helps them. If you do not wish to become such an outlaw, to aid downtrodden commoners and to fight against corrupt officials, then you should leave this place! Go!
> Hong Gildong: Great Master! Now I finally understand your meaning. I will become a great righteous outlaw who fights on behalf of the oppressed.[24]

When Hong meets the bandits he will lead, they assure him that "Once we were thieves, but now we have become honorable warriors who want to save the country."[25] By portraying the corrupt officials they are fighting against as the true enemies of the state, Hong Gildong and the Hwalbindang claim to be the champions not only of the common people but of the country, which is endangered by misrule and greed.

In the original *The Story of Hong Gildong*, the main purpose of the protagonist's actions is the demonstration of his great abilities and marvelous powers. Even the good that he does for the people is primarily for showing what an excellent official he would have made had he been allowed to work for the government. Bak Taewon's hero, on the other hand, acts out of genuine concern for the sufferings of the people and sets out to destabilize the status quo by attacking the *yangban* in all eight provinces. Shin Dong Wu's Hong Gildong, by contrast, is a moderate rebel who regards his role as essentially a supporter of his country who seeks to correct the harm done by corruption and oppression. This figure, less egotistical and radical than the previous incarnations, was probably deemed a more appropriate hero for the young readership of the comics. It can also be seen as a product of its historical period, when South Korea was undergoing massive economic and social changes under the presidency of Park Chung-hee. Hong Gildong, in the time of the "economic miracle on the Han River," is someone concerned with social justice, but he is also a patriot with a healthy respect for law and order. He keeps in check the chaotic impulses of Chadolbawi, who is constantly berated by Hong for wanting to exact personal vengeance and to keep some of the plundered wealth for himself. While the story can still be read as a work of social criticism, the potentially radical elements are toned down significantly. Hong Gildong does not dream of ruling his own kingdom or seek to destabilize the existing one through a concerted attack on its ruling class.

Shin Dong Wu's older brother Shin Dong Heon (1927–) became an artistic pioneer in the 1960s as the premier producer of animation for television commercials. In 1967, he brought out his greatest achievement as the director of the first full-length animated movie in Korea, the film version of his brother's *Hong Gildong* (fig. 5.3). Shin Dong Wu wrote the script and oversaw the artistic production. The storyline generally follows that of the comics, concluding with Hong rescuing his parents from the clutches of the evil minister of military affairs and finally receiving permission from his father to address him as Father.

The film was a great success, becoming the second-highest-grossing movie of 1967.[26] Later in the same year, Shin Dong Heon quickly put out another animated work entitled *Hopi and Chadolbawi* (*Hopi wa Chadolbawi*), starring two characters from Shin Dong Wu's comics. Two years later, Segisanga, the production company responsible for the movie, released a sequel called *General Hong Gildong* (*Hong Gildong janggun*, 1968, directed by Yong Yusu), without the involvement of the Shin brothers. The film tells a nationalist and essentially conservative story, one utterly devoid of

Figure 5.3. Poster for the 1967 movie *Hong Gildong*, directed by Shin Dong Heon. Chadolbawi and Gopdani are portrayed on the right, Master Baekun on the top left, and the villain Eom Gajin on the bottom left.

subversive elements. Invaders from the northern frontier of Joseon are devastating the country's defenses. Hong Gildong's father, who is still in service at the royal court, suggests to the king that they summon his secondary son to lead the army against the foreigners, since he possesses great martial skills. Hong Gildong is in the countryside with his mother and engaged to Gopdani, living a happy life as a farmer (something the character of the original work would never have been content with). An evil official, who is secretly collaborating with the commander of the invading army because he wants to be king, seeks to prevent Hong's appointment. When the military situation becomes desperate, Hong Gildong is finally granted leadership of the Joseon army, which he leads against the foreigners. Hong ultimately fights a duel with the barbarian chieftain Ya Yaengbo, who is also a magician and can transform himself into an eagle and a dragon. After Hong defeats him in single combat, the film concludes with the wedding of Hong and Gopdani. Here the outlaw rebel has been completely transformed into a patriotic nationalist and a defender of the established order.

Almost three decades after the opening of the animated film *Hong Gildong*, Shin Dong Heun made another sequel, *Return of the Hero Hong Gildong* (*Doraon yeonggung Hong Gildong*, 1995), from an original story by Shin Dong Wu, who had unfortunately passed away the year before its release. The film, illustrated by mostly Japanese artists, utilized the latest techniques, which significantly improved the quality of animation.[27] It begins with a "reboot" of the Hong Gildong story, the hero leaving home out of frustration at his secondary-son status and meeting Chadolbawi and Gopdani on the road. The rest of the narrative is about his struggle against an evil demon named Golban Dosa ("Master Rock Head"), who goes about in the guise of a mystical priest, spreading a plague that turns people into monstrous animals. By turning the hero into a fighter of monsters, Shin Dong Heun made the inexplicable choice of not having him engage in any act of righteous outlawry, which was what he was best known for. Despite the high quality of the animation and the voice acting by some of South Korea's most famous actors, including Kim Minjong, Chae Shira, and Shin Hyunjun, the movie did not succeed at the box office. It failed to do anything innovative with the old characters, who were of little interest to a new generation of young audience, which held no nostalgia for 1960s animation.

In the history of Korean cinema, *The Story of Chunhyang*, the rival to *The Story of Hong Gildong* as the most beloved story from classic literature, was made into a series of important films. The 1923 version, by the Japanese director Hayakawa Koshū, was a key work of the silent era; the 1935 work by Yi Myeongu, who would also direct the 1936 *The Story of Hong Gildong*, broke new ground as the first talkie produced in Korea; the 1955 version by the celebrated director Lee Gyuhwan inaugurated the golden age of 1950s and 1960s cinema;[28] and the 2000 version by the great Im Kwontaek, which brilliantly incorporated the performance of *pansori* narration into the film, is a masterpiece of contemporary cinema. And those were only the most notable among countless others that were made of the story. In contrast, *The Story of Hong Gildong* was never made into a successful live-action movie. There is evidence that the 1935 film was popular, but the two colonial-era films about the hero had little lasting influence. Likewise, the 1958 *The Extraordinary Hong Gildong* (*Ingeol Hong Gildong*), directed by Kim Ilhae; the 1969 *The Righteous Outlaw Hong Gildong* (*Uijeok Hong Gildong*) by Im Wonsik; and the 1976 *Hong Gildong* by Choe Inhyeon all failed to make a significant mark in the history of Korean cinema. Because it was the animated *Hong Gildong* of 1967 that became the most successful rendering of the story on film, the outlaw's story proliferated in the realm of movies and comic books for juvenile audiences. Consequently, many Koreans now think of the narrative as one intended for children. This view has been solidified by the appearance of other Hong Gildong–themed movies that were either animated versions for children (for example, *Space Warrior Hong Gildong* [*Ujujeonsa Hong Gildong*], 1983; *Hong Gildong 2084*, 2011) or satires in the mode of slapstick comedy (for example, *Super Hong Gildong*, 1987, starring the comedian Shim Hyungrae, and its sequels; and *Mixed-Up Hong Gildong* [*Jjambbong Hong Gildong*], 1990, with the comedian Lee Changhoon). The role of Hong Gildong in the realm of South Korean juvenile film and literature starting from 1965 is perhaps a subject that warrants a more detailed study.

THE IMPOSSIBLE HERO

Hong Gildong in South Korean Literature, 1965–1985

As the comic book Hong Gildong became firmly established as a major icon in Korean popular culture, some of the most important literary writers in South Korea utilized the figure of the righteous outlaw in their works. He is evoked as a potent cultural symbol in short stories including Nam Jeonghyeon's "Land of Excrement" ("Bunji," 1965), Han Seungwon's "The Story of the New Gildong" ("Sin Gildong jeon," 1978), Yi Munyol's "In Search of Hong Gildong" ("Hong Gildong eul chajaseo," 1985), and Seo Hajin's "Hong Gildong" (1998). Other writers, such as Bak Yangho and Jeong Biseok, followed Bak Taewon's example in writing full-length novels about the character. As with the cinematic and literary retellings, the authors created their own versions of the hero's story for various literary and ideological purposes. In the works produced from the 1960s to the 1990s, three significant characterizations of Hong Gildong appeared. First, Hong Gildong as a righteous rebel whose spirit is needed in the contemporary world by people who are oppressed, subjected to injustice, and made to suffer the everyday humiliations of living in modern society. Second, Hong Gildong as the embodiment of a masculine ideal that is impossible to achieve by today's everyman, including would-be rebels who model themselves on him but who prove to be hopelessly inadequate in comparison. And third, Hong Gildong as a symbol of traditional Korea, embodying the values of the bygone era that have been lost through the country's entrance into modernity.

In April 1960, the increasingly autocratic regime of South Korea's first president Syngman Rhee fell after a popular uprising. The brief period of hope for the establishment of a genuinely democratic state was dashed in May of the following year by the coup d'état of General Park Chung-hee, who would head the government until his assassination in 1979. Nam Jeongheyon (1939–) emerged as one of the most vociferous voices of opposition to the regime in the literary world. He published scathing works that criticized not only the government but also the United States for its support of Park's regime.[29] In 1965, he earned the unfortunate distinction of becoming the first major writer to be prosecuted by the state for publishing a work that was deemed to violate the National Security Law.[30] The writing that landed him in trouble was the short story "Land of Excrement" ("Bunji"), which was characterized as anti-American. That, the prosecutor argued, made it a seditious work. Nam was found guilty and handed a sentence of seven years in prison, but he was released in 1967, with the rest of the term suspended. His work, however, remained banned until 1988, when censorship of literature ended with the establishment of democracy.

"Land of Excrement" is a harrowing tale of a deranged man who exacts horrific vengeance for a lifetime of humiliations. It is also a bitter allegory of the state of the nation and of Korean manhood that has been emasculated and driven to enraged madness by modern history. The story is told in the form of a letter written by a man named Hong Mansu and addressed to his deceased mother in the afterlife. Hong's status as the representative Korean man is affirmed not only through his descent from Dangun, the mythic first king of Korea, but also his claim that he is the tenth-generation descendant of Hong Gildong.[31] Hong Mansu is hiding in a mountain surrounded by an elite division of American troops who, Hong imagines, have ten thousand missiles and cannons trained on him. He further claims that the Pentagon, which is directly involved in the operation, is ready to destroy the entire mountain with a nuclear bomb just to make sure he is killed. Despite the dire situation he is in, he assures his dead mother that he will survive and triumph over his enemies, since he dares not die a meaningless death and face his great ancestor Hong Gildong in the afterlife.

> My progenitor is Hong Gildong, the chief of the Hwalbindang who commanded the wind and the rain with his magic and used his supernatural powers to appear and disappear at will, scaring the wits out of the royal court's followers. I plan to make full use of his secret skills to make my parents proud, even though you have already passed away. My heart trembles at the prospect of achieving the purpose.[32]

The story then reveals how he became a mortal enemy of the US military.

When Hong Mansu was a child, his mother announces one day that the country has been liberated from the Japanese, thanks to the Americans, and that his fugitive father will soon return home. True to the rebellious tradition of Hong Gildong, his father is an independence activist on the run from the colonial authorities. The mother's joy is short-lived, however, as her husband never returns, and she is gang-raped by American soldiers. The assault drives her insane, subjecting Mansu to the sight of her naked body as she tears off her clothes and goes about ranting in deranged outrage. He is haunted especially by the image of her violated genitals, which would have driven him insane too, had he not been helped by "the blood of Hong Gildong which flows serenely throughout my body."[33] His mother dies not long after.

After fighting in the Korean War, he comes home to find that his sister Buni has become the mistress of an American soldier by the name of Master Sergeant Speed, who very well could have been one of the soldiers who had raped their mother. At Buni's urging, Mansu makes his living by selling American products like milk, butter, chocolate, and chewing gum provided by Sergeant Speed from his base. That puts him in the agonizing position of being unable to do anything as he listens to the American abuse his sister verbally and physically, berating her for not living up to the standards of his American wife. Mansu gets a chance for revenge when he learns that Sergeant Speed's wife, whose name Mansu claims is Bitch (비취), is coming to Korea for a visit. Under the pretext of giving her a tour of the area, he lures her to an isolated spot and rapes her.

Despite the predicament he ultimately finds himself in, imagining that the Pentagon will resort to using a nuclear bomb to kill him for having violated a white woman, Mansu remains confident that he will somehow prevail over the Americans and prove he is worthy of having descended from the great hero of the past.

> To those who have heard only of the miracles of Jesus, I will revive with the greatest pleasure the extraordinary wonders performed by my ancestor Hong Gildong. And so I will break their spirit in an instant and shake them to their cores. They will naturally fall into panic. When that time comes, I bid you, mother, to give me your ardent applause.
>
> Only ten seconds remain. Yes. Soon I will take this stained T-shirt and cut it into the shape of the *taeguk* [the blue and red yin-yang in the center of the Korean flag] and turn it into a radiant flag. I will then ride a cloud to cross the ocean. On the great continent beyond, there will be women with serenely glistening milk-colored skins, which I have had a taste of, sprawled out all over the land. I will plant my magnificent flag devotedly into their bellybuttons. Believe me. Mother, I am not lying. Ah, you are still shaking, doubting my words. How pitiful you are. Here, look at me. At my glaring, protruding eyes. Do you think that someone like me could die so easily? Hahaha.[34]

The theme of the defense of the female body from violation as the essential test of masculinity, which appeared in previous revisions of the Hong Gildong story, is brought to the foreground in this work. The sense of humiliation and impotence felt by the Korean man is depicted in terms of his inability to prevent his mother's rape and his sister's exploitation. And the United States, which supports the repressive regimes of postwar South Korea, is indicted in the form of the American soldiers who perpetrate the violations. The foreigners also stand for modernity, the name of

Master Sergeant Speed denoting the breakneck pace of the political and economic changes the country was undergoing. Unlike the previous incarnations of Hong Gildong, his descendant Hong Mansu utterly fails to defend his mother and sister; nor can he avenge them by punishing the people who committed the acts against them. All he can do is resort to eye-for-an-eye retribution by raping one of their women. As Kelly Y. Jeong has put it in her incisive analysis of the themes of gender and misogyny in postwar South Korean fiction:

> Such narrative violence is rooted in [the displacement] of male resentment and powerlessness against foreign dominance onto women, who are doubly victimized in the situation.
>
> Through an abject oversexualization of woman, postwar writers respond to the sense of crisis and threat the Korean male subject feels in the neo-colonial predicament of postwar South Korea, where Korean women prostitute themselves to American soldiers.[35]

Despite the protagonist's constant references to his famed ancestor and his certainty that he will one day measure up to his heroic status, it is painfully clear that he is no modern-day Hong Gildong. He tries to emulate the hero, but he lacks the magical powers and martial prowess of his ancestor. So he can only watch helplessly as the female bodies that represent the motherland and its purity are violated by foreigners. What marks the narrative as essentially masculine is the fact that the sufferings of women in the story are depicted primarily in terms of their effect on Mansu's sense of his manhood. That blindness to the effect of the violations on their direct victims is what allows him to imagine that a proper response would be for him to perpetrate the act on a woman who belongs to the violators. After he attacks the American's wife, discharging the rage of his lifetime, he dreams of using his ancestor's power of flight not to find an island where he can establish a good kingdom but to conquer more such women with his phallic flagpole. That is how he imagines he can recover his damaged manhood. It is apparent, however, that he will not succeed as he is nothing but a hapless fugitive with no special powers. Even for a direct descendant of Hong Gildong, the invincible and righteous outlaw of the past has become an impossible hero in the modern world.

Another failed Hong Gildong figure appears in the short story "The Story of the New Gildong" ("Sin Gildong jeon," 1978) by Han Seungwon.[36] The narrator, a high school teacher in the southern city of Gwangju, describes the questionable character of a colleague, a math teacher named Yi

Chungil. Yi has earned the nickname "the New Gildong" because of his wily and illicit ways. Educational authorities are cracking down on the private tutoring of high school students for the college entrance examination, which schoolteachers are prohibited from engaging in. Yet Yi somehow manages to make good money from the practice without ever getting caught. A fellow teacher reports him to the authorities, even drawing them a map to the house where Yi secretly meets with his students at night. When the inspectors go to the place, they find him in his sleeping clothes and discover no trace of students, despite conducting a thorough search. The teacher who reported him is then disciplined for making a false accusation. Rumors circulate afterward that Yi owns an enormous wardrobe that he bought specifically for the purpose of hiding his pupils.

The narrator makes it clear, however, that when Yi is referred to as the New Gildong, it means something debased and lowly. "His colleagues called him that in an ironic manner, referring only to the fact that he was quick as a rabbit and sly as a fox, going about his business here and there using his clever trickery. Such was his personality and his way of life."[37] Han is pointing to the established view of Hong Gildong as not only a clever outlaw but also a moral exemplar of high ideals. The humorous nature of describing Yi, who is nothing more than a crooked educator, as a modern-day Hong Gildong lies in the identification of the petty person with such a lofty figure solely on the basis that they are both outlaws who cleverly evade the authorities. So the character is depicted from the outset as a substandard version of the hero.

Yi Chungil is not completely devoid of virtues, however, as he is known to be devoted to an old woman who may be his mother or his mother-in-law, though no one knows their exact relationship. The narrator, who has always been suspicious of his wily colleague, gains an opportunity to discover his true identity when he travels to the island of Usan, where Yi Chungil comes from. A chance meeting with a fisherman who used to know Yi leads to the discovery of incriminating things about his past. It turns out that Yi's true name is Jeongsu, not Chungil; that his father was a notorious thief on the island; and that he did not even finish middle school, never having attended the educational college he claims to have graduated from. Despite the revelation of Yi as an utter fraud, the narrator cannot help being impressed with what he calls Yi's "Hong Gildong–like ability" to advance himself in society.[38]

In the conversation with the fisherman, the narrator finds out Yi's greatest secret, which infuriates him. During the Korean War, Yi was engaged in "flag-waving as the head of propaganda for the village."[39] In the initial phase of the war, when North Korean troops managed to take over much of the peninsula in a matter of weeks, some South Koreans quickly put themselves in their service ("flag-waving" was a euphemism for active collaboration with the communists). Some of them did so because they were communist sympathizers from the outset, while others were opportunists who mistakenly thought the invaders were there to stay. There were also malcontents who enthusiastically greeted the end of a society they despised. In the short time that the collaborators found themselves in power, they went after people in their communities for ideological as well as personal reasons, some of them even committing atrocities. When the North Koreans were pushed back across the border, many of their southern supporters had to leave with them, and those who did not were hunted down by the authorities. The fisherman does not elaborate on what Yi actually did as "the chief of propaganda" for the communists, but he marvels at how he managed to thrive afterward when many others like him ended up being imprisoned or executed.

Yi Jeongsu survived by taking on the identity of Yi Chungil, another resident of the island. The father of the real Yi Chungil was a policeman who might have died at the hands of the North Koreans at the beginning of the war, or he might have been a collaborator who killed many people before being executed after the communists left—the fisherman is unsure. His widow, who made a living by selling cabbages and rice cakes, made sure that her son received a decent education, and it was her son who graduated from the educational college that Yi lied about having attended. Unfortunately, he died of some disease not long after he finished his studies, which allowed Yi to take over his identity. Considering his remarkable ability to survive through that tumultuous period, the fisherman also declares that Yi is "a true equal of Hong Gildong."[40]

The narrator's rage at finding out about Yi's wartime activities comes from the fact that his own father was murdered by "flag-wavers." Despite the fact that his father owned only a modest tract of land, he was accused by communist collaborators of being an oppressive landlord and was executed by them. The teacher returns to Gwangju, resolved to expose Yi and all his lies.

At home, he is told by his wife that Yi has been trying to reach him, the fisherman having tipped Yi off that his past has been discovered. The story ends with a meeting between the two teachers, during which Yi confesses his crimes before making a plea.

"I will live in anxiety to the day I die, constantly afraid that my lie will be found out. I wish I could reveal everything, and live just as I am. But I cannot do that. Not after all that I've done," he said in a tearful voice. "But Teacher Choe, please wait a little. Until my mother passes away. She's a truly unfortunate person. Did she not live her life only for the sake of her son? You might have guessed already, but the woman that I serve as my mother is actually the mother of the deceased Yi Chungil."[41]

We never find out if the narrator decides to extend him that mercy. Like Hong Mansu of "Land of Excrement," this failed Hong Gildong also turns out to be a victim of history, one who had to resort to fraud in order to find himself some dignity in life.

In the beginning of the story, the narrator makes it clear that the characterization of Yi as a modern Hong Gildong is an ironic one, as he has the hero's cleverness without his ideals. The comparison becomes even more problematic once his past is revealed. He was a half-educated son of a thieving outcast on the island, so perhaps it was understandable that he worked on behalf of the communist invaders who promised to turn the country into a socialist utopia. In fact, leftist intellectuals like Kim Taejun and Bak Taewon would likely have approved of such actions by a modern-day Hong Gildong. Even after he took on another person's identity, he continued to engage in illicit acts that made people consider him a new Gildong. But far from a humorous tale of a wily trickster, the story is steeped in the tragedy of modern Korean history. The narrator will never see justice done for what happened to his father, but he seeks to allay some of his anger by seeing that Yi is exposed. But the story concludes with Yi's confession that he is already being punished for his past deeds, as he is doomed to lead a life of constant anxiety. Despite the resourcefulness of Yi Chungil, or Yi Jeongsu, that rivals that of Hong Gildong, he leaves his home on Usan Island but never reaches his own Yul Island where he can live in peace. Hong Gildong has not only become an impossible hero, but his happy ending has also become unavailable to his modern emulators.

The first major retelling of the hero's story in a full-length novel since Bak Taewon's 1947 work appeared in the crucial year of 1979 (the last year of Park Chung-hee's regime, before his assassination in October), in a story that takes place during another pivotal period in South Korean history, from the end of the Korean War in 1953 to the April 19 revolution of 1960 that brought down President Syngman Rhee. The novel *Hong Gildong of Seoul* (*Seoul Hong Gildong*) by Park Yangho (1948–) tells the story of the twentieth-generation descendant of Hong Gildong. The style of the narrative is reminiscent of Bak Taewon's novels, in that both take place in specific historical contexts for the purpose of highlighting their political themes. Just as the earlier work featured lengthy passages detailing the abuses of power committed by the mad king Yeonsan and his cronies, *Hong Gildong of Seoul* describes the corruptions of the Rhee government, including the measures the president took to steal the 1960 election. But unlike Bak Taewon's leftist revolutionary hero, Park Yangho's Hong Gildong is a fiercely anticommunist patriot. The rebellious figure battles various authorities associated with the government, but he does so for the purpose of saving the nation from corrupt power holders, in the same manner as Shin Dong Wu's comic book Hong Gildong.

The novel opens in a humorous manner, in a parody of the sensationalistic descriptions of Hong Gildong's abilities in the original work. The eighteen-year-old Hong is a resident of Gyeryong Mountain in Chungcheong Province, a place famous to this day as a site of powerful spiritual forces, frequented by mystics of shamanistic, Buddhist, and Daoist persuasions.[42] He is a student of a Buddhist master named Muhanjeong ("No Limits"), who teaches him magic and martial arts. Hong has the taekwondo skills of a sixth-degree black belt, he can put a nail into a tree with his forehead and take it out with his teeth, and he can use hypnosis to make a pig do a disco dance.[43] He possesses the agility of the Olympic gymnast Nadia Comăneci and has the physique of Mister Universe from *The Man with Two Faces* (the Korean title for the 1970s television show *The Incredible Hulk*, so the reference is to the actor and bodybuilder Lou Ferrigno).[44] Later on, he is also described as having the looks of the French actor Alain Delon, the toughness of the American Charles Bronson,[45] and the voice of the Italian opera singer Enrico Caruso.[46] In addition to his magical and martial skills, he has also mastered the Confucian classics, political theory, economics, and the English language.

In the course of the story, it is revealed that ten years ago he had to flee to Gyeryong Mountain after committing murder. Like the father of Hong Mansu in Nam Jeonghyeon's "Land of Excrement," this Hong Gildong's father was also an anti-Japanese activist during the colonial period. Hong's uncle was a policeman and a collaborator who reported his own brother to the Japanese, resulting in his arrest, torture, and death. Hong Gildong tried to avenge his father but ended up killing his uncle's son by mistake.[47]

As in the comic book story, Hong gains his skills not through his own studies but under the tutelage of an old master of uncanny powers. After ten years of training, his teacher tells him he has taught him all he knows and exhorts him to go down to the world to help the people of the country, which is still in disarray after the occupation by the Japanese and the war waged by the communists. On his way down the mountain, Hong runs across a group of soldiers and beats them up for being rude to him, but he then regrets it when he finds out that they are looking for communist insurgents who may be hiding in the area. As he apologizes to the soldiers, "I have done you wrong. My master told me that there is no one in the world more wicked than red commies, and instructed me never to discuss morality or faith with them. I have behaved in an excessive manner to you, when all you were trying to do is capture such people."[48]

Hong Gildong arrives in Seoul in September 1953, only a few months after the end of the Korean War, and finds the city in a chaotic state, with its impoverished denizens trying desperately to survive in the ruins of bombed-out buildings. He goes to the lair of a street gang and takes over its leadership by beating its chiefs in a fight. He renames the gang Hwalbinhoe (Convention for Aiding the Impoverished) and creates a ten-point agenda for the group, which is cleverly worded so that each of the Korean letters for the numbers one through ten corresponds to a key word in the agenda:[49]

One [il]: Let us despise the Japanese [il is the first letter of the Korean word for Japan—Ilbon].

Two [i]: Let us kill fleas [flea = i; Hong explains that by fleas he means all harmful vermin, including human vermin, that are harming the nation].[50]

Three [sam]: Let us inherit the spirit of the March First Movement [March = third month, samwul].

Four [sa]: Let us show no mercy [literally, allow no "exceptions"— "sajeong"].

Five [o]: Let us eliminate the communist Fifth [o] Column.

Six [yuk]: Let us beat up cursed [yuksiral] bastards [Hong explains he is thinking specifically of politicians who engage in factional fights instead of looking after the welfare of the people].[51]

Seven [chil]: Seven times seven is forty nine [Hong explains that for the leadership of the gang, he means to pick seven men to act as his chief followers and have each of them pick seven of their own, for a total of forty-nine leaders].[52]

Eight [pal]: Let us never put our loyalty up for sale [to sell = palda].

Nine [gu]: Let us help destitute [guchahan] people.

Ten [sip]: Let us work at our task for ten years.

After Hong Gildong successfully converts the street thugs into righteous outlaws, he follows his ancestor's ways in stealing from the rich, taking on the guises of important government authorities to make fools out of corrupt officials (including his uncle, who is still a high-ranking policeman), and targeting Buddhist monks. In the latter act, instead of robbing Haein

Temple, Hong Gildong takes advantage of a contemporary controversy within Korean Buddhism over the legitimacy of sects that allow monks to marry and have children. Hong pretends to be a government official sent by President Rhee to help settle the issue and takes bribes from partisans on both sides.[53]

With the wealth he accumulates through such activities and the take-over of a business association in charge of selling used American goods, he buys land in Jamsil District, south of the Han River (decades before the place became valuable real estate, as the author explains). There he builds a self-sufficient community for his men and their families, as well as for homeless people and orphans, with factories that produce matches and yeot candy. In a conversation with a rich man about his reasons for becoming an outlaw, he explains:

> "Because of the war fought by countrymen against countrymen, which none of us wanted to fight, our nation is teeming with countless orphans, beggars, disabled veterans, war refugees, and the old who lost their children, all wandering lost in the streets. They need so much help, but our nation is not paying enough attention to them. So they have no choice but to become thieves. The country bears the responsibility for this, and so the people of the nation are at fault for the situation. I am putting all my efforts into improving their condition. And I am spending all the money I made into the cause."
>
> "Even through illegal means?"
>
> "What exactly is illegal and legal? If it is illegal to take away the wealth of those who accumulated their riches through illegal means, to selfishly eat well and live comfortably by themselves, what exactly is legal?"[54]

Hong also gets involved in a series of conflicts with the infamous real-life mob boss Yi Jeongje (1917–1961), who became the most powerful gangster in the city after putting his thugs at the service of the Rhee regime in intimidating political opponents, helping steal elections, and beating up protesters at antigovernment rallies. Despite their antagonism, Hong and Yi cooperate on one occasion, to threaten officials from Czechoslovakia who are in the country under the protection of the US military as international inspectors. Hong and other vociferous anticommunists are convinced that the foreigners, who are described as "long-nosed red commies," are actually spies who are in the country to probe for its weaknesses. As the outlaws plan to break into the US military base to threaten the foreign communists into leaving the country at once, Hong gives strict instructions not to harm any American soldiers, since they are allies of

South Korea.[55] Unlike Hong Mansu of "Land of Excrement," this descendant of Hong Gildong has no animosity toward Americans.

Like many modern revisions of the Hong Gildong story, *Hong Gildong of Seoul* features episodes dealing with the hero's love life. In this case, however, the two female characters who appear are described in terms of the traditional whore/virgin dichotomy in a rather literal way and for an initially comic purpose. After Hong takes over the leadership of the street thugs, he loses his virginity to a prostitute who calls herself Sim Cheong, a name given to her by the brothel madam because she entered into the profession to take care of her blind father.[56] This is a reference to the well-known folktale of a girl who offers herself as human sacrifice for the sake of her blind father. Hong thinks he is in love with her, but then he meets Kim Sukyeong, the educated and sophisticated daughter of a rich but generous man who becomes an ally of the outlaw. After Hong takes Sukyeong's virginity, they get married, though the ceremony is disrupted by the jealous Sim Cheong.[57] Sim then turns on her former lover, becoming a police informant.

In the last part of the novel, which takes place in the second half of the 1950s, Hong gets further involved in the historical events of the time. He attends the famous May 1956 speech by the celebrated independence activist and opposition party politician Sin Ikhui (1892–1956), who exhorted the people to stand up to the Rhee regime. Hong is inspired by his words and becomes distraught when he hears of Sin's untimely death only days after the speech. When he is approached by an acquaintance in Military Intelligence about getting involved in a coup d'état, Hong declines only because he feels that the time is not yet ripe for a political action. That moment comes in April 19, 1960, when students and laborers rise up in protest against the thoroughly corrupt elections that had just taken place. Hong mobilizes his men to protect the students in the streets from the onslaught of Yi Jeongje's gangsters, who are working for the government. They successfully beat back the thugs and receive the gratitude of the protestors, but when the police show up and open fire on the crowd, Hong Gildong is hit by a bullet. As he is surrounded by his followers, he leaves them with a final declaration: "I will not die. I will only disappear for a while."[58]

Park Yangho's novel cleverly inserts the traditional hero into a crucial moment in South Korean history for the purpose of political criticism. Ever since Nam Jeonghyeon became the first major literary figure to be persecuted by President Park Chung-hee's regime in 1965, writers, artists, and filmmakers continued to be subjected to strict censorship. By setting *Hong Gildong of Seoul* in 1953 through 1960, detailing the abuses of the authorities during the time of Syngman Rhee, the author comments on similar problems in his own time without overtly indicting the current government, pointing to the 1970s in references to popular culture, like disco music, the television show *The Incredible Hulk*, and the movies of Charles Bronson. Park Chung-hee's regime also engaged in election stealing and used gangsters to intimidate and assault political opponents and protesters. It is significant that the modern Hong Gildong is portrayed as an ardent patriot who abhors the Japanese and the communists and regards American soldiers as allies, in stark contrast to Bak Taewon's social revolutionary Hong Gildong and Nam Jeonghyeon's anti-American Hong Mansu. Despite the depictions of the corruptions of the dictatorial government and the glorification of the hero's outlaw activities, it defies a censor to characterize the work featuring such a patriotic protagonist as subversive. In addition to the thinly veiled criticism of the Park regime, *Hong Gildong of Seoul* is quite radical in its articulation of the idea that fighting against the crooked, tyrannical, irresponsible state, even through illegal means, is in fact the highest act of patriotism. The novel, therefore, functions as both a historical novel of the 1950s and a political exposé of the state of the nation in the 1970s.

Jeong Biseok (1911–1991) was one of the most successful popular novelists of his time, best remembered today for the controversial 1954 bestseller *Madame Freedom* (*Jayu buin*), about the wayward wife of a professor. The work, along with the equally controversial film version of 1956 (directed by Han Hyeongmo), played a significant role in the "New Woman" debate of the time.[59] In the last phase of his long career, Jeong turned to writing historical fiction set in premodern Korea and China and to producing bowdlerized versions of classic Korean and Chinese novels for popular readership. In 1985, he published *Hong Gildong the Novel* (*Soseol Hong Gildong*) in two volumes. In the introduction, Jeong explains his purpose in writing the work:

> Hong Gildong—when the name is uttered, people commonly think of the figure as a historical one, but in reality he is a completely imagined character created by Heo Gyun, who lived during the reign of Gwanghae, for his fictional work *The Story of Hong Gildong*. Despite that fact, Hong Gildong feels closer to us than any real-life figure. That is due to the strenuous effort, the high-minded ideals, and the bold combativeness with which the character tried to right the wrongs of the world and to create a society in which all people could live in prosperity, if only in a novel.
>
> Since all would welcome the advent of such a world, it is understandable that ever since *The Story of Hong Gildong* was written, the name of Hong Gildong has been evoked and his ideas shouted out in times of trouble. One

could even say that "Hong Gildong" has become synonymous with righteousness. For that reason, contemporary people should be familiar with the classic work *The Story of Hong Gildong*. There are, however, many aspects of the work that modern readers would find problematic.

As those who are familiar with the story are aware, much of the content of the classic *Hong Gildong* is rather absurd, making many elements of the plot difficult for the scientifically minded modern reader to accept. There is the additional problem of the story taking place during the time of King Sejong the Great, which was the most peaceful time in the five-hundred-year history of the Joseon dynasty. Having Hong Gildong commit his acts in the period of tranquility creates the possibility of his figure being seen merely as a treacherous subject who brings confusion to the world by deluding the people.

In the effort, then, to write my own *The Story of Hong Gildong*, about a great hero of his time worthy of the endless veneration of the people, I have borrowed the historical period of the reign of Yeonsan, when the political situation of Joseon was at its darkest and most disorderly moment, utilizing real-life figures and the tumultuous events of the time. While there is not an iota of divergence in the ideology behind the classic *The Story of Hong Gildong* and my own work, most readers will see that there is a great deal of difference in the plot itself. I have taken the ideals represented by the name Hong Gildong and created a new story which resulted in this work, *Hong Gildong the Novel.*[60]

There are a number of points in the introduction that are of interest in analyzing this work. Jeong points to the widespread familiarity among Koreans of Hong Gildong as a representative figure of righteous rebellion against oppression as well as of the desire for a just society for all. He also asserts, however, that the original work does an inadequate job of presenting the protagonist as such by setting the story in the time of the benevolent King Sejong, apparently unaware that some versions of *The Story of Hong Gildong* take place during the reigns of King Sejo and the fictional King Seonjong. Jeong's rationale for moving the story to the dark period of King Yeonsan's rule is to highlight the truly heroic and righteous nature of the hero's actions. This view stands in interesting contrast to Bak Taewon's 1947 novel, which also takes place in the time of Yeonsan.

Jeong Biseok does not mention Bak's work, which was still banned in South Korea at the time he published the novel. It is clear, however, that Jeong was quite familiar with the work, since he freely makes use of episodes from it, sometimes to the point of outright plagiarism. To give a few examples, in Bak Taewon's novel, there is an early episode, not in the original work, in which the young Hong Gildong takes a walk outside the family compound and comes across a group of young noblemen engaged in an archery competition. At their behest, Hong takes part and beats them all, including the son of a powerful and corrupt official, who ridicules the secondary son by saying, "How unfortunate that such a skill will go to waste, since you can only reach the fifth rank in government service."[61] The statement infuriates Hong, who almost gets into a fight with him, but he restrains himself and walks away. In Jeong Biseok's novel, the scene is repeated almost exactly.[62] Also, in Bak's novel, there is the aforementioned comic scene in which Hong's gang takes over the office of the magistrate of Seonsan, imprisons its guards and officials, puts on their clothes, and distributes money and food to the people.[63] Jeong describes the same scene after Hong's band takes over the magistrate's office in the town of Geumhwa. At the end of the episode in both novels, when the infuriated magistrate plans to go after Hong Gildong, his advisors urge him to let the matter go, as stories of their ordeal would bring great embarrassment upon them. They use the same exact words in dissuading the magistrate: "I bid you to regard the insult you have suffered at their hands in the same way as you would a bite you received from a mad dog, and please calm yourself. I think it would be best to cover up the entire matter."[64] Also, both Bak and Jeong aimed to create realistic historical narratives by denigrating the magical elements in the original work and providing mundane explanations for them.[65] And finally, both novels feature a number of extended descriptions of King Yeonsan's abuses of power in similar or identical words. What Bak Taewon and Jeong Biseok never mention is the reference to the real-life bandit Hong Gildong in the *Sillok* royal records of the year 1500, surely something that Jeong, had he been aware of it, would have pointed to as a further justification for having the story take place in the time of Yeonsan.

Despite such similarities—which sometimes amount to plagiarism on the part of Jeong Biseok—there are significant and crucial ideological differences between the two works. In Bak Taewon's novel, Hong Gildong comes to realize that the problem facing Joseon is not just a matter of abuses perpetrated by individual power holders but the entire feudal system based on the absolute rule of the greedy and corrupt—"Some were more corrupt and others less, but every single one of the bastards was nothing more than a filthy government official."[66] That is the reason Hong decides to create a Hwalbindang group in every province, so there will be no place that the ruling class can feel safe. Even Hong Gildong's father, Minister Hong, is implicated as a typically corrupt and lascivious *yangban*. In direct contrast to the original work, Hong Gildong does not bother to help his father when he is imprisoned, even after his half-brother, who is also portrayed as a corrupt official, implores him to do so. The leftist

Bak denied the feasibility of the Confucian ideal of a country ruled by a morally upright intellectual class that benevolently works for the welfare of the common people. The feudal system is inherently inequitous, so it must fall if the people are to have a chance at living in a truly just and egalitarian society. The expression of such ideas in Bak's novel makes its ending all the more disappointing as Hong Gildong doesn't participate in the downfall of Yeonsan's regime, and the hero abruptly disappears without carrying on the fight—and after hailing the new monarch.

Jeong Biseok, while taking the basic framework of Bak's work and appropriating many of its episodes, alters Hong Gildong's ideological alignment. He does so by making use of the idea from Shin Dong Wu's comic book *Hong Gildong* and Park Yangho's *Hong Gildong of Seoul*: the depiction of the struggle against the unjust as an act of patriotism. Jeong also has Hong Gildong attain his martial prowess by learning from an old master, represented by the Buddhist priest Grand Master Hakjo ("Learned Ancestor"), a historical figure who lived during the second half of the fifteenth century. After the teacher deems Hong to be ready to achieve his great purpose in the world, he sends him to a place where there are men who are already ready to follow him. Unlike in the original work, Hong does not need to change them from being mere bandits to righteous outlaws, because the Buddhist master has already done so. In the same exact way that Shin Dong Wu's comic Hong Gildong meets a sturdy, bearded chieftain by the name of Teopseok Buri ("Bushy Beard"), who immediately relinquishes command of his men to him, Jeong Biseok's hero encounters a sturdy, bearded chieftain named Beomsu, who becomes his second-in-command.

Despite Jeong's professed effort to write a realist historical novel, he commits a number of glaring anachronisms in the process of turning his Hong Gildong into a patriotic rebel. Just as the Hwalbindang men in the Shin Dong Wu comic book declare their commitment to becoming "great warriors in the cause of saving the nation,"[67] Beomsu identifies his people as "patriots" (*aegukja*) who "think nothing of their lives in their struggle for righteousness."[68] In a scene in which Hong addresses the Hwalbindang men, he asserts that while he may be their chieftain, he exists only for their sake.[69] Kings and officials should also exist only for the sake of the common people, but that is unfortunately not the case in the current state of the country. The powerful rule over the people as if they are their slaves. It is the purpose of the Hwalbindang to rectify the situation. After the speech, Jeong explains Hong Gildong's views in the following way: "At the time the word 'democracy' that we use today did not exist, of course. Yet the view held by Hong Gildong was the same democratic ideal that we speak of in our time. And he was a true hero of democracy who sought to realize that ideal in the world."[70] But even as Hong Gildong expresses discontent at the social system that divides people into *yangban* and commoners,[71] Jeong says that "Hong Gildong was not someone who was fond of revolution" but one who preferred to "set things right in a rational manner while avoiding an outright revolt."[72] Through most of the novel, Hong is indeed presented as a reformer rather than a revolutionary, doing the work of an upright official by punishing the corrupt and returning their ill-gotten wealth to the people.

The situation changes in the last part of the narrative, when he becomes convinced, just like Bak Taewon's Hong Gildong, that King Yeonsan must be toppled for the sake of the suffering people. Unlike Bak's protagonist, however, Jeong's hero actually participates in the ensuing coup d'état, leading his men into the capital to help righteous ministers dethrone the monarch.[73] In a strikingly ironic scene, however, Hong reveals his most conservative side after his victory, when some people express the wish that he become the new king of Joseon.[74] He falls into depression, overwhelmed with the guilt he feels from having acted beyond what is fitting to his social station, by playing a key role in the downfall of the king. He confides in his old master Hakjo about the matter.

> "Master, I am suffering so much at the thought that I have committed an act of treason. What must I do?"
>
> "Hmm . . . , I understand your feelings. Your concerns are justified if you consider your situation in light of the principle of propriety between the ruler and his subjects. But you should also take into account the fact that you also achieved an act of enhancing goodness and suppressing evil, and see that there is no reason to trouble yourself."
>
> "That may be so, but still, I, a mere subject, dared to expel His Majesty from his throne, so how can that not be a crime?"[75]

This sudden conservatism on Hong's part, which did not bother him at all earlier when he decided to take part in the coup, provides Jeong with a convenient way of ending the novel. To atone for what he views as a crime, he disbands the Hwalbindang before he takes his parents and his love interest, a girl named Yamjeon ("Modest One")—who plays a disappointingly minor role in the story despite the fact that she is also taught martial arts by Master Hakjo—and goes into voluntary exile in Geumgang Mountain. So the "hero of democracy" proves himself to be a traditional Confucian at the end, abandoning the affairs of the world and leaving the country's social and political system intact.

The most interesting aspect of this popular novel about a very familiar subject is how Jeong Biseok took many of his narrative ideas from Bak Tae-won's leftist work but made crucial changes to turn it into a significantly more conservative tale. While Jeong's Hong Gildong is described as a champion of protodemocratic ideals who abhors the status system of Joseon, he is first and foremost a patriot who ultimately bows down to the Confucian principles of propriety and order. For that reason, he can neither take the throne for himself nor carry on the fight to transform his country into a more egalitarian state devoid of the privileges of class and wealth.

THE NORTH KOREAN HONG GILDONG

One of the most bizarre episodes from the surrealistic dystopia that North Korea has become is the kidnapping of the South Korean filmmakers Shin Sang-ok and Choi Eun-hee in 1978. Before Kim Jong-il became the supreme leader of North Korea in 1994, he oversaw the cultural and artistic development of the country, especially in the realm of cinema, in which he had a special interest.[76] From the mid-1960s onward, Kim reportedly put a great deal of personal effort into building up a film industry, even writing a textbook entitled *On the Art of the Cinema* (1973), which inevitably became the essential guidebook for all North Korean filmmakers.[77] By the second half of the 1970s, however, Kim apparently became frustrated by the persistently low quality of the industry's domestic products and took a rather drastic measure to rectify the situation.

Choi Eun-hee (1926–2018), a celebrated South Korean actress, and her ex-husband Shin Sang-ok (1926–2006), one of the South's most successful directors, were kidnapped by North Korean agents in Hong Kong and forced to make films for Kim Jong-il.[78] Starting in 1983, Shin and Choi ran the central production company in North Korea until March 1986, when Kim Jong-il allowed them to travel to Austria on a business trip, where they managed to elude their minders and flee to the US embassy, where they received asylum.[79]

The Shin Sang-ok and Choi Eun-hee period of 1983–1986 represents the only golden era of North Korean cinema, when Shin, Choi, and directors under their supervision produced the best films ever made in the country. This was thanks not only to their filmmaking talents but also the considerable leeway Kim Jong-il afforded them in artistic expression. As spelled out in no uncertain terms in Kim's textbook on cinema, all North Korean films had to feature "correct" political themes in the works, including the support of the central *juche* ("self-reliance") ideology of the country's founder Kim Il-sung, the depiction of the inequities of feudal Joseon, and the exposure of the evils of the Japanese, Americans, and

South Koreans. While such ideas are apparent in the works directed or supervised by Shin and Choi, they were allowed to be relegated to the background, to let the central narratives unfold in a naturalistic manner.

One of the films Shin supervised in 1986 was *Hong Gildong*, directed by Kim Gilin and written by Kim Seryun, which was released after Shin's departure (fig. 5.4). The work is essentially a martial arts movie, and it enjoyed success not only domestically but also in a number of Soviet-bloc Eastern European countries.[80] The requisite ideological criticism of Joseon-dynasty feudalism is featured in the work but does not dominate the narrative. The plot element that is most characteristically North Korean is also the film's most original feature, namely, the sudden appearance of Japanese ninjas whom Hong and his men battle in the last part of the film, reflecting the country's endemic xenophobia.

The story begins in the familiar manner, with the birth of Hong by the lowborn concubine of Minister Hong. The baby grows up to become an extraordinarily talented boy. Hong Gildong's father is an honest official who informs the king that many people in the northern province of Pyeongan have turned to banditry because of hardship brought on by the corruption of local officials. Through the connivance of a rival in the royal court, Minister Hong is dispatched to the troubled province to deal with the chaotic situation.

Hong Gildong and his mother decide to join him, but on their way north they are ambushed by a group of bandits hired by Minister Hong's wife to murder them. Their servants are killed, but Hong and his mother are saved by a mysterious old man who paralyzes the bandits with

Figure 5.4. Ri Yeongho as Hong Gildong in the North Korean film *Hong Gildong* (1986).

touches to their pressure points. The old man takes the boy and his mother to his mountainside abode, where he agrees to teach martial arts to Hong. It is clear in the ensuing scenes that the work was influenced by Shin Dong Wu's comic books, probably from Shin Sang-ok's familiarity with them. In Shin's comics, Master Baekun has Hong practice his jumping skills by leaping over a corn stalk that grows taller and taller. Eventually, Hong can jump so high he is able to fly through the air.[81] In the North Korean film, the old man orders the young boy Hong to jump repeatedly over a sapling. The scene then cuts neatly to years later: the sapling has become a tall tree, and the fully grown Hong can fly over it.

The young man goes to a rural inn on an errand and encounters the same bandits who tried to kill him and his mother. In the fight that ensues, he kills their chieftain and rescues a girl named Yeonhwa ("Lotus Flower"), who turns out to be the daughter of a political rival of Hong's father. Their love blooms, but Hong's teacher forces him to return the girl to her family, since his training is not complete. Eventually, the teacher tells Hong that he has taught him all that he knows and that he must go forth to "defend the country and save the people from misery." Hong and his mother return to Minister Hong's house, to the shock of everyone who thought them dead, especially the minister's wife, who plotted their murder. Once it is revealed that Hong was Yeonhwa's savior, her father arranges for them to marry, but when he finds out that he is a secondary son, he cancels the wedding. Hong is subjected to another murder attempt by the assassin Teukjae, who turns out to be the brother of the bandit chieftain Hong killed, but is saved by a warning from his half-brother Inhyeong. After that, Hong leaves the household.

Out in the world, Hong learns of the greed, corruption, and depravities of the nobility and the sufferings of the common people. When he wonders how learned men could be capable of such cruelty, a peasant tells him that "all *yangban* are cruel." He then embarks on rescuing unjustly persecuted commoners, punishing corrupt noblemen, and distributing their ill-gotten wealth to the people. After Hong gathers a group of righteous outlaws to work with him, including the reformed Teukjae, a new enemy appears. Mysterious men in black, referred to as the Black Shadow Group, kidnap young women and steal treasures from the royal palace. Hong's half-brother Inhyeong, now a government official, is in charge of stopping them. After a series of violent confrontations, the black shadows are exposed as Japanese ninjas who are arranging for a ship to take them and their booty out of Joseon. In the climactic battle that follows, the film alternates from a scene at a beach, where government soldiers led by Inhyeong and bandits under the command of Teukjae cooperate in fighting the ninja army, to Hong Gildong going after the chief ninja and his men. In a series of well-executed martial arts sequences, Hong Gildong, Inhyeong, and their men triumph over the foreigners. Once again, the kidnapped women represent the nation's purity and integrity, which must be protected from violation at the hands of nefarious outsiders.

When the heroes are brought to the royal court, the king tells Hong that he will grant him anything he wishes as a reward for his service to the country. Hong responds that he desires nothing for himself but asks that the monarch help the common people. Inhyeong, however, steps forward to request that the king grant his half-brother permission to marry Yeon-hwa, despite his low birth. But Yeonhwa's father objects that allowing such a thing would lead to the confusion of classes. The king agrees with the father, reneging on his promise to Hong. The film ends with Hong and his men, along with his mother and Yeonhwa, leaving Joseon on a ship. A narrator describes how they are leaving Joseon in search of a land without class discrimination and poverty but then asks whether such a place of equality and plenty will really be waiting for them beyond the sea.

As previously mentioned, the film is mostly a martial arts action movie, with only a modicum of political and social criticism of Joseon in the depictions of the contemptuous treatment Hong has to endure because of his lowborn status and of the corrupt behavior of the nobility. The appearance of ninjas in the final act is a cliché of Japanese villainy, a familiar theme in North Korean cinema. It is only in the ending that the film makes its antifeudal message explicit.

Despite the ideologically "correct" conclusion of the narrative, however, the political content of the work is less radical than Bak Taewon's 1947 novel. In Bak's work, all *yangban* officials, including Hong's father and half-brother, are corrupt and lascivious men who are complicit in Joseon's feudal order. The North Korean film, on the other hand, follows the original work in portraying Minister Hong and his legitimate son as upright and honest officials, despite the claim by a peasant that all *yangban* are cruel. In addition, when the king reneges on his promise to reward Hong, the hero makes no protest at the injustice and meekly withdraws to leave the kingdom.

The surprising weakness of the political message may stem from the double-edged nature of portraying a heroic rebel against tyrannical authority. Hong Gildong's activities might give viewers the opportunity to question the nature of oppression in their own society and inspire resistance to it. I will elaborate on this point further when I compare the film to the South Korean television show *Sharp Blade Hong Gildong* (*Kwaedo Hong Gildong*, 2008), which features a conclusion with a much more radical political message.

CHAPTER SIX

South Korea, 1994–Present

The Republic of Korea's spectacular rise to economic prosperity and its attainment of democracy in 1988 hardly made the classic figure of the righteous outlaw irrelevant. As seen in the previous chapters, many writers who retold the Hong Gildong story in the twentieth century deployed the figure in opposition to contemporary tyranny, from the Japanese colonial authorities to the dictatorial regimes of Syngman Rhee and Park Chung-hee. But even in the period of dynamic economic growth, representative politics, and free expression, persistent problems remained, including the economic disparity among the classes, the corruption of politicians and *chaebol* corporations, and the perpetually tense situation with North Korea. In the new age, many South Korean cultural figures continued to be inspired by the rebel hero from the past. But with the changing times, the image and significance of Hong Gildong underwent a transformation as well. Two literary stories published in the 1990s provide good examples of the novel ways in which the righteous outlaw was utilized in the era.

HONG GILDONG IN A TIME OF PROSPERITY
AND DEMOCRACY

Yi Munyol (1948–) emerged in the 1980s as one of the most important South Korean writers. In 1994 he published a short story collection that included "In Search of Hong Gildong" ("Hong Gildong eul chajaseo"). The narrative is a family drama concerning a Joseon-dynasty scholar from a prominent *yangban* family who is lauded for his erudition. He is particularly famous for his mastery of the Chinese classic of divination *Zhouyi* (the *I Ching*), the book that Hong Gildong learned his magic from, which allows him to tell a person's fortune with uncanny accuracy. At an advanced age, he sees the birth of his only daughter, whom he loves deeply. He educates her personally, delighting in her display of extraordinary intelligence. But just as Hong Gildong's father lamented that his secondary son's talents would go to waste because he is lowborn, the scholar regrets her gender, saying, "This is the limit of my fortune in life. If you had been born a man, I could have raised you to become a great scholar."[1]

After the girl grows up, marries a young man from a respectable family, and becomes pregnant with her first child, she comes to visit her childhood home. Despite her father's objection, she insists on staying there to give birth in a closed-up room that is reputed to be a place of concentrated vital energy, in the hope that it will give her an extraordinary child. She has a healthy boy and returns to her husband's household, and her father comes to see the child. When the boy's paternal grandfather asks him to use his divinatory skills to tell the baby's fortune, he declines. When his in-law insists, he reveals the truth of what he sees—"Do not put too much hope in this child. He is not long for this world. You should see about getting yourself a second grandchild."[2] The dire pronouncement creates a rift between him and his in-laws as well as his daughter, who becomes estranged from him. They only see each other again eight years later, at the funeral of the daughter's father-in-law. She tells her father that despite his prediction her son is alive and well, to which he replies, "I have heard that was so, but eight years is not enough time to know how things will turn out." Indeed, the boy dies of illness a year later, and then the narrator relates the decline and fall of both families. The relevance of the story's title is not revealed until the very last paragraph.

> At this point, there will be those who wonder why I decided to tell such a story, in the form of literary fiction, no less. Would it be very strange for me to answer them by saying—"In order to search for Hong Gildong"? What I mean by that is, I wanted to see if I could revive the traditional characteristics of works like *The Story of Hong Gildong*, *The Story of Sim Cheong*, and *The Story of Janghwa and Hongryeon* in modern fiction. To explain further, the feeling of nostalgia that is aroused by stories from a traditional family history and the unique charm of such narratives, they inspired me to write this strange and formless tale.[3]

Despite the title, Hong Gildong himself never appears, though the traditional genre of the family drama harkens back to the first part of *The Story of Hong Gildong*. The figure, nevertheless, plays a symbolic role as the

touchstone of Korean tradition embodied in classic literature. In the introduction to the story collection, Yi Munyol characterizes "In Search of
Hong Gildong" as "an experimental work dealing with the tradition of
national literature."[4] The conclusion of the story points to the gulf between classic and modern Korean fiction, which also speaks of the sudden and violent intrusion of modernity in the country's history. Yi, in
telling this seemingly old-fashioned story, which is actually a hybrid of
classic and modern elements, attempts to explore the possibility of heal-
ing the rift between the old and the new. This is in contrast to many revisions of the Hong Gildong story in which authors make use of the
righteous outlaw by altering, updating, and modernizing him in order to
make his story relevant to contemporary concerns. Rather than forcing
the old to accommodate itself to the new, Yi wants to transform the new
through the revitalization of the old. Can we still tell the kinds of tales
that entertained our ancestors through the medium of modern fiction in a
way that would be meaningful to contemporary readers? Yi admits that
this particular story may be one that has not found its proper form, but he
suggests that modern Korean literature could find a great deal of inspiration in the attempt to establish a connection with the literature of the bygone era. The true relevance of *The Story of Hong Gildong* is Yi's use of the
work as the representative example of classic fiction, the spirit of which
has been lost in the modern period but could be found again.

The 1998 story "Hong Gildong" by Seo Hajin (1960–) is the first work
written by a female writer to make symbolic use of the hero.[5] Seo makes it
clear at the outset that the title is an ironic one, in a similar way to Han
Seungwon's "The Story of the New Gildong." Given the image of Hong
Gildong as a heroic and righteous figure, it is comical that he is associated
with the narrator of the story, who is an ordinary middle-aged man living
in contemporary Seoul. He is an everyman whose life and psychology
make it impossible to live up to the ideal of the great hero. But unlike the
other would-be Hong Gildongs who appeared earlier, his feeling of inad-
equacy does not come from his failure to defeat tyrannical rulers, corrupt
officials, or foreign invaders who are oppressing the people and endan-
gering the dignity of the women in his life. As a man living in an age of
prosperity and democracy, one who has met the social requirements of
having a respectable job and a stable family, his problems stem from his
sense of leading an essentially meaningless existence in the midst of the
monotonous bustle of modern life. He is, in fact, depressed to the extent of
considering suicide, and the only thing keeping him from that course is
the fear of how it would affect his loved ones. He goes to a therapist, but
the sessions do not go well as he walks out of the office whenever he is

confronted with issues he finds too difficult to face. In the course of the story, a number of things are revealed that shed light on his current condition. His midlife crisis may be exacerbated by a condition he inherited from his father, who committed suicide when the protagonist was seven years old. The true cause of his death was kept a secret, with the official story of an accidental drowning while fishing. But he remembers the terrible repercussions of his father's action on his family, for which his grandmother condemned him as a "disgraceful son."[6] This makes him reluctant to cause the same distress to his own family.

He also had a mistress with whom he had a passionate but guilt-ridden affair. He used his position as an executive in the broadcasting industry to advance her career. But once she became a successful talk-show host, she cut off contact with him, sending him into despair. In this time of crisis, the narrator dreams every night of Hong Gildong. The hero is evoked not as a figure of righteous rebellion but for a specific magical power he demonstrates in the classic novel.

> Hong Gildong . . . who made exact replicas of himself out of straw. What if I were to disappear and a person just like me—if indeed we can call something like that a person—remained there to do everything I had ever done? Someone who, instead of me, went to work in the morning, did my job, joked with my coworkers, went home to listen to my wife's nagging, and every once in a while slept with her, making a seamless transition after my disappearance. No one notices I've evaporated. I could sell my soul for a replica. I was sick of it—pushing my phantom of a self when I no longer had the energy to sustain myself in this world.
>
> Every night I dreamt of Hong Gildong. Dreams where with one breath I stand tall, a straw man; the breath cools and I fall limp. I creep in like smoke and disappear without a trace. A point in time before my birth. I wanted to return to a life unconceived, to primal fluid spilled, a kernel smaller than the first of seeds.[7]

If he could create a replica of himself, that would be the perfect solution to his problem, since then he could disappear from existence without leaving his family to deal with the consequences of his death. Perhaps then he could make a fresh start through reincarnation.

At the end of the story, when he is actually confronted by his doppelgänger, who is willing to take his place, the narrator suddenly becomes uncertain about the prospect of disappearing from the world. His agonizing ambivalence and the ultimate loss of sanity are represented in the confused way he tries to communicate with his double, whom he sees across a street.

I raised my hand. He waved in greeting. "I don't need you anymore—you can disappear," I mumbled in his direction. He said something too; I think it was, "I can't; you are the one who ought to disappear." I said, "I'll explain." The other I said, "No, you can't explain." I said, "Nothing happened. It's over now." The other I said, "That's not important. Come over here."

"No, I'll go over there." I took a step toward him. He took a stride toward me, and at that very moment I saw him grin. He seemed featherlight. Out of his pockets popped his hands, and his arms unfurled like wings. The tails of his trench coat flapped and he seemed ready to fly away.[8]

The scene is rife with uncertainty about whether he is encountering a magical straw man version of himself or if the other is the real Hong Gildong and the narrator has been a straw man replica all along. The man across the street seems about to fly into the air, but the narrator also feels like he is growing ever lighter and has the sense that he is "scattering like straw."[9] He steps onto the street to meet his double, only to be hit fatally by a car.

One of the recurring themes in contemporary South Korean literature is the sense of alienation that an everyman character feels from the stressful grind and the repetitive monotony of modern life. The fear of falling into dire poverty or being subjected to political oppression may have lessened during the era of prosperity and democracy, but there is a clear sense in the literary depictions of the modern Korean condition that the attainment of financial security and social respectability fails to address essential issues of personal happiness and fulfillment. Works that tackle the topic often employ imagery of birds, wings, and flight, in fantasies of escape from the life of quiet desperation. In Seo Hajin's story, the protagonist has been so beaten down by stress and depression that he can think of Hong Gildong only in terms of how possessing his power to make replicas of himself would allow him to escape into death.

In contemporary fiction, the figure of Hong Gildong remains relevant as an ideal to hearken back to. He is the representative of the traditional world that has passed as well as of the haunting figure of invincible masculinity that the modern Korean man longs for in fantasies of flight and regeneration.

HONG GILDONG IN THE AGE OF *HALLYU*

Sharp Blade Hong Gildong (2008) and *The Descendants of Hong Gildong* (2009)

Although the Hong Gildong story continued to be retold in popular culture, it became apparent in the 1990s that the old narrative had to be infused with a novel sensibility to attract a new audience. Koreans had become too familiar with the story, having memorized its plot and its cultural significance for school examinations and watched different media versions of it throughout their childhood and youth. When the director Shin Dong Heun made a sequel to the 1967 animated film and released it under the title of *Return of the Hero Hong Gildong* (*Doraon yeongung Hong Gildong*) in 1995, it proved to be a box-office failure. Likewise, when the television network SBS aired a new *Hong Gildong* series that ran from July to September of 1998, a standard costume drama taking place during the reign of King Yeonsan, it did not reach a significant audience. The public indifference to such works might have led producers to conclude that the old story has been told too many times to be revisited again. Indeed, no major version of the Hong Gildong narrative appeared for a decade after the SBS show. In the same period, however, South Koreans found significant opportunities to export their cultural products beyond the domestic market in the phenomenon that has earned the name of *hallyu*.

The term, meaning "Korean Wave," was coined by Chinese journalists in the late 1990s to denote the spectacular success of South Korean entertainment products, particularly television dramas, pop music, and movies, across East Asia.[10] The phenomenon began with early successes such as the drama *What Is Love Anyway* (*Sarangi mwogille*, 1991), which was a hit in China and other countries, and the spy-thriller film *Shiri* (1999), an international blockbuster. The *hallyu* phenomenon expanded even more in the first decade of the new century, with shows such as *Winter Sonata* (*Gyeoul yeonga*) and *The Great Janggeum* (*Dae Janggeum*) dominating numerous television markets and Korean pop music (K-pop) finding a massive audience among the young not just in Asia but also in Europe and South America. It has been a limited phenomenon in the United States, but Korean films have made significant inroads, with such works as *Old Boy* (2003), *Memories of Murder* (2003), and *The Host* (2006) receiving critical approbations as well as cult followings. The ubiquitous playing of the rap song "Gangnam Style" by the singer Psy in late 2012, from a viral video on YouTube, marks the first mainstream success of Korean pop music in the United States.

In January 2008, the television network KBS began to air *Sharp Blade Hong Gildong* (*Kwaedo Hong Gildong*; English release title: *Hong Gildong, the Hero*), which played for the next three months, over twenty-four episodes. This fresh and innovative take on the Hong Gildong story was created as a *hallyu* product, and it proved to be successful domestically and abroad.[11]

The narrative departs completely from *The Story of Hong Gildong* and the historical reality of Joseon society, and it engages in flagrant and deliberate anachronisms. Modern objects including a telescope, sunglasses, and golf clubs appear in the show, which also features K-pop songs as background music and young characters interacting like modern-day youths. Such ahistorical elements are part of the show's *hallyu* strategy in addressing an international audience that has no inherent interest in the essential "Koreanness" of the narrative. The anachronisms, furthermore, are sometimes used to brilliant effect in addressing social and political issues of contemporary relevance and as a series of postmodern commentaries on the Hong Gildong tradition.

The show is an example of a recently developed genre called "fusion historical drama" (*fusion sageuk*), denoting a narrative set in premodern Korea but with little concern for historical accuracy or specificity and featuring modern elements. It purportedly takes place during the Joseon dynasty and when China was under Qing rule, an odd choice given that the putative author Heo Gyun lived when China was still Ming. The two kings featured in the story are not named, and the plotline of the second one's overthrow of the first is entirely fictional, since no such coup occurred in Joseon after the establishment of the Qing dynasty in 1644. The first king is an amalgam of both Joseon-dynasty monarchs who were dethroned, Yeonsan and Gwanghae, as he is portrayed as a lunatic, like the former, and as a killer of his half-brother, like the latter.

Figure 6.1. Advertisement for the KBS television show *Sharp Blade Hong Gildong* (*Kwaedo Hong Gildong*, 2008) with Hong Gildong (center, played by Kang Jihwan), his love interest Heo Inok (center right, Sung Yu Ri), and the prince-in-exile Yi Changhwi (center left, Jang Geunseok). The other four are key members of the Hwalbindang.

The first episode opens in a comically anachronistic manner, at a party where corrupt *yangban* are entertained by dancers doing hip-hop moves to a Korean rap song. A young woman flies into the palace on a giant kite and joins the dance. She is Heo Inok (played by Sung Yu Ri, whom *hallyu* consumers would recognize as a former member of the popular K-pop girl group Fin.K.L.), a Hwalbindang outlaw. The other bandits then crash the party, led by a conspicuously modern-looking Hong Gildong (played by Kang Jihwan) sporting a pair of sunglasses and a stylish haircut. They defeat the soldiers at the scene, bring the noblemen to their knees, and are greeted with cheers by the common people. A flashback takes the audience to several years before, to show how Hong became the chief of the righteous outlaws.

In the rest of the episode, the obligatory scenes from Hong's life at home are shown quickly, starting with his exclusion from the household ritual of paying respect to the monumental tablets of ancestors because he is a secondary son. Hong also remembers his childhood, when he was forbidden from addressing his father as Father and his older brother as Brother. The story then departs from the original *The Story of Hong Gildong*. It is revealed that his mother was killed when he was a child because she tried to run away to give him a better life somewhere. A Buddhist priest by the name of Master Haemyeong takes him under his wing and teaches him martial arts. Despite his teacher's attempt to turn him into a righteous champion of the powerless, Hong becomes a street thug who terrorizes local merchants and shopkeepers by causing disturbances in the city streets and stealing their goods. He spends much of his time getting drunk, gambling, and sleeping with prostitutes. His ultimate plan is to gather enough money to make his way to Qing China, where he can start a new life. The first episodes are mostly humorous in nature, with many scenes of broad physical comedy that can be easily comprehended across cultures.

As the story proceeds, it departs even further from the original, becoming more complex with the arrival from China of a mysterious young man named Yi Changhwi (played by the popular *hallyu* actor and model Jang Geunseok), who is actually a prince in exile and the rightful heir to the throne of Joseon. He is returning to the country to topple the mad usurper king, his half-brother. Also on the ship is an old man named Heo (Jeong Gyusu) and his adopted granddaughter, Inok, who deal in Chinese medicine. Three distinct plotlines unfurl in the ensuing episodes, first of Hong Gildong coming to understand the inequities of Joseon society and becoming the leader of righteous outlaws, second of Yi Changhwi planning his revolution against the king, and third of the blossoming romance between Hong and the ditzy but pure-hearted Inok.

In addition to the use of modern music, the appearance of anachronistic fashion and objects for their "coolness" effect, and the casting of young, attractive actors, some of them already known internationally, the show bolsters its *hallyu*-ness with references to foreign languages and cultural icons. In an early episode, not long after Hong and Inok first meet, he asks her to give him lessons in Chinese. Inok obliges by teaching him the Mandarin expression *jia you*, literally meaning "put more gas" (that is, in a car), which is commonly used as a cheer to urge a person or a sports team on. Both Hong and Inok utter the phrase throughout the show. Inok also tells a member of the Hwalbindang that she has seen Westerners in China utter the English phrase "I love you" before hugging and kissing each other. She says it a number of times to Hong because she is too embarrassed to express her feelings in Korean. In yet another scene, Hong and Inok get into an argument about whether the Korean virgin-girl ghost or the Chinese vampire-zombie *jiangshi* is more frightening, with visual representations of both creatures. When Hong Gildong joins four outlaws who will go on to become the core members of the Hwalbindang, their characteristics evoke the members of Japanese children's shows like the *Super Sentai* series (reedited as *Mighty Morphin Power Rangers* in the United States) and *Kagaku ninjatai gatchaman* (*G-Force* in the United States, *Doksuri ohyeongje* in Korea). The heroes in these shows are usually five in number,

Figure 6.2. Hong Gildong in the age of *hallyu*. Kang Jihwan as Hong Gildong and Sung Yu Ri as Heo Inok in *Sharp Blade Hong Gildong*.

consisting of a male leader, a female, a large obese man, a thin sharp-featured man, and a young boy, which is reflected in *Sharp Blade Hong Gildong* by the characters Hong Gildong, Jeong Malnyeo, Yeon Ssi, Sim Sugeun, and Gomi, respectively. This creates a sense of familiarity for the international audience who may not know the Hong Gildong tradition but grew up watching the Japanese shows, which were popular throughout East Asia.

The early episodes are comedic and modern in their pop-culture sensibility, designed to entertain young *hallyu* audiences with only a superficial resemblance to the original story of Hong Gildong. As the narrative unfolds, the anachronisms characteristic of fusion historical dramas are sometimes used in a surprisingly creative manner, especially in references to contemporary social and political concerns. In one scene, a corrupt *yangban* official shows off his luxurious foreign-made sedan chair, though he admits that as a government official he should buy a domestic product, as a modern politician might with his expensive automobile. In another episode, the same official discusses his nefarious plans while playing golf with wooden clubs of faux-Joseon design. And in another scene, in a conversation between a minister and a noblewoman, the former discusses the arrival of an envoy from Qing China. He points out that when a large and powerful empire like China demands things of a small country like Joseon, there is little choice but to comply. As an example, he mentions that the government was obligated to send soldiers to fight in Arabia despite the people's objections. This is a reference to the participation of several thousand South Korean troops in the recent US wars in Iraq and Afghanistan.

The show also makes a series of clever postmodern commentaries on the Hong Gildong tradition. After Hong Gildong turns into a righteous outlaw and becomes beloved by the common people, Inok's grandfather, Heo the medicine salesman, entertains a crowd by telling them the fantastic story of Hong's early life, how his father had a vision of a dragon that compelled him to have intercourse with a servant girl, and how Hong grew up to become a master of martial arts and magic. Much of the fantastic tale, including Hong's supernatural powers, is exaggerated by the old man, who is trying to attract an audience for the purpose of selling his medicine. To emphasize the invented nature of his story, the visual representation of his narration shows Hong dressed in the familiar manner of the figure from the 1960s Shin Dong Wu comics, complete with a blue vest and a small hat.

When Master Haemyeong, Hong's martial arts teacher, asks Heo what his personal name is, his answer is a terrific joke that references a number of famous figures with the family name of Heo. The old man confesses that because he is involved in a number of trades, he uses a different name for each of them. When he sells medicine, he calls himself Heo Jun, the celebrated Joseon-dynasty doctor of the late sixteenth and early seventeenth century; when he is engaged in business, he calls himself Heo Saeng, the fictional scholar from a story by the eighteenth-century writer Bak Jiwon, who becomes rich through shrewd dealings in goods; when he acts as a storyteller, he calls himself Heo Gyun, the putative author of *The Story of Hong Gildong*; and when he exercises for the sake of physical fitness, he calls himself Heo Jae, who was South Korea's most famous basketball player during the late 1980s and 1990s.

Toward the end of the show, after Hong Gildong rejects the love of Seo Eunhye, the daughter of the evil Minister Seo, she tries to get back at him by writing the work *The Story of Hong Gildong* and arranging for it to be circulated among the common people. She does this to get him into trouble with the "subversive" story of a secondary son who becomes a king. This is an original notion of the classic work being authored by a jilted woman.

Given the light tone of much of the show, the rather serious and radical turn of the last two episodes comes as a surprise. After an initially antagonistic relationship, Hong Gildong and the prince Yi Changhwi form an alliance, following Hong's realization that the mad king has to be toppled for the sake of the common people. Yi promises Hong that if they succeed, he will become a benevolent king who works for the welfare of all his subjects. They start a revolution, which ends with the king being dethroned and Yi becoming the new ruler of Joseon. The story could very well have ended there, as did the novels by Bak Taewon and Jeong Biseok, with Hong disbanding the Hwalbindang to live happily ever after with his beloved Inok, but the narrative then unexpectedly takes a dark and complicated turn.

Soon after Yi Changhwi ascends the throne, he finds out that what he thought was the proof of his rightful claim to kingship was a fabrication. His deceased mother had ordered the maker of the royal sword to engrave a message on the blade that falsely claimed that it was the wish of Changhwi's father that he succeed him. Ruthless noblemen who become privy to the information use it not only to maintain their power under the new monarch but also to prevent him from enacting reforms that would help the common people. Hong Gildong comes to the despairing Yi and criticizes him for retaining all the corrupt officials in his court. When Yi tells him about the situation he is in, Hong exhorts him to forget about court intrigue and establish his legitimacy by doing well by the people. Yi tries to do so by appointing Hong as the minister of military affairs and then as the head of the Office of the Inspector General. But he is soon forced to dismiss Hong from both posts when his officials vehemently protest the upstart's forcible drafting of noble sons into the army (a reference to the contemporary scandal of inordinate numbers of sons from wealthy and politically connected families avoiding mandatory military service) and his confiscation of the ill-gotten wealth of corrupt officials.

When Hong Gildong comes to take leave of Yi Changhwi, to rejoin the Hwalbindang in a mountain lair, the king confronts him about the work *The Story of Hong Gildong*, which has become so popular that it has attracted the attention of powerful people. The following exchange takes place between them.

Yi Changhwi: This story is about a hero named Hong Gildong who is lowborn, but becomes the minister of military affairs, and finally a king.

Hong Gildong: I did not write it.

Yi: I know that, but this has become a big problem. It contains ideas that call for the destruction of the monarchy as well as the entire social system. Someone is dreaming up these notions, and the people are greeting them with enthusiasm.

Hong: All that is completely different from what I want. Even if I were to create a new place like the country on Yul Island, I would not become its king nor make someone else its king.

Yi: Are you saying that you wish to live in a world that has no need of a sovereign?

Hong: Every country needs a ruler. But a king is someone who comes to power as if he dropped from the heavens, whether the people want him or not. But things would be different if the common people got to choose their ruler according to their true desire.

Yi: That would not be a king. That is not how one becomes a king. Is it your desire to destroy the monarchy and the social system of this country?

Hong: Even if kings and *yangban* were to disappear, another group of powerful people would rise under a different name. And beneath their power, there will also be the lowborn and the enslaved. There may not be any world out there where every person is equal. But people below will continue to harbor the dream of such a world and carry on the struggle to realize it. The Hwalbindang and I live among such people and exist for them.

Yi: Are you saying that you will continue to fight until you create that world?

Hong: Only through struggle can some changes be realized.

Yi: Stop now. If you do not find a way to stop, you will find yourself going against the country, of which I am the protector.

Hong: I will not be broken by such a fight. In fact, I will fight until all that I confront is broken. I know that this is hard for you to accept, but you promised me once that you would try to understand and trust me. I know for certain that I am going to a better world.

This constitutes another postmodern commentary on *The Story of Hong Gildong*, in that Hong Gildong denies harboring the literary character's ambition to become a king of his own country. In contradiction to the tradition of describing Yul Island as an egalitarian utopia, Hong rightly points out that if he became a king of such a place, it would be an act of replicating the Joseon political and social system, with all of its inherent inequities. By denigrating the conclusion of *The Story of Hong Gildong*, he presents himself as a much more radical figure than the protagonist of the original work. In this *hallyu* version of the story, Hong is a protodemocrat who believes that a country's ruler should be chosen by the people.

After much agonizing over the situation, the king decides that he has no choice but to send an army to the lair of the Hwalbindang and force them to disband. They refuse to do so, and government troops completely surround the home of the righteous outlaws. That night, Hong, his beloved Inok, and the remaining Hwalbindang gather together for the last time before waves of fire arrows fall upon them, destroying their home and everyone in it. The show ends with scenes of Joseon's capital city turning into modern-day Seoul, with the voice of Master Haemyeong claiming that Hong Gildong is immortal and that he will still be alive in a hundred years, in five hundred years, always watching over this world divided between the powerful and the powerless. The last image is of Hong Gildong standing atop a skyscraper, armed with his staff and dressed in red (the color of revolution), gazing down at the streets of the metropolis.

As a *hallyu* product designed to appeal mainly to a young audience, this serious and politically engaged conclusion comes as a surprise. The North Korean film version of the Hong Gildong story features the requisite criticism of Joseon society, but the issue is dealt with only briefly and in a more cautious manner than in *Sharp Blade Hong Gildong*.[12] The two works are informed by different political ideologies, the northern one displaying the xenophobia of *juche* (self-reliance) and the southern one pointing to modern democracy. But it is the South Korean show that ends up presenting its political viewpoint in a much more overt and radical manner.

In the conclusion of the North Korean film, when the king refuses to let Hong Gildong marry a nobleman's daughter, the hero leaves Joseon without complaining to his sovereign about his broken promise. In contrast,

the South Korean show has Hong confront the king, argue with him vocif-
erously, and ultimately fight to the death against his army. It is also significant that the North Korean film features good and honest officials like
Hong's morally upright father and half-brother, despite a peasant's declaration that "all *yangban* are cruel." Bak Taewon, in his social-realist novel of
1947, took the more radical step of condemning the entire *yangban* class as
hopelessly corrupt, including Hong's greedy and lascivious father and
half-brother. *Sharp Blade Hong Gildong*, interestingly, follows Bak's example
in portraying all noblemen as villains. Hong's father is the chief advisor to
the mad king who tries to stop Yi Changhwi's revolution, and his half-
brother Inhyeong is a bumbling and cowardly fool who constantly tries to
bring Hong down, motivated by jealousy after finding out that his love
interest, the noble daughter Seo Eunhye, has fallen for the outlaw. Even the
officials who throw their support behind Yi Changhwi in toppling the
mad king turn out to be staunch conservatives who thwart the new monarch's reforms that would benefit the common people.

The fact that the South Korean television show ends on a much more
overtly political note than the North Korean film is indicative of the
greater measure of the freedom of expression in the democratic South,
where people feel less wary of criticizing those in positions of power. The
North Korean filmmakers may very well have been concerned about going too far in showing scenes of defiance against political authority, even
in the context of the old feudal order. That points to the double-edged
nature of the subversive potential of the Hong Gildong story, as it has
been utilized so many times in modern retellings. The righteous outlaw
could be deployed as a figure of rebellion against any tyrannical entity
that one may wish to criticize and subvert, which is dangerous in a country run by a dictatorship that demands absolute obedience and unques-
tioning loyalty from its people. The North Korean Hong Gildong fights
against corrupt officials, but when he stands before the king, he raises no
protest at his ultimate mistreatment. The hero of *Sharp Blade Hong Gildong*,
on the other hand, fights and ultimately dies for what he believes in. Even
then it is declared at the end that his spirit is alive and well today. The
presence of such a radical theme, even in a mass media show like *Sharp
Blade Hong Gildong*, points to the creative potential of South Korean culture in the age of prosperity, democracy, and global influence.

Another revision of the Hong Gildong story for a *hallyu* audience with
a similar modern sensibility is the 2009 film *Descendants of Hong Gildong*
(*Hong Gildong ui huye*, directed by Jeong Yonggi; US release title, *The Righteous Thief*). Its plot revolves around a seemingly ordinary family in contemporary Seoul who are secretly righteous thieves who steal from the

corrupt rich and give the plunder to charity because they are descendants of the Joseon-dynasty hero. In this version, the original Hong Gildong does not leave Joseon to found his own kingdom. On his deathbed, he expresses regret to his sons that despite all of his efforts, he failed to set the country in proper moral order. When his sons pledge to continue the fight, the dying hero gives them strict rules to abide by, including stealing only from the unjust and never keeping the loot for themselves.

Unlike the serious and politically charged stories of modern-day descendants of Hong Gildong by Nam Jeonghyeon ("Land of Excrement") and Park Yangho (*Hong Gildong of Seoul*), this version is comedic and action oriented. The Hong family targets Yi Jeongmin, a corrupt and murderous corporate chairman. In an early scene, Yi discovers that thieves have emptied his safe, leaving a piece of paper with the name Hong Gildong written on it. Hong Muhyeok (played by Yi Beomsu), the older son of the family,

Figure 6.3. Poster for the 2009 film *The Descendants of Hong Gildong* (US release title: *The Righteous Thief*). Hong Muhyeok (center, played by Yi Beomsu) leads a family of righteous thieves who are descendants of the Joseon-dynasty hero. They take on the evil corporate chairman Yi Jeongmin (center left, Kim Suro), who is also pursued by the upright prosecutor Song Jaepil (left, Seong Dongil), whose sister, Song Yeonhwa (right, Yi Siyeong) is in love with Muhyeok.

works as a schoolteacher during the day. He finds out that his girlfriend's brother is an upright prosecutor who is not only pursuing Yi Jeongmin but also the elusive thief who has been stealing from the villain. Given the complexities of the situation, Muhyeok decides that he must part with his beloved Yeonhwa (interestingly, the same name, meaning "lotus flower," as Hong Gildong's love interest in the North Korean film).

The funniest scene in the film occurs after Muhyeok rescues Yeonhwa from the henchmen of Yi Jeongmin, who is trying to find out the identity of the "Hong Gildong" thieves tormenting him. Muhyeok realizes that he must tell Yeonhwa the real reason he broke up with her, so she can understand why she is in danger. As soon as he confesses the truth, she responds by slapping him in the face. The following dialogue ensues:

> Song Yeonhwa: Are you saying you had to break up with me because you are the eighteenth-generation descendant of Hong Gildong, and you are also active as a righteous outlaw?
> Hong Muhyeok: Yes.
> Song: You mean, Hong Gildong who wasn't allowed to address his father as Father? Hong Gildong who flew around on a cloud, and appeared in the west and then in the east, punishing corrupt officials?
> Hong: Sure. But the real story of Hong Gildong is quite different because that writer Heo Gyun exaggerated things a lot to make it more entertaining.
> Song: Are you kidding me?

After many action sequences and endangerments, Yeonhwa realizes that Muhyeok has told her the truth. Instead of letting him go, however, she ends up joining the family as a participant in their outlaw activities.

HONG GILDONG AS HISTORICAL FANTASY

Seol Seonggyeong and Jeong Cheol's *The Real-Life Hong Gildong* and Kang Cheolgeun's *Country of Humanity*

In direct contrast to *Sharp Blade Hong Gildong* and *Descendants of Hong Gildong*, with their attempt at an international *hallyu* appeal, another narrative concerning Hong Gildong was constructed in the late 1990s that represents a retrograde attempt at infusing a renewed nationalist perspective into the hero's significance. In 1998, Seol Seonggyeong, a professor of classic Korean literature, published a book entitled *The Real-Life Hong Gildong* (*Siljon inmul Hong Gildong*), cowritten by Jeong Cheol, a journalist. Seol followed the work with two additional texts, *The Life of Hong Gildong and the Story of Hong Gildong*

(*Hong Gildong ui sam gwa Hong Gildong jeon*, 2002) and *Secret of the Story of Hong Gildong* (*Hong Gildong jeon ui bimil*, 2004), in which he further elaborated on his ideas.

What those books purport to demonstrate is not only that Hong Gildong was a historical figure, as it is known through his appearance in the *Sillok* royal records, but that the fictional story about him is a generally accurate recounting of his actual life story. In other words, Seol claims in *The Real-Life Hong Gildong* that he has found evidence that the historical Hong was indeed a secondary son of a government minister who led a band of righteous outlaws in Joseon, then left the country with his men to conquer a foreign island that he ruled over as king. The narrative he unfurls is not so much history as pseudohistorical fantasy based on a series of wild speculations, free manipulation of evidence, and filling gaps in the records with convenient fictions. Unfortunately, given its sheer entertainment value as well as its power to arouse nationalist pride in its depiction of Hong's adventures abroad, Seol's ideas have found a following in South Korea, which led to the establishment of Jangseong County in South Jeolla Province as the official "home" of Hong Gildong. His claims have also appeared uncritically in English-language scholarly works. Robert J. Fouser has written that Seol Seonggyeong

> uncovered detailed information on the historical Hong Gildong. According to Sol, Hong Kildong was born in Changsong County in South Cholla Province in 1443. He led a number of peasant rebellions, including a major rebellion in 1495 in Yonsan County, South Ch'ungch'ong Province. . . . In an attempt to escape Korea, he traveled south in 1500 to Haterumajima, a small island between Okinawa and Taiwan that is part of the Ryuku Island chain. He traveled extensively in the Ryuku Islands and died in 1510 on Kumejima. Memorial tablets and folklore relating to Hong Kildong exist on several of the islands today. This information confirms the arguments of those who believe that the story, whether authored by Ho Kyun or not, developed from folk tales about a real person named Hong Kildong.[13]

Suk-young Kim, in her discussion of the North Korean film, asserts that

> Hong Gil-dong has been known as a fictional invention of the writer Heo Gyun, but recently, scholars from both South Korea and Japan, including Seol Seolgyeong [*sic*] and Gadena Shodoku, who conducted extensive research at the Japanese Yaeyama Archive in Okinawa, have concluded that Gil-dong was an actual historical figure.[14]

As previously pointed out, it has long been known that a real-life bandit by the name of Hong Gildong operated during the reign of King Yeonsan and was captured in the year 1500. But what Seol claims to have discovered beyond that needs to be examined in some detail.

The Real-Life Hong Gildong begins by attempting to reconcile the few records of the historical bandit Hong Gildong in the *Sillok* with the legend of a runaway half-brother of the official Hong Ildong from the eighteenth-century work *Enlarged Edition of Extraordinary Events of Haedong* (*Jeungbo Haedong ijeok*) by Hwang Yunseok (1729–1791). This tale was discussed in chapter 3, but it would be useful to revisit it at this point.

> I have once heard that in the mid-period of the Joseon dynasty there lived a person by the name of Hong Gildong who was an illegitimate younger half-brother of High Minister Hong Ildong, who lived in Achagok of Jang-seong County. He was confident in his talent and vigor which made him magnanimous in spirit, but due to his status as a secondary child the laws of the land prevented him from pursuing distinction through the attainment of a government position. So he suddenly ran away one morning. At a future time, an emissary returning from Ming China said that an envoy from a country across the sea came to Beijing, bearing a letter from the king of that country whose family name is Gong. The *gong* had the ideogram *su* beneath it, so what kind of a character was this? One might suspect that perhaps this was a subtle mixing up of the character "Hong" by Gildong. Gildong then suddenly appeared, coming alone on a horse to see Ildong and to congratulate him on his birthday. He stayed with him for a few days, but when it came time for him to leave, he wept and said, "Once I go, I will never be able to return," before he quickly departed. Given the overall grandness of his character and the restlessness of his actions, he must have resolved never to live beneath the power of another, so he ran away to some foreign place where he made himself king.[15]

Seol takes this fairy tale–like story of a runaway boy who becomes the king of a foreign land and accepts it uncritically as a historical fact that needs to be reconciled with other corroborating evidence of Hong Gildong's existence. As mentioned in chapter 3, Hong Ildong of Jangseong County was indeed a historical figure, the son of a government minister by the name of Hong Sangjik, who died in the 1420s. Seol claims to have found evidence that Hong Ildong did have a half-brother named Gildong, a secondary son of Minister Hong Sangjik, in *Comprehensive Clan Records of Myriad Families* (*Manseong daedongbo*). The text is a 1931 compilation of the genealogy of major *yangban* families based on their clan records (*jokbo*). In the section on the line of the illustrious Hong family of Namyang, there is a record of "Gildong," son of Sangjik, with a note that says that he was "known as a magician."[16] For historians who deal with such records, this bit of information appears to be rather farcical, since the original Hong family *jokbo* that was used for the compilation makes no mention of Gildong. In fact, there is no record of Gildong the secondary son of Sangjik and half-brother of Ildong anywhere other than the legend recounted in the eighteenth century and the *Comprehensive Clan Records of Myriad Families*, which was published in the twentieth century. Seol explains away the absence of the name in the original Hong family *jokbo* by claiming that it was omitted because of his secondary-son status, but he offers no evidence of this. What is probably the case is that the editors of the *Comprehensive Clan Records of Myriad Families* were familiar with *The Story of Hong Gildong* and *Enlarged Edition of Extraordinary Events of Haedong* and inserted the name, with the obvious allusion to the story in describing the figure as a magician, possibly as a humorous literary reference.

Seol then tries to account for another difficulty that I have also discussed previously. In the *Sillok* of 1428, there is mention of the widow of Minister Hong Sangjik having completed the mourning period for the death of her husband.[17] That means that Minister Hong died in 1426 or slightly earlier, but not later. Even if his secondary son was born in the year of his death, Hong Gildong would have been, at the youngest, seventy-four when he was captured in 1500. Given the sheer absurdity of the idea of such an elderly bandit, Seol resorts to the first of his many fantastic speculations. Without offering a single piece of real historical evidence, he claims the following: Hong Sangjik, the father of the real Hong Gildong, must have faked his death in the 1420s for political reasons and lived on, at least until 1450, and saw the birth of his secondary son sometime in the 1440s.[18]

To reiterate, there is no evidence to justify such a speculation. Seol's certainty of it, however, is based on his idée fixe that the legend of the runaway son in *Enlarged Edition of Extraordinary Events of Haedong* is a true story and that its protagonist is the same person as the bandit leader who appears in the *Sillok*. The name of the outlaw in the royal records is written as 洪吉同, while the name in *Enlarged Edition of Extraordinary Events of Haedong* appears as 洪吉童, with a different last character. Seol concludes that the name must have been written differently in the *Sillok* in order to protect the Hong family from the disgrace of having produced an outlaw.[19]

Having established, at least in his imagination, the origin of the real-life Hong Gildong, Seol goes much further in "discovering" the hero's adventures. He points out that while the *Sillok* does show that Hong Gildong was captured in 1500, it makes no mention of him being punished for his crimes. The absence of such a record allows him to assert that Hong must have escaped and fled abroad or that he was deliberately sent away in exile.[20] His favorite theory is that Hong made a secret deal with the Joseon government, in which he and his men would pretend to be captured so that the authorities could take credit for having gotten rid of the bandit scourge, but then they would be secretly released and allowed to leave the kingdom. His main evidence for this scenario is that it matches the account in *The Story of Hong Gildong* of the hero making such a deal with the king, in which he promises to leave the country in return for a royal pardon. Needless to say, no evidence for any of that is presented, other than an argument that the lack of a definite record of Hong's execution must mean that he was in fact not executed and to point out that the stories found in both *The Story of Hong Gildong* and *Enlarged Edition of Extraordinary Events of Haedong* show that Hong Gildong went abroad to become a king. In the *Sillok* records of the reign of King Yeonsan, there are five mentions of Hong Gildong, most of them in relation to discussions on the appropriate punishment for the high-ranking official Eom Gwison, who was known to have aided Hong's bandits. The fact that Hong's capture is mentioned at all indicates the seriousness of his crimes, but there is no reason to expect that his punishment was such an important thing that it would have been recorded in the *Sillok*. The real-life outlaw Hong Gildong, unlike his collaborator Eom Gwison, was someone of no importance in terms of his social status, so he was probably executed without fuss. For Seol, however, the absence of a record of his execution provides the opportunity to build a fantasy of Hong's further adventures.

The issue that Seol then tackles is the question of where Hong Gildong could have gone to after he left Joseon. He asserts that his destination must have been the Ryukyu Islands (Okinawa) because there were diplomatic contacts between the Ryukyu Kingdom and Joseon, so Hong and his followers could have taken the ship of an envoy from the islands.[21] Korean for Ryukyu, furthermore, is Yuguguk, which is close to the name Yuldoguk ("the country of Yul Island"). Seol then attempts to bolster this assertion by claiming actually to have found evidence of Hong Gildong and his activities on the islands. In the year 1500, Oyake Akahachi, the chieftain of Ishigaki Island, raised a revolt against the central authority of the Ryukyu Kingdom, which was based in the city of Shuri on Okinawa.[22] Despite the fact that Akahachi was known to have been born on the island of Hateruma, Seol claims that he was, in fact, none other than Hong Gildong, mainly because one of his alternate names was Hongkawara.[23] Seol admits, however, that it is improbable that Hong Gildong could have escaped from Joseon, taken on the new identity as the chief of Ishigaki, and then led a rebellion within the single year of 1500. His solution to this problem is to claim that the record of the year of the revolt must be wrong, since there is also a record of the Ryukyu Kingdom sending diplomatic missions abroad and engaging in a major construction project for a royal grave around that time, which they could not have embarked on in the midst of a war, so the more likely date of the commencement of the Aka-hachi Hongkawara rebellion is 1504. The historical records also say that the rebellion was crushed in 1500, but Seol refuses to believe that this was the end of the hero. Since there is no definitive account of when and how Akahachi Hongkawara met his end, he must have survived to rule over another island, the best candidate for such a place being the island of Kumejima because there is a local legend that the island was conquered and ruled over by a foreign king around that time.[24] To all this, Seol adds one final risible fantasy, that Hong Gildong taught the people of Okinawa martial arts, which became karate, which in turn returned to Korea during the colonial period to become taekwondo.[25] Seol affirms the traditional attribution of *The Story of Hong Gildong* to Heo Gyun, but he ignores the issue of how Heo could have learned of his hero's Okinawan adventures. In Seol's 2004 book *The Secrets of the Story of Hong Gildong*, he points to passages in Heo Gyun's writings that demonstrate his knowledge of the Ryukyu Kingdom and claims that as "proof" that he had the place in mind when he wrote of Hong Gildong's adventures on Yul Island.[26] Some of the assertions concerning Hong's travel to the Ryukyus are taken from the writings of the Japanese scholar Gadena Shodoku, whose ideas may have risen out of confusion created by the 1921 Japanese translation of *The Story of Hong Gildong*, which has the last part of the narrative take place in Ryukyu instead of Yul Island.

This entertaining, albeit utterly groundless, narrative of the "real-life" adventures of the "historical" Hong Gildong provides a fiction of retroactive vengeance against the Japanese for their colonization of Korea from 1910 to 1945. In brief, in the sixteenth century, a great Korean hero went to the islands that would become part of the Japanese empire in the nineteenth century, raised a rebellion in one, and then conquered another to rule over as king. He, furthermore, introduced the fighting technique that the Japanese mistakenly think is their own, when it was really a Korean export that was destined to be imported back to Korea to become a world-famous martial art and now an Olympic event. The story may have its attractions for Koreans of nationalist bent, but it is hardly history in any legitimate sense of the word. The proper perspective on Seol's work is that it is a pseudohistorical fantasy based on sheer speculation for the purpose of supporting an attractive predetermined thesis. It is comparable to books like Erich von Däniken's *Chariots of the Gods?* (1968), which claims that archaeological evidence points to contacts between ancient civilizations and space aliens, and Gavin Menzies's *1421: The Year China Discovered the World* (2002), which asserts that Chinese explorers reached America before Columbus. But Seol's writings have inspired the most recent novelistic treatment of the Hong Gildong story.

Kang Cheolgeun, who is, appropriately enough, a scholar of the *hallyu* phenomenon, published a novel entitled *Country of Humanity* (*Saramui nara*) in 2010, with a declaration on its cover stating: "Hong Gildong was a historical figure. In pursuit of the rebirth of Hong Gildong as a hero of South Japan (Okinawa)." In the introduction to the work, Kang affirms the findings of Seol Seonggyeong, pointing to the inspiration provided by Seol's *The Life of Hong Gildong and the Story of Hong Gildong*.[27] The book also features photographs of texts that supposedly contain evidence of the historical Hong Gildong, places in Janseong County where the hero is thought to have hailed from, and views of Okinawan islands where he ended up.

All the major retellings of the Hong Gildong narrative that I have examined mostly ignore or explain away the last part of *The Story of Hong Gildong* on his adventures abroad. In the novels by Bak Taewon and Jeong Biseok, Hong disappears after King Yeonsan is toppled; Shin Dong Wu's comic book hero stays in Joseon and continues his fight against corrupt officials and diabolical criminals; and in the television show *Sharp Blade Hong Gildong*, he meets his death in the final battle. Kang's *Country of Humanity* is unique in that most of its narrative is about Hong's foreign adventures.

Kang's novel opens at a time when the righteous outlaw group Hwalbindang, led by Hong Jungsan (Gildong's pseudonym, the necessity of which is unexplained), has been operating so successfully that the king, Yeonsan, mobilizes the Joseon army to destroy them. Hong is confident that he could win a battle against the army, but he worries that a war would bring much suffering to the common people.[28] So he asks a corrupt *yangban* by the name of Eom Gwidong (based on Eom Gwison, the official implicated in the *Sillok* records as a collaborator of Hong Gildong) to open secret negotiations with the government. Kang's story closely follows Seol's baseless theories as the minister of military affairs Yi Gyesun agrees to an arrangement in which Hong and his men will pretend to be captured by soldiers, Yi taking credit for the arrest, and then discreetly leave Joseon. Hong Jungsan persuades diplomatic envoys from the Ryukyu Kingdom to take him, his followers, and their families to the southern islands. After they pay their respects to the king of Ryukyu at his capital, they go to a small island on the far end of the archipelago where they establish their home, eventually giving it the name of Yul Island.

An interesting aspect of the narrative is the disagreement that ensues over the kind of state they should build on their new home. I have previously discussed how there is no textual evidence to support the view of Yul Island under Hong Gildong's rule as an egalitarian utopia. In Kang's novel, Hong Jungsan is portrayed as a protodemocrat, similar to the hero of Jang Biseok's 1985 novel and *Sharp Blade Hong Gildong*, whose ideas come into conflict with those of his strategist and father-in-law Jang Jeokin. In an early episode, Hong saves a young woman from the clutches of bandits who subsequently become his followers. Her father, Jang Jeokin, not only consents to their marriage but also becomes Hong's strategist. While Jang plays an essential role in the rise of Hong as a successful leader of righteous outlaws, he finds himself at odds with him when the Hwalbindang community establishes itself on Yul Island.

Jang advises Hong to create a monarchy and a Neo-Confucian social system in his realm, based on the ideas of the philosopher Zhu Xi. Hong, along with most members of the Hwalbindang, are appalled at the idea of creating another Joseon on the island. Hong counters his suggestion with his own vision.

> The new country will have no need of a king or *yangban* officials. It must not have a status system. Every person under Heaven is a human being who is equal to others. For practical reasons we will have representatives, but the positions will be rotated among different people once every few years. Instead of *yangban* officials, there will be just the right number of representatives to do the necessary work for the country. For instance, it will be enough to have a few people who will train our soldiers and others who will take care of official documents. And on matters of importance to the entire country, a council of elders and representatives will meet and make decisions together. On each island, people will volunteer to become representatives and work for the sake of the people. And those positions will be rotated among different people as well.[29]

Jang Jeokin thinks that such radical ideas are not feasible and that the state of Yul Island is doomed to collapse without the stability and order that only a monarchy and strict social hierarchy can provide. The disagreement between Hong and Jang creates such a rift between them that the latter ends up leaving Yul Island.

After Hong and his followers settle down in their new home, they find that the Ryukyu monarch is becoming increasingly tyrannical, imposing ever greater taxes and causing great suffering to the people. Hong realizes that he may have to go to war against Ryukyu, so he makes alliances with the discontented people of other islands and begins to train an army and build a naval fleet. When the conflict begins, Jang Jeokin betrays Hong by offering his services to the king of Ryukyu. But Hong is able to anticipate Jang's strategy and soundly defeats the forces of Ryukyu in battle. After the great victory, Hong allows all the islands to become independent and to choose their own leaders, and he forms a friendly federation with them. The novel ends on a rather dark historical note, describing how the people of the islands lived in harmony and prosperity for a hundred years after the arrival of Hong, until the Japanese invasion of 1609, when they had to submit themselves to that foreign power.

This novel both follows the historical fantasy created by Seol and is in line with Kim Taejun's view of the hero as a radical egalitarian who dreams of a classless utopia. The work goes even further by eventually making a villain out of Jang, who advocates what Hong actually does in the original work, namely, recreate a traditional monarchical state on Yul Island. It is significant that it is in the latest versions of the hero's story, in the *hallyu* television show *Sharp Blade Hong Gildong* and in the *hallyu* scholar Kang Cheolgeun's novel *Country of Humanity*, that Hong becomes the most overt advocate of democracy. In both works, he is conspicuously modern in character, as is the pseudohistorical fantasy of Seol Seong-gyeong. Seol claims to have discovered the secret history of Korea's greatest hero in the remote past, but the narrative he unfurls is very much an invention of the contemporary era.

HONG GILDONG TOURISM

Janseong County's Home of Hong Gildong and Hong Gildong Theme Park

In 1998, a minor but interesting controversy erupted in South Korea over the issue of the trademark right to use the figure of Hong Gildong for the purpose of merchandising and tourism. It began when Jangseong County in South Jeolla Province protested the television network SBS's plan to create a cartoon figure of the hero and other characters to advertise the Hong Gildong show that was set to air in July.[30] Jangseong officials claimed that SBS would be violating the county's exclusive right to use Hong Gildong for commercial purposes. Their claim to Hong Gildong is based on the place being the site of the old lineage home of the illustrious Hong family. I have shown that Seol Seonggyeong connected the historical outlaw to the old *yangban* family through two documents of little value as historical evidence—the legend of a runaway secondary son in *Enlarged Edition of Extraordinary Events of Haedong* and the record of

Hong Gildong's name (with a different last character from the name of the bandit in the *Sillok* records) in the 1931 *Comprehensive Clan Records of Myriad Families*. Despite the weakness of the connection, the county's claim to be the hometown of Hong Gildong was endorsed by Seol Seonggyeong.[31]

The matter became more complicated when the city of Gangneung in Gangwon Province jumped into the fray, as it too claimed to possess a trademark right to the Hong Gildong "character," the word signifying a cartoon or stylized design figure. Gangneung's justification for its exclusive use of the hero's image was that it was the hometown of Heo Gyun, the purported author of *The Story of Hong Gildong*. SBS avoided further complications by curtailing its plans, but Jangseong County and Gangneung City eventually went to court. The case was not settled until 2009, in favor of Jangseong. It turned out that Gangneung did file for an exclusive trademark earlier than Janseong but failed to renew it at the end of its ten-year period, giving Jangseong the opportunity to obtain a new trademark.[32] A September 2009 article in a Gangwon Province newspaper entitled "Gangneung Lost Its 'Hong Gildong Character' to Janseong County" bitterly regretted the outcome, noting how the city could no longer make use of its Hong Gildong figure, which had been the city's mascot for the last ten years (fig. 6.4).[33]

For a decade before the final settlement of the case, Jangseong County invested heavily in its image as the hometown of Hong Gildong. This was part of a government campaign in the 1990s to boost internal tourism by encouraging towns to develop travel venues with distinct themes. As Okpyo Moon has pointed out, after "the introduction of the local government system in the mid-1990s, South Korean municipalities have endeavored to build distinct local characters, partly for tourism purposes and partly to increase financial viability by drawing more

Figure 6.4. The city of Gangneung's Hong Gildong mascot figure that could no longer be used for commercial purposes after the legal case of 2009.

subsidies from the central government."[34] In addition to creating its rival Hong Gildong character, the county organized an annual Hong Gildong Festival with parades, traditional entertainments, and conferences. It also began the construction of the Hong Gildong Theme Park around the site of the Hong family's Joseon-dynasty compound. The park was completed in 2012, where the fourteenth annual Hong Gildong Festival was held (fig. 6.5).

Timothy Tangherlini, in his insightful essay on the significance of the Korean Folk Village (*Minsokcheon*) in Yongin, which claims to be a recreation of a traditional Joseon-dynasty village, points to the tourism destination's proximity to the amusement park Everland.[35] In explicating the connection between the two places, Tangherlini refers to the anthropologist Nelson Gradburn's observation that in contemporary society "the long-held distinction between theme parks and amusement parks on the one hand and museums and cultural centres on the other—between the popular and the authoritative—is blurring fast."[36] The Hong Gildong Theme Park provides a perfect example of such blurring, as an artificial construct of an imaginary vision of Korea's premodern past that claims to be an authentic representation of tradition based on a famous literary work.

The railway station of Jangseong is decorated with advertisements declaring the place to be the hometown of Hong Gildong, with cartoon

Figure 6.5. Map of the Hong Gildong Theme Park from its brochure, with Hong Gildong (bottom right) and his companions.

drawings and statues of the hero's character and that of his Hwalbindang companions (fig. 6.6). The theme park itself is a massive complex featuring a reconstructed *yangban* family compound, a Hwalbindang "lair" where people can stay overnight, a children's activity area, a sports field, the Home of Hong Gildong, and a Hong Gildong museum. The museum displays Joseon-dynasty artifacts found in the area and enlarged reproductions of pages from old texts that are presented as evidence for the historical Hong Gildong. A monitor screen continuously plays a documentary on the subject, with Seol Seonggyeong providing much of the narration. A billboard at the parking lot displays a massive painting of Hong Gildong with his companions, who are newly imagined characters—but they closely resemble the Japanese anime-inspired group of five, consisting of the male hero, a female, a large obese man, a thin sharp-featured man, and a young boy, just as they were featured in the television show *Sharp Blade Hong Gildong*. To these five, an additional female was added, making it a group of six. The Home of Hong Gildong, supposedly the historical element of the park, is at the farthest end from the entrance to the park, where a Joseon-dynasty-style house was built to represent the place where the hero grew up. At the front of the house are two figures, a painted mannequin of an elderly *yangban* representing Hong Gildong's father, Minister Hong, and a bronze statue of Hong Gildong kneeling before him (figs. 6.7 and 6.8). A placard behind the statue explains that Minister Hong is exhorting his son to go forth and become the champion of the downtrodden.

Figure 6.6. Sign at the Jangseong railway station: "A place of dreams and hope, the hometown of Hong Gildong, Jangseong."

Figure 6.7. The Home of Hong Gildong.

As a prominent representation of what supposedly took place at that historical site, the image of the father and son seriously distorts the original Hong Gildong story. In *The Story of Hong Gildong*, the hero leaves home in defiance of his father and in protest at his treatment at home because of his status as a secondary son. The builders of the Hong Gildong Theme Park altered that episode to its opposite. Now the hero's adventures stem from filial obedience, giving the impression that Hong Gildong launched his career as a righteous outlaw at the command of his father. As an example of the blurring of the distinction between an amusement park and a historical site, that change reflects the fact that the place was designed mainly for children, with its cartoon figures, entertainment and sports activities, and places for overnight stays on school trips. *The Story of Hong Gildong's* portrayal of the hero as a runaway child who leaves home in defiance of his parents was apparently deemed problematic. He was, consequently, turned into an obedient son who goes on his adventures under the orders of his father to help the downtrodden, a moral exemplar who not only fights for the powerless but who also abides by the Confucian virtue of filial piety. This was, no doubt, seen as a more appropriate and edifying message for young visitors to the site.

In his work on the Korean Folk Village, Tangherlini has also pointed to the problematic nature of the place's claim to provide a true experience of a traditional village, given that it was built in the 1970s at a site of no historical significance. The cases of both the Folk Village and the Hong Gild-

Figure 6.8. Statue of Hong Gildong kneeling before his father.

ong Theme Park point to the central paradox inherent in the use of tradition and history for a commercial purpose, as the demands of the quintessentially modern industry of tourism invariably jeopardize the very authenticity that is advertized as an essential element of a particular site's attraction. Just as Seol Seonggyeong built his wild theories on the historical Hong Gildong by filling gaps in the historical records with his fantasies, the Home of Hong Gildong was newly built on the approximate site of the old Hong family house. Despite the wholly modern and artificial nature of the place, it was necessary that a strong historical claim be made for it to become a viable tourist destination. And Seol's pseudohistorical fantasy provided the necessary "scholarly" support, for he wholeheartedly endorsed the notion of Jangseong as the hometown of the famous fictional hero.

There is no doubt that the essential motivation for the development of Jangseong County as the hometown of Hong Gildong is commercial in nature, since the actual historical justification for both the historical Hong Gildong and his connection to Jangseong is questionable at best. Yet the significant investment the county put into the effort, as well as Seol Seonggyeong's ideas, point to the undeniable fact that even today the famous righteous outlaw functions as a figure of admiration, desire, and nostalgia for modern Koreans, in the diverse realms of literature, history, and fantasy.

(While preparing this manuscript, two more Hong Gildong adaptations have been shown in South Korea. May 2016 saw the release of the movie *Detective Hong Gildong: The Village That Disappeared* [*Tamjeong Hong Gildong: Sarajin maeul*; US release title, *Phantom Detective*], directed by Jo Sung-hee, a stylish noir movie in which Hong Gildong is a private detective in 1970s South Korea. He unearths a conspiracy by a secret organization to massacre the people of a rural village for political purposes. In January 2017, the television network MBC began airing the show *Rebel: Thief Who Stole the People* [*Yeokjeok: Baekseong eul humchin dojeok*], another Hong Gildong drama set in the time of King Yeonsan. What is interesting about this adaptation is that it may be the first major historical production to do away with the idea of Hong as a secondary son of a *yangban*, discarding the iconic lament that he cannot address his father as Father and brother as Brother. In this story, his father is a slave in a nobleman's household who manages to emancipate himself before founding a rural criminal organization. After his death, Hong Gildong takes over its leadership and eventually challenges the king himself in a popular rebellion.)

Epilogue

The Joseon-dynasty literary character Hong Gildong is very much alive and thriving in contemporary Korean culture. There are, however, not one but many Hong Gildongs who have appeared here and there, east and west, in the sky and on the earth, in fiction, comic books, film, and television over the course of the modern era: the colonial-era nationalists' Hong Gildong, who embodied the Korean spirit that had to be preserved during the time of subjugation; Hong Gildong the champion of the poor and the oppressed against the rapacious rich and corrupt power holders in modern society; Hong Gildong the rebel fighting against the tyrannical state and foreign imperialism; Hong Gildong the hero of children's comics and animated films; Hong Gildong the masculine ideal, which today's everyman finds impossible to live up to; and Hong Gildong the symbol of traditional values that have become lost with the onset of modernity. These new versions of the figure have kept his story alive, but they have also obscured the significance of the original work, like the false Gildongs that the hero made out of straw and animated with his magic to evade and confuse the authorities out to capture him. The Hong Gildong the vast majority of modern Koreans think they know is actually not the hero of the classic literary work *The Story of Hong Gildong* but an amalgam of the many new versions of him that they read about in a modern novel or a comic book or saw in a movie or a television drama. Despite the fact that people are overly familiar with the story of the secondary son who laments that he cannot address his father as Father and his older brother as Brother, who leaves home to become the chief of righteous outlaws, and who becomes the king of his own realm, the exact details as well as the true significance of the original work is familiar only to a few scholars. A typical South Korean would have read a short passage from the original text in a school textbook and memorized some facts for the college-entrance examination, including that it was written by Heo Gyun in the seventeenth century, that it protested the Joseon-dynasty policy on secondary sons, and that it was written to criticize the kingdom's feudal order. This has led to the misunderstanding of *The Story of Hong Gildong* not just among the public but also academics, who perpetuate these myths in their lectures and writings.

As I have endeavored to demonstrate in the course of this book, it is improbable that *The Story of Hong Gildong* was written in the seventeenth century by Heo Gyun. Even if Heo's former student Yi Sik was right that Heo wrote a work about the real-life outlaw Hong Gildong, it is highly unlikely that it is the extant work. The original text was probably written around the middle of the nineteenth century, by an anonymous writer of secondary or commoner status who was seeking to profit from the burgeoning market for popular fiction aimed at a general readership. There are themes and episodes in the work that can be regarded as subversive, in its featuring of an outlaw hero who makes fools out of magistrates and soldiers and who dares to dream of becoming a king himself. They are, however, hardly revolutionary in nature, since the hero would have liked nothing better than to have served his country as a righteous official and replicates the dynastic monarchical system of Joseon when he founds his own realm. The work's primary aim was to entertain, and whatever political ideology it was thought to represent was largely imposed on it by modern interpreters from Kim Taejun onward, who wanted it to feature messages important to the times they lived in.

The Story of Hong Gildong is, no doubt, a great work of traditional Korean literature. But its greatness has to be appreciated in terms of what it was for its author and its original audience. It was not written by a *yangban* writer for *yangban* readership to demonstrate his composition skills and erudition through the classic perfection of his writing and learned allusions to philosophy, history, and high literature. Nor was it a work so ahead of its time that only modern nationalists and leftists could fully comprehend its radical and revolutionary ideas. It was, first and foremost, a commercial work written for the common reader, a fantasy of exciting adventures embarked on by a boy of marvelous talents who manages to break through the social constraints of his time to realize his ambitions in the world. In that sense, *The Story of Hong Gildong* can be regarded as a genuine example of people's literature, that is, literature informed by the hopes and frustrations of commoners living during the tumultuous period of the dynasty's decline. Historical evidence points to its popularity at a time when one age was coming to a disastrous end but the terrifying shape of the following one could not yet be discerned. It would be unwarranted to link the work directly to historical events like the Donghak Rebellion and the Gabo Reforms of 1894 that sought to address the problems of Joseon society, but the story does represent a major cultural expression of that troubled era.

My initial interest in this project came from the recognition of my childhood hero in Eric Hobsbawm's description of the universal figure of the noble robber. When I delved into the text of *The Story of Hong Gildong*, I was surprised that its protagonist was significantly different from the character I remembered from comic books and animated shows. I found the Hong Gildong of the original story less charitable and more narcissistic, as he seemed to do good mainly for the purpose of demonstrating what a great official and general he would have made had he been allowed to serve in the government, but also less moralistic and blandly idealistic than the cartoon character. My reaction was not one of disappointment but fascination, as I had outgrown the need for perfect heroes, real or imagined. In fact, in the course of my career as a historian, I have come to regard all idealized figures with suspicion, seeing behind them the distortion of historical evidence through wishful thinking and ideological manipulation. Like the nostalgia for a bygone golden age that never actually existed, the desire for a flawless hero is a symptom of the lack of a mature and realistic understanding of the world on the part of both an individual and an entire culture. History is replete with disasters and atrocities committed by those holding onto what amount to juvenile fantasies about their heroes, their people, their belief system, and their nation.

The fascination I felt as a historian came from the discovery of the work as a window into the popular culture of late Joseon. The dynasty can boast of a rich and illustrious literary tradition of poetry, philosophy, and history by *yangban* writers, but it only produced modest achievements in prose fiction, which the noble literati did not consider a respectable literary genre. So it is highly significant that the work that is arguably the most important achievement of premodern fiction was one written for commoners. That is at the essence of the reason that, even after the decline and collapse of the political and social order dominated by the *yangban*, the story remained one of the best-known narratives in the modern era, featuring themes that still resonate with contemporary Koreans.

The Joseon dynasty fell, but Hong Gildong lived on, a figure familiar to the people of the peninsula well over a century after his creation. As the legacy of his story persists into the future, his significance can be made even richer by better understanding his first manifestation as the invincible and righteous outlaw who dreamed of a better life beyond the walls of his family's home and beyond the land of his birth.

Extant Manuscripts of
The Story of Hong Gildong

The following descriptive listing of the thirty-four extant manuscripts of *The Story of Hong Gildong* is based on the works of Lee Yoon Suk. Lee published his findings on twenty-eight variant texts in his 1994 article "*Hong Gildong jeon* wonbon hwakjeongeul wihan siron" (An essay on the determination of the original text of *The Story of Hong Gildong*), which he expanded in his 1997 book *Hong Gildong jeon yeongu: seoji wa haeseok* (Research on *The Story of Hong Gildong*: texts and interpretation) with one additional text (the handwritten Jeong Urak 37/23).[1] Since then, Lee has found an additional five texts (*gyeongpan* 17, *wanpan* 34, Yi Subong 30, Jeonnam University 43, and Jeong Gyubok 66), for a total of thirty-four discovered so far. As an introduction to this technical discussion of the manuscripts, I need to reiterate some of the points already made in the introduction.

Of the thirty-four extant texts, nine were printed and twenty-five handwritten. The printed works were produced in the three centers of the printing industry in the nineteenth and early twentieth century—Gyeongseong (today's Seoul), Wanju (today's Jeonju in North Jeolla Province), and Anseong (in Gyeonggi Province, south of Seoul). They are, therefore, referred to as *gyeongpan*, *wanpan*, and *anseongpan* texts (the syllable *pan* denoting the wooden or metal printing plate). The numerals indicate the number of standard-size sheets used, providing a general idea of the length of the narrative. For example, the *gyeongpan* 24 is a printed text in twenty-four sheets that was published in Gyeongseong, while the *wanpan* 36 is thirty-six pages and was published in Wanju. The *gyeongpan* and *wanpan* texts are distinguished from each other not only by the fact that they were produced in different cities but also because the works in each group share similarities in content and style (the two *anseongpan* texts are so similar to the *gyeongpan* texts that they are categorized together). This indicates that the variants in each group are closely related.

The handwritten texts are referred to by the names of their owners or the institutions where they are housed. For example, the Park Sunho 86 is a handwritten text of eighty-six sheets in the private collection of Park Sunho, while the Tōyō bunko 31/31/33 is a work in three volumes of thirty-one, thirty-one, and thirty-three sheets at the Tōyō bunko (Asian studies) library in Tokyo, Japan. Most of the handwritten texts also share similarities in content and style with either the *gyeongpan* or the *wanpan* printed texts and so are categorized as *gyeongpan*-related handwritten texts or *wanpan*-related handwritten texts. Lee Yoon Suk has pointed to eight of the handwritten works that do not fit into either the *gyeongpan* or the *wanpan* groups but share distinctive characteristics with one another. He asserts that they should be considered a third category of texts, giving them the name of *pilsa* (handwritten) works. So the three categories, comprising thirty-four texts, are organized into five groups: *gyeongpan* printed texts (including the two *anseongpan* texts), *gyeongpan*-related handwritten texts, *wanpan* printed texts, *wanpan*-related handwritten texts, and *pilsa* texts (handwritten texts distinct from the *gyeongpan* and the *wanpan*).

In the effort to establish the sequence of their production, the immediate difficulty a scholar faces is the fact that only fifteen variants identify their publication dates (all handwritten texts, with the single exception of the Deokheung seorim 37, which is unique in its use of the new print style and features the publication date of 1915). The dates range from 1893 (the Yi Gawon 21 *gyeongpan*-related text) to 1936 (the Jeong Urak 37/23 *pilsa* text). But a plausible hypothesis on their history can be made through the consideration of the commercial practices of the printing industry at the time. In the nineteenth century and early twentieth century, Korean printers did not solicit original works from authors but published printed versions of handwritten works that already enjoyed popularity. Once a work proved successful, both copiers of handwritten texts and publishers of printed texts produced abbreviated versions of the work in order to cut down on the cost of production, especially of paper. Given such practices, the longer handwritten texts can generally be regarded as older, with shorter, printed versions as later shortened variants.

Of the *gyeongpan*, the *wanpan*, and the *pilsa* groups, the works of the last category are probably the closest copies and variants of the first *The Story of Hong Gildong* because they were all handwritten and because one of them (the Kim Donguk 89) is the longest extant version. The Tōyō bunko *gyeongpan* version in three volumes has the highest sheet count (ninety-five), but the Kim Donguk 89 has the highest character count (the former features an average of fourteen characters per line at eleven lines per page; the latter features twenty characters per line at ten lines per page). Seven *pilsa* texts (out of eight) identify their dates of publication, two of them featuring the latest years 1934 and 1936 (the Park Sunho 86 and the Jeong Urak 37/23, respectively), but the Kim Donguk 55 bears the second-to-earliest date of 1894 (the earliest is the Yi Gawon 21 *gyeongpan*-related text, 1893). Based on these points, Lee Yoon Suk has asserted that the Kim Donguk 89, the longest among all the extant manuscripts, is a copy of the original work or one that is closest in content to the ur-text.

Of the two other categories of texts, the *gyeongpan* and the *wanpan*, the former is probably the earlier group because the range of publication dates on the handwritten manuscripts and the one printed one (the Deukheung seorim 37) are earlier (*gyeongpan*: 1893, 1901, 1912, 1915; *wanpan*: 1900, 1909, 1913, 1915, 1927).

To summarize, according to the most plausible history of writing and publication of the different variants of *The Story of Hong Gildong* constructed by current scholars, most notably Lee Yoon Suk, the original work of around eighty-nine sheets was written sometime in the middle of the nineteenth century, or not many decades before, in handwritten form. As the story gained popularity among readers, a number of abbreviated handwritten copies (from eighty-six sheets to eighteen) were made in the course of the second half of the nineteenth century and into the twentieth, the last of them appearing in the mid-1930s. Those are the texts of the *pilsa* group.

In the last decade of the nineteenth century, a significantly shorter version (half to a third as long as the earliest *pilsa* works) was produced, featuring a number of changes (the monarch of the story as King Sejong and the highest governmental position achieved by the hero's father as the minister of personnel). This version also proved to be popular, not only spawning many handwritten copies of various lengths (from forty-seven sheets to twenty-one) but also compelling printers in Gyeongseong (Seoul) and Anseong to publish printed versions ranging from thirty sheets to seventeen, from the 1890s to the 1910s. Those handwritten and printed works are collectively the *gyeongpan* texts.

In the first decade of the twentieth century, a third version appeared, also with some changes, including the additions of an overtly anti-Buddhist passage related to the raid on Haein Temple and a more detailed description of the war on Yul Island. As it too spawned a number of handwritten copies varying in length from seventy to twenty-eight sheets (from 1900 to 1927), printers in the city of Wanju (Jeonju) began to put out abbreviated versions in print, in thirty-six to thirty-four sheets. All the variants are mostly or entirely in *hangeul*, with the single exception of the *pilsa* text Seogang University 30, which is entirely in literary Chinese, published in 1909.

What follows is a preliminary list of the thirty-four variants, categorized in the order of *pilsa* texts, *gyeongpan*-related handwritten texts, printed *gyeongpan* texts, *wanpan*-related handwritten texts, and printed *wanpan* texts (with the year of publication for ones that provide the information), followed by a descriptive listing with detailed information on each of the texts. I have indicated with an asterisk the five texts that Lee Yoon Suk has recently discovered, the descriptions of which have not been published previously.

Preliminary List

Pilsa Texts

1. Kim Donguk 김동욱 89
2. Kim Donguk 김동욱 55 (1894)
3. Seogang University 서강대 30 (1909)
4. Jo Jeongeop 조정업 31/33 (1910)
5. Kim Donguk 김동욱 18 (1919)
6. Jeong Myeonggi 정명기 77 (1933)
7. Park Sunho 박순호 86 (1934)
8. Jeong Urak 정우락 37/23 (1936)

Gyeongpan-Related Handwritten Texts

9. Park Sunho 박순호 53
10. Kang Jeonseop 강전섭 51
11. Yonsei University 연세대 48
12. Jeonnam University 전남대 43
13. Yi Subong 이수봉 30*
14. Sungsil University 성실대 19
15. Yi Gawon 이가원 21 (1893)
16. Tōyō bunko 동양문고 (東洋文庫) 31/31/33 (1901)
17. Kim Donguk 김동욱 47 (1912)

Gyeongpan Texts—Printed

18. Gyeongpan 경판 30 (early 1892 or before—see descriptive note)
19. Gyeongpan 경판 24
20. Gyeongpan 경판 23
21. Anseongpan 안성판 23
22. Gyeongpan 경판 21
23. Anseongpan 안성판 19
24. Gyeongpan 경판 17*
25. Deokheung seorim 덕흥서림 37 (1915)

Wanpan-Related Handwritten Texts

26. Park Sunho 박순호 41
27. Kang Jeonseop 강전섭 34
28. Jeongsin Munhwawon 정신문화원 68 (1900)
29. Park Sunho 박순호 52 (1909)
30. Jeong Gyubok 정규복 66 (1913)*
31. Guknip Doseogwan 국립도서관 70 (1914)
32. Kim Donguk 김동욱 28 (1927)

Wanpan Texts—Printed

33. Wanpan 완판 36
34. Wanpan 완판 34*

Descriptive List

Pilsa Texts (All Handwritten)

1. Kim Donguk 89—김동욱 89

Location: Danguk University, Yulgok Memorial Library (단국대학교 율곡기념 도서관) (originally from the private collection of the late Kim Donguk).
Publication: Typescript edition appeared in *Hanguk jeontong munhwa yeongu* 7 (한국전통문화연구 제7집).
Textual Description: Mixture of *hangeul* and Chinese characters; 89 sheets, 10 lines per page, average of 20 characters per line. Longest extant manuscript of *The Story of Hong Gildong*.
Date: Unknown.

The Name "Hong Gildong" in Chinese Characters: 洪吉洞 (the Kim Donguk 55 is the only other text with the same last character, all others featuring the name in Chinese use the character 童, with the single exception of the recently discovered *wanpan* 34, which writes it uniquely as 東).

2. Kim Donguk 55—김동욱 55

Location: Danguk University, Yulgok Memorial Library (단국대학교 울곡기념도서관) (Collection of the late Kim Dongwook).
Publication: Unpublished.
Textual Description: Originally in 55 sheets, but it is apparent that an additional sheet has been added later. Most of the text features 12–14 lines per page, 22–28 characters per line, but the first two sheets (the later additions) have 7 lines per page with 13–18 characters per line.
Date: Gabo 갑오 (Blue Horse Year, 1894).
The Name "Hong Gildong" in Chinese Characters: 洪吉洞.

3. Seogang University 30—서강대 30

Location: Seogang University Library (서강대학교 도서관).
Publication: *Seogang eomun* 6 (서강어문 제 6 집).
Textual Description: The only text that is entirely in Chinese characters; 30 sheets, 11 lines per page, average of 25 characters per line.
Date: A marginal note indicates that it was begun on Mushin 무신 (Yellow Monkey Year, 1908), twelfth month, second day, and completed on Giyu 기유 (Yellow Fowl Year, 1909), first month, fourth day.
The Name "Hong Gildong" in Chinese Characters: 洪吉童.

4. Jo Jongeop 31/33—조종업 31/33

Location: Private collection of Jo Jongeop.
Publication: Unpublished.
Textual Description: Originally in three volumes; third volume is missing. The first volume in 31 sheets, the second in 33, both 11 lines per page, average of 15 characters per line.
Date: Gyeongsul 경술 (White Dog Year, 1910), fourth month, twenty-fifth day.
The Name "Hong Gildong" in Chinese Characters: 洪吉童.

5. Kim Donguk 18—김동욱 18

Location: Danguk University, Yulgok Memorial Library (단국대학교 울곡기념도서관) (Collection of the late Kim Donguk).

Publication: Unpublished.

Textual Description: Originally in 20 sheets, but two sheets missing—16 lines per page, average of 25 characters per line.

Date: Gimi 기미 (Yellow Sheep Year, 1919), ninth month, ninth day.

The Name "Hong Gildong" in Chinese Characters: None.

6. Jeong Myeonggi 77—정명기 77

Location: Private collection of Jeong Myeonggi.

Publication: Translated into modern Korean and published in *Hanguk jeontong munhwa yeongu* 8 (한국전통문화연구 제 8집).

Textual Description: 77 sheets, 11 lines per page, 15–21 characters per line.

Date: Gyeyu 계유 (Black Fowl Year, 1933), second month, second day.

The Name "Hong Gildong" in Chinese Characters: 洪吉童.

7. Park Sunho 86—박순호 86

Location: Private collection of Park Sunho.

Publication: Photographic reproduction in Park Sunho, ed., *Hangeul pilsabon gososeol jaryo chongseo* (한글필사본고소설자료총서); translated into modern Korean and published in *Gukmunhak yeongu* 14 (국문학연구 제 14 집).

Textual Description: 86 sheets, 9 lines per page, average of 19 characters per line.

Date: Gapsul 갑술 (Blue Dog Year, 1934), first month.

The Name "Hong Gildong" in Chinese Characters: None.

8. Jeong Urak 37/23—정우락 37/23

Location: Private collection of Jeong Urak.

Publication: Unpublished.

Textual Description: In two volumes of 37 and 23 sheets, first volume with 12 lines per page, 20–28 characters per line, the second volume with 10 lines per page, 18–22 characters per line.

Date: Byeongja 병자 (Red Rat Year, 1936).

The Name "Hong Gildong" in Chinese Characters: None.

Gyeongpang-Related Handwritten Texts

9. Park Sunho 53—박순호 53

Location: Private collection of Park Sunho.

Publication: Unpublished.

Textual Description: 53 sheets, 9–10 lines per page, 16–21 characters per line.

Date: Unknown.

The Name "Hong Gildong" in Chinese Characters: 洪吉童.

10. Kang Jeonseop 51—강전섭 51

Location: Private collection of Kang Jeonseop.

Publication: Unpublished.

Textual Description: Unknown.

Date: Unknown.

The Name "Hong Gildong" in Chinese Characters: Unknown.

11. Yonsei University 48—연세대 48

Location: Yonsei University Library (연세대학교 도서관).

Publication: Unpublished.

Textual Description: 48 sheets, 11 lines per page, average of 18 characters per line.

Date: Unknown

The Name "Hong Gildong" in Chinese Characters: None.

12. Jeonnam University 43*—전남대 43

Location: Jeonnam University Central Library (전남대학교 중앙도서관).

Publication: Unpublished.

Textual Description: 43 sheets, 11 lines per page, average of 20 characters per line.

Date: Eulchuk 을축 (Blue Ox Year, 1925).

The Name "Hong Gildong" in Chinese Characters: None.

13. Yi Subong 30*—이수봉 30

Location: Private collection of Yi Subong.

Publication: Unpublished.

Textual Description: 30 sheets, 13 lines per page, 22–27 characters per line.

Date: Gyesa 계사 (Black Snake Year, 1893).

The Name "Hong Gildong" in Chinese Characters: None.

14. Sungsil University 19—숭실대 19

Location: Sungsil University Library (숭실대학교 도서관).

Publication: Photographic reproduction in *Sungsil eomun* 7 (숭실어문 제 7집).

Textual description: 19 sheets, 12 lines per page, average of 32 characters per line.

Date: Unknown.

The Name "Hong Gildong" in Chinese Characters: None.

15. Yi Gawon 21—이가원 21

Location: Danguk University Yulgok Memorial Library (단국대학교 율곡기념 도서관) (from the personal collection of Lee Gawon).

Publication: Photographic reproduction in the journal *Yeolsang gojeon yeongu* 2 (열상고전연구 제2집).

Textual Description: 21 sheets, 14–15 lines per page (with one 12-line page, one 13-line page, and one 16-line page), average of 25 characters per line on the first two sheets and 30 characters on all other pages.

Date: Gyesa 계사 (Black Snake Year, 1893), first month.

The Name "Hong Gildong" in Chinese Characters: 洪吉童.

16. Tōyō bunko 31/31/33

Location: Tōyō bunko, 동양문고 (東洋文庫), Tokyo, Japan.

Publication: Unpublished.

Textual Description: 3 volumes; first volume—31 sheets, second volume—31 sheets, third volume—33 sheets; 11 lines per page, average of 14 characters per line.

Date: Sinchuk 신축 (White Ox Year, 1901), twelfth month.

The Name "Hong Gildong" in Chinese Characters: None.

17. Kim Donguk 47—김동욱 47

Location: Danguk University, Yulgok Memorial Library (단국대학교 율곡기념 도서관) (originally from the private collection of the late Kim Donguk).

Publication: Unpublished.

Textual Description: 47 sheets, 11 lines per page (some pages with 10 or 12 lines), average of 20 characters per line.

Date: Imja 임자 (Black Rat Year, 1912), twelfth month, tenth day.

The Name "Hong Gildong" in Chinese Characters: 洪吉童.

Gyeongpan Printed Texts

18. Gyeongpan 30—경판 30

Location: L'École des langues orientales, Paris, France.

Publication: Kim Donguk, ed., *Yeongin gososeol pangak jeonjip* 5 (영인고소설 판각전집 제5집).

Textual Description: Oldest known printed text; 30 sheets, 14 lines per page, average of 24 characters per line.

Date: No date in the text but sometime before February 1892 (when the French diplomat Maurice Courant departed Korea). Courant discusses this version of *The Story of Hong Gildong* in his 1894–1896 work *Bibliographie coréene*.

The Name "Hong Gildong" in Chinese Characters: None.

19. Gyeongpan 24—경판 24

Location: Guknip jungang doseogwan (국립중앙도서관) (National Library).

Publication: Kim Donguk, ed., *Yeongin gososeol pangak jeonjip* 3 (영인고소설판 각전집 제3집); also photographic reproduction in a number of publications.

Textual Description: 24 sheets, in the first 20 sheets, 14 lines per page with 21 characters per line; in sheets 21–24, 15 lines per page, average of 24 characters per line.

Date: Unknown.

The Name "Hong Gildong" in Chinese Characters: None.

20. Gyeongpan 23—경판 23

Location: Private collection of O Hangeun (오한근).

Publication: Kim Donguk, ed., *Yeongin gososeol pangak jeonjip* 3 (영인고소설 판각전집 제3집).

Description: 23 sheets, 15 lines per page, average of 25 characters per line.

Date: Unknown.

The Name "Hong Gildong" in Chinese Characters: None.

21. Anseongpan 23—안성판 23

Location: Tōyō bunko, 동양문고 (東洋文庫), Tokyo, Japan.

Publication: Kim Donguk, ed., *Yeongin gososeol pangak jeonjip* 3 (영인고소설 판각전집 제3집).

Textual Description: Identifies itself as having been printed in the city of Anseong; 23 sheets, 15 lines per page, average 25 characters per line.

Date: Unknown.

The Name "Hong Gildong" in Chinese Characters: None.

22. Gyeongpan 21—경판 21

Location: Private collection of Ha Dongho (하동호).
Publication: Kim Donguk, ed., *Yeongin gososeol pangak jeonjip* 5 (영인고소설
판각전집 제5집).
Textual Description: 21 sheets (15th sheet missing), 15 lines per page, aver-
age of 28 characters per line.
Date: Unknown.
The Name "Hong Gildong" in Chinese Characters: None.

23. Anseongpan 19—안성판 19

Location: Guknip jungang doseogwan국립중앙도서관 (National Library).
Publication: Kim Donguk, ed., *Yeongin gososeol pangak jeonjip* 3 (영인고소설
판각전집 제3집).
Textual Description: Identifies itself as having been printed in the city of
Anseong; 19 sheets. In sheets 1 and 2, 14 lines per page, average of 21
characters per line; in sheets 3–14, 14 lines per page, average of 21 char-
acters per line; in sheets 15–19, 16 lines per page, average of 31 characters
per line.
Date: Year unknown, but the copyright page indicates that the first edi-
tion was published sometime during the Japanese imperial era of
Daisho (大正, 1912–1926), June 11.
The Name "Hong Gildong" in Chinese Characters: None.

24. Gyeongpan 17*—경판 17

Location: Ppuri gipeun namu Museum, Suncheon, South Jeolla Province
(뿌리깊은나무 박물관, 전라남도 순천시).
Publication: Unpublished.
Textual Description: 17 sheets, 15 lines per page, 21–32 characters per line.
Date: Unknown.
The Name "Hong Gildong" in Chinese Characters: None.

25. Deokheung seorim 37—덕흥서림 37

Location: Unknown.
Publication: published in *Guhwaljabon gososeol jeonjip* 17, Incheon University Minjok munhwa yeonguso (구활자본고소설전집 제 17집, 인천대학 민족
문화연구소 편).
Description: Unique among the printed texts as the only one in the new
print style; 37 pages, 17 lines per page, 34 characters per line, with Chinese characters included parenthetically.

Date: Written in the modern numerical style as 1915.
The Name "Hong Gildong" in Chinese Characters: 洪吉童.

Wanpan-Related Handwritten Texts

26. Park Sunho 41—박순호 41

Location: Private collection of Park Sunho.
Publication: Unpublished.
Textual Description: 41 sheets, with about 3 pages missing, 12 lines per page, average of 24 characters per line.
Date: Unknown.
The Name "Hong Gildong" in Chinese Characters: 洪吉童.

27. Kang Jeonseop 34—강전섭 34

Location: Private collection of Kang Jeonseop.
Publication: Unpublished.
Textual description: Unknown.
Date: Unknown.
The Name "Hong Gildong" in Chinese Characters: Unknown.

28. Jeongsin Munhwawon 68—정신문화원 68

Location: Jeongshin munhwa yeonguwon (정신문화연구원).
Publication: Unpublished.
Textual Description: 68 sheets, 8–10 lines per page, average of 16 characters per line.
Date: Gyeongja 경자 (White Rat Year, 1900), tenth month.
The Name "Hong Gildong" in Chinese Characters: 洪吉童.

29. Park Sunho 52—박순호 52

Location: Private collection of Park Sunho.
Publication: Park Sunho, ed., *Ibonryu hangeul pilsabon gososeol jaryo chongseo* (이본류 한글필사본고소설자료총서).
Textual Description: 52 sheets, sheets 1–33, 10 lines per page; sheets 34–52, 11 lines per sheet, irregular number of characters per line, ranging from 20 to 28.
Date: Giyu 기유 (Yellow Fowl Year, 1909), second month, seventh day.
The Name "Hong Gildong" in Chinese Characters: None.

30. Jeong Gyubok 66*—정규복 66

Location: Private collection of Jeong Gyubok.
Publication: Unpublished.
Textual Description: 66 sheets total; sheets 1–14 indicate that a number of people wrote the text, as they feature irregular numbers of lines and characters per line. A single person seems to have written from sheet 15 onward, as they consistently have 10 lines per page and an average of 19 characters per line.
Date: Gyechuk 계축 (Black Ox Year, 1913).
The Name "Hong Gildong" in Chinese Characters: None.

31. Guknip doseogwan 70—국립도서관 70

Location: Guknip jungang doseogwan 국립중앙도서관 (National Library).
Publication: Unpublished.
Textual Description: 70 sheets, 9 lines per page, average of 20 characters per line.
Date: Gapin 갑인 (Blue Tiger Year, 1914), second month, third day.
The Name "Hong Gildong" in Chinese Characters: None.

32. Kim Donguk 28—김동욱 28

Location: Danguk University, Yulgok Memorial Library (단국대학교 율곡기념도서관) (originally from the private collection of the late Kim Dongwuk).
Publication: Unpublished.
Textual Description: 28 sheets, 15 lines per page (some sheets with 16 lines), 30 characters per line.
Date: Jeongmyo 정묘 (Red Rabbit Year, 1927), eleventh month, first day.
The Name "Hong Gildong" in Chinese Characters: 洪吉童.

Wanpan Printed Texts

33. Wanpan 36—완판 36

Location: Guknip jungang doseogwan (국립중앙도서관) (National Library).
Publication: Photographic reproduction in Kim Donguk, ed., *Yeongin gososeol pangak jeonjip* 3 (영인고소설판각전집 제3집); and a number of printed editions.
Textual Description: 36 sheets, 15 lines per page, average of 25 characters per line.
Date: Unknown.
The Name "Hong Gildong" in Chinese Characters: None.

34. Wanpan 3*—완판 34

Location: Private collection of Kim Namdon (김남돈).

Publication: Jang Jeongryeong, *Heo Gyun gwa Gangneung* 허균 과 강릉 (Gangneung City, 강릉시, 1998).

Textual Description: 34 sheets (first two sheets missing), 15 lines per page, 25–30 characters per line.

Date: Unknown.

The Name "Hong Gildong" in Chinese Characters: 洪吉東—this text uniquely writes the last character of the name with the ideogram for "east."

Notes

Introduction

1. Douglas Fairbanks—*Robin Hood* (1922, dir. Allan Dwan); Errol Flynn—*The Adventures of Robin Hood* (1938, dir. Michael Curtiz and William Keighley); animated fox—*Walt Disney's Robin Hood* (1973, dir. Wolfgang Reitherman); Kevin Costner—*Robin Hood: Prince of Thieves* (1991, dir. Kevin Reynolds); Russell Crowe—*Robin Hood* (2010, dir. Ridley Scott).

2. For an introduction to Chunhyang, see Peter H. Lee, *Anthology of Korean Literature: From Early Times to the Nineteenth Century* (Honolulu: University of Hawai'i Press, 1981), 257–284; and the film *Chunhyang* (2000, dir. Im Kwon-taek).

3. See Viet Thanh Nguyen, *Nothing Ever Dies: Vietnam and the Memory of War* (Cambridge, MA: Harvard University Press, 2016), 129–155; and Kil J. Yi, "The Making of Tigers: South Korea's Military Experience," in *The Australian Army and the Vietnam War, 1962–1972,* ed. Peter Dennis and Jeffrey Grey (Canberra: Army History Unit, 2002), 152–179. Two leading Korean writers, Ahn Jungho and Hwang Sok-yong, both veterans of the war, have written powerful novels on the subject, available in English translation. Ahn Junghyo, *White Badge: A Novel of Korea* (New York: Soho Press, 1989); and Hwang Sok-yong, *The Shadow of Arms*, trans. Chun Kyung-Ja (Ithaca, NY: Cornell East Asia Series, 1994). For an interesting discussion of the impact of the war on Korean culture, see Remco Breuker, "Korea's Forgotten War: Appropriating and Subverting the Vietnam War in Korean Popular Imaginings," *Korean Histories* 1, no. 1 (2009): 36–59.

4. Warren Wilkins, *Grab Their Belts to Fight Them: The Viet Cong's Big-Unit War Against the U.S., 1965–1966* (Annapolis, MD: Naval Institute Press, 2011), 226.

5. Eric Hobsbawm, *Bandits* (New York: The New Press, 2000), 47–48.

6. Lee, *Anthology of Korean Literature*, 119–147.

7. After the death of King Seonjo (r. 1567–1608), he was given the posthumous "temple name" of Seonjong until it was changed to Seonjo by his son and successor Lord Gwanghae in 1616. It is highly unlikely, however, that the reference in the *pilsa* 89 version of *The Story of Hong Gildong* is to that monarch, who was known by that name for only a few years. "Seongjong" may have been a mistake, but it is possible that the author made up the king to create a fictional time for the story.

8. For my English translation of the text, see *The Story of Hong Gildong*, trans. Minsoo Kang (New York: Penguin, 2016). For the *pilsa* 89 in the original, see Lee Yoon Suk, *Hong Gildong jeon pilsabon yeongu* (Research into the handwritten manuscripts of *The Story of Hong Gildong*) (Seoul: Kyung-in, 2015), 165–244.

9. Only handwritten texts feature dates, with the single exception of the Deokheung *seorim* 37, which is unique in its use of the new print style and features the publication date of 1915.

10. Lee Yoon Suk, "*Hong Gildong jeon* wonbon hwakjeongeul wehan siron" (An essay on the determination of the original text of *The Story of Hong Gildong*), *Tongbang hakji* 85 (January 1994): 247–285. For an expanded descriptive listing of twenty-nine of the variants, see Lee Yoon Suk, *Hong Gildong jeon yeongu: seoji wa haeseok* (Research on the story of Hong Gildong: texts and interpretation) (Seoul: Gyemyeong daehakgyo chulpanbu, 1997), 33–42.

11. Horace Newton Allen, *Korean Tales* (New York: G. P. Putnam's Sons, 1889), 3.

12. Ibid., 170–193.

13. Ibid., 170.

14. Ibid., 175.

15. Ibid., 178.

16. Ibid., 181.

17. Ibid., 189.

18. See Hŏ Kyun, "The Tale of Hong Kil-tong," trans. Marshall R. Pihl Jr., *Korea Journal* (July 1, 1968): 4–21; and Lee, *Anthology of Korean Literature*, 119–147.

19. Lee, *Anthology of Korean Literature*, 122.

20. Ibid., 146.

21. Ibid., 140.

22. No translator is given credit in the book except for the Korean Classical Literature Institute—*Hong Kil-tong chon / The Story of Hong Gil Dong* (Seoul: Baekam, 2000).

23. "The Story of Hong Gildong," trans. Minsoo Kang, *Azalea: Journal of Korean Literature & Culture* 6 (2013): 220–320.

Chapter 1: The Phantom of Hong Gildong in the Fog of Myth

1. For more on the ideology behind the founding of the Joseon dynasty, see the two major classics on this topic in English: Martina Deuchler, *The Confucian Transformation of Korea: A Study of Society and Ideology* (Cambridge, MA: Harvard University Asia Center, 1992); and John Duncan, *The Origins of the Chosŏn Dynasty* (Seattle: University of Washington Press, 2000).

2. For the use of the concept of "status" rather than "class" to describe the Joseon-dynasty social hierarchy, see Eugene Y. Park, *Between Dreams and Reality: The Military Examination in Late Chosŏn Korea, 1600–1894* (Cambridge, MA: Harvard University Asia Center, 2007), 5–9.

3. For a detailed study of illustrious noble lineages of the Joseon dynasty, see Martina Deuchler, *Under the Ancestors' Eyes: Kinship, Status, and Locality in Premodern Korea* (Cambridge, MA: Harvard University Asia Center, 2015).

4. Kyung Moon Hwang, *Beyond Birth: Social Status in the Emergence of Modern Korea* (Cambridge, MA: Harvard University Asia Center, 2004).

5. At the beginning of the Joseon dynasty, an offspring of a concubine could not claim any part of the father's inheritance unless there was no surviving issue by the legitimate wife. In laws promulgated in 1405 by King Taejong, illegitimate children were given some consideration as a son of a commoner-status concubine was given a tenth of his father's property and a son of a lowborn concubine was given a seventh. Deuchler, *The Confucian Transformation of Korea*, 208–209.

6. See Yi Sŏngmu, "The Influence of Neo-Confucianism on Education and the Civil Service Examination System in Fourteenth- and Fifteenth-Century Korea," in *The Rise of Neo-Confucianism in Korea*, ed. Wm. Theodore de Bary and JaHyun Kim Haboush (New York: Columbia University Press, 1985), 125–160.

7. For details, see Edward J. Schultz, *Generals and Scholars: Military Rule in Medieval Korea* (Honolulu: University of Hawai'i Press, 2000).

8. See Park, *Between Dreams and Reality.*

9. For details on laws concerning the status of secondary children, see Martina Deuchler, "'Heaven Does Not Discriminate': A Study of Secondary Sons in Chosŏn Korea," *Journal of Korean Studies* 6 (1988–1989): 121–163.

10. In addition to Deuchler, "Heaven Does Not Discriminate," see JaHyun Kim Haboush, *A Heritage of Kings* (New York: Columbia University Press, 1998), 94–95.

11. For details on the essential role people of secondary status played in the modernization of Korea, see Hwang, *Beyond Birth.*

12. See Samuel Hawley, *The Imjin War: Japan's Sixteenth-Century Invasion of Korea and Attempt to Conquer China* (Berkeley: Institute of East Asian Studies, 2005), 82–87.

13. For a general introduction to the history of the *Sillok*, see George M. McCune, "The Yi Dynasty Annals of Korea," *Transactions of the Korea Branch of the Royal Asiatic Society* 29 (1939): 87–92. For a general introduction to historical practice in traditional Korea, see Yŏng-ho Ch'oe, "An Outline History of Korean Historiography," *Korean Studies* 4 (1980): 1–27. Recently, Harvard University Press published the English translation of the annals of King Taejo, translated by Byonghyon Choi: *The Annals of King T'aejo: The Founder of Chosŏn Dynasty* (Cambridge, MA: Harvard University Press, 2014).

14. See the official *Annals of the Joseon Dynasty* website: http://sillok.history.go.kr/main/main.jsp.

15. It should be noted, however, that Danjong did not receive his temple name until 1648, almost two centuries after his death.

16. For a concise introduction to King Sejong and the intellectual innovations under his reign, see Young-Key Kim-Renaud, ed., *King Sejong the Great: The Light of Fifteenth-Century Korea* (Washington, DC: International Circle of Korean Linguistics, 1992).

17. Gary K. Ledyard, *The Korean Language Reform of 1446* (Seoul: Singu munhaksa, 1998), 127–153.

18. See Ledyard, *The Korean Language Reform of 1446.* This work was originally completed in 1965 by Ledyard as his dissertation and was published in book form in 1998 by a Korean press. The text contains Ledyard's English translations of both the *Hunmin jeongeum* and the *Hunmin jeongeum haerye.* For more on the subject, see Kim Jeongsu, *The History and Future of Hangeul, Korea's Indigenous Script*, trans. Ross King (Folkestone: Global Oriental, 2005); and Young-Key Kim-Renaud, ed., *The Korean Alphabet: Its History and Structure* (Honolulu: University of Hawai'i Press, 1997).

19. My own translation of the famous declaration. For a slightly different rendering, see Ledyard, *The Korean Language Reform of 1446*, 277.

20. For details on the systems, see Ledyard, *The Korean Language Reform of 1446*, 44–67.

21. Ledyard, *The Korean Language Reform of 1446*, 320.

22. Ki-Moon Lee, "The Inventor of the Korean Alphabet" in Kim-Renaud ed., *The Korean Alphabet*, 11–30.

23. Ledyard, *The Korean Language Reform of 1446*, 140–146.

24. Ledyard, *The Korean Language Reform of 1446*, 151.

25. See Peter H. Lee, *Anthology of Korean Literature: From Early Times to the Nineteenth Century* (Honolulu: University of Hawai'i Press, 1981), 73–78.

26. For an English translation of the work, see *The Memoirs of Lady Hyegyŏng*, trans. Ja-Hyun Kim Haboush (Berkeley: University of California Press, 1996).

27. JaHyun Kim Haboush, *The Great East Asian War and the Birth of the Korean Nation* (New York: Columbia University Press, 2016), 109–111.

28. For details, see Vipan Chandra, *Imperialism, Resistance, and Reform in Late Nineteenth-Century Korea: Enlightenment and the Independence Club* (Berkeley: Institute of East Asian Studies, 1988), 104–125.

29. See Andre Schmid, *Korea Between Empires, 1895–1919* (New York: Columbia University Press, 2002), 72–78.

30. Hwang, *Beyond Birth*, 249.

31. Kim, *The History and Future of Hangeul*, 38–41.

32. See the *New York Times* article on this development: http://www.nytimes.com/2009/09/12/world/asia/12script.html.

33. For details on these policies and its eventual failure, see Duncan, *The Origins of the Chosŏn Dynasty*, 204–213.

34. Ki-baik Lee, *A New History of Korea*, trans. Edward W. Wagner and Edward J. Schultz (Seoul: Ilchokak, 1984), 202–204.

35. Edward Willett Wagner, *The Literati Purges: Political Conflict in Early Yi Dynasty* (Cambridge, MA: Harvard University Press, 1974), 67.

36. Jungjong—eighteenth year (1523), second lunar month, tenth day. From this point on, references to the *Sillok* records will be simplified by the reign year, modern year, lunar month, and day. For example, in this case, Jungjong 18 (1523), 2/10.

37. For a total of ten records: five in King Yeonsan's reign, four in King Jungjong's, and one in Seonjo's—Yeonsan 6 (1500), 10/22; 10/28; 11/6; 11/28; 12/29. Jungjong 8 (1513), 8/29; 18 (1523), 2/10; 25 (1530), 12/28; 28 (1531), 1/1. Seonjo 21 (1588), 1/5.

38. Yeonsan 16 (1500), 12/21.

39. Jungjong 26 (1531), 1/1.

40. Yeonsan 6 (1500), 10/28.

41. Jungjong 8 (1513), 8/29.

42. Seonjo 21(1588), 1/5.

43. For a historical study of the concept of the Three Bonds and Five Relationships, see Hsu Dau-Lin, "The Myth of the 'Five Relations' of Confucius," *Monumenta Serica* 29 (1970): 27–37.

44. Hong Myong-Hee (1880–1968), a major writer among the first generation of modern novelists, began to publish a fictional account of the life of Im Kkeukjeong in serial form in the newspaper *Joseon ilbo* from 1924 until it was shut down by the Japanese authorities in 1940, leaving the work unfinished. Hong, a committed communist who moved to North Korea after liberation, turned the bandit into a protosocialist rebel. The work is currently published in seven volumes and is regarded as one of the finest examples of historical fiction in early modern Korean literature. In South Korea, Hwang Suk-Young, one of the country's most important contemporary writers, completed a ten-volume cycle of *Jang Gilsan* in 1984.

45. Yi Ik, *Seongho saseol* (Essays of Seongho) (Seoul: Minjok munhwa chu jinhwoe, 1995), 219.

46. In English, a short essay on Heo Gyun's life and works can be found in Jae-Yung So, "The Life of Hŏ Kyun and the Features of His Literary Works," *Journal of Social Sciences and Humanities* 52 (1980): 1–17; and translations of some of his poetry in *Borderland Roads: Selected Poems of Hŏ Kyun*, trans. Lan Haight and T'ae-yŏng Hŏ (New York: White Pine, 2009).

47. Heo Gyun, "Songoksanin jeon" (The story of the scholar Songok [Songok was Yi Dal's hometown and his literary name]) in Heo Gyun, *Hong Gildong jeon / Heo Gyun sanmunjip* (*The Story of Hong Gildong* / Collection of Heo Gyun's writings) (Seoul: Hanyang chulpan, 1996), 137–141.

48. Heo, *Hong Gildong jeon / Heo Gyun sanmunjip*, 110–113.

49. Heo, *Hong Gildong jeon / Heo Gyun sanmunjip*, 111.
50. Heo, *Hong Gildong jeon / Heo Gyun sanmunjip*, 120–123.
51. Heo, *Hong Gildong jeon / Heo Gyun sanmunjip*, 121.
52. Heo, *Hong Gildong jeon / Heo Gyun sanmunjip*, 122.
53. Yi Sik, *Gukyeok Taekdang Jip* (Translated collected writings of Taekdang) (Seoul: Minjok munhwa chujinhoe, 1996), 6:236.
54. Kim Taejun, *Joseon soseolsa* (Seoul: Doseo chulpan, 1989), 10. The quotation is from the American scholar William J. Long's *English Literature: Its History and Its Significance for the Life of the English-Speaking World* (Boston: Ginn and Co., 1909), 344. Lee Yoon Suk has pointed out, however, that Kim Taejun did not take the quote directly from the book but translated it into Korean from a Japanese translation, from a Japanese book on modern literature. See Lee Yoon Suk, "Kim Taejun 'Joseon soseolsa' geomto" (An examination of Kim Taejun's 'History of Joseon fiction'), *Dongbak hakji* 161 (March 2013): 403–442, 434.
55. Kim, *Joseon soseolsa*, 10.
56. Kim, *Joseon soseolsa*, 71–78.
57. Lee Yoon Suk, "*Hong Gildong jeon* wonbon hwakjeongeul wihan siron" (An essay on the determination of the original text of *The Story of Hong Gildong*), *Tongbang hakji* 85 (January 1994): 247–285, 254–256.
58. Yi Myeongseon, *Yi Myeongseong jeonjip* (Complete works of Yi Myeongseon) (Seoul: Bogosa, 2007), 3:244. For details on this issue, see Lee Pok-kyu, "Chogi gukmunsoseol ui jonjae yangsan" (The mode of existence of early Korean novels), *Gukjae eomun* 21 (2000): 25–44, 26–29.
59. Kim, *Joseon soseolsa*, 77.
60. For instance, Kim Ki-dong, in his 1956 work *Survey of Classical Korean Prose Fiction* (*Hanguk godae soseol gaeron*), much of which is based on Kim Taejun's *History of Joseon Fiction*, affirms that *The Story of Hong Gildong* was the first *soseol* to be originally written in *gukmun* (national script). Kim Ki-dong, *Hanguk godae soseol gaeron* (Seoul: Daechang munhwasa, 1956), 327. In 1958, Pak Song-eui published *History of Classic Korean Fiction* (*Hanguk godae soseolsa*), which also owes a great deal Kim Taejun's pioneering work. The 1992 edition of the work, with a slightly different title of *Theory and History of Classical Korean Fiction* (*Hanguk godae soseollon gwa sa*), includes an English-language summary of the book, in which it is asserted once again that "*Hong Kil-tong-jŏn* is the first novel written in Han-gŭl not by an anonymous author, but by Hŏ Kyun (1969–1618)." Pak Song-eui, *Hanguk godae soseollon gwa sa* (Theory and history of classical Korean fiction) (Seoul: Jimundang, 1992), 9 (from the back of the book).

Chapter 2: Elusive Traces of Hong Gildong in History

1. James Shapiro, *Contested Will: Who Wrote Shakespeare?* (New York: Simon & Schuster, 2010).
2. See Lee Yoon Suk, "*Hong Gildong jeon* wonbon hwakjeongeul wihan siron" (Essay on the determination of the original text of *The Story of Hong Gildong*), *Tongbang hakji* 85 (January 1994): 247–285, 249–250.
3. Paik Sung-Jong, "Gososeol *Hong Gildong jeon* ui chohak e daehan jaegumpto" (Some problems of *The Tales of Hong Kiltong*, an old novel), *Chindan Hakhoe* 80 (December 1995): 307–331; Lee Pok-kyu, "Chogi gukmunsoseol ui jonjae yangsan" (The mode of existence of early Korean novels), *Gukjae eomun* 21 (2000): 25–44, 26–29.
4. Yi Sik, *Gukyeok Taekdang jip* (Translated collected writings of Taekdang) (Seoul: Minjok munhwa chujinhoe, 1996), 6:236.
5. Ch'ên Shou-yi, *Chinese Literature: A Historical Introduction* (New York: Ronald Press Company, 1961), 471; Way-yee Li, "Full-Length Vernacular Fiction," in *The Columbia History*

of Chinese Literature, ed. Victor H. Mair (New York: Columbia University Press, 2001), 620–658, 621.

6. On the four great novels of the Ming dynasty, see Andrew H. Plaks, *The Four Master-works of the Ming Novel* (Princeton, NJ: Princeton University Press, 1987).

7. Kim Hŭnggyu and Peter H. Lee, "Chosŏn fiction in Korean," in *A History of Korean Literature*, ed. Peter H. Lee (Cambridge: Cambridge University Press, 2003), 273–287, 273–274.

8. Ch'ên, *Chinese Literature*, 471.

9. Heo Gyun, *Seongso bubugo* (Minor writings of Seongso) (Seoul: Minjok munhwa chujinhoe, 1985), 2:242.

10. Peter H. Lee, "Literary Criticism," in *A History of Korean Literature*, ed. Peter H. Lee (Cambridge: Cambridge University Press, 2003), 316–335, 333.

11. In the eighteenth century, a few literary figures acknowledged the moralistic and aesthetic values of some refined works, such as *Sassi namjunggi* (Record of Lady Sa's journey south) and *Guunmong* (Nine cloud dream). Lee, "Literary Criticism," 332–335.

12. Heo, *Seongso bubugo*, 335.

13. Paik, "Gososeol Hong Gildon ui chohak e daehan jaegumpto," 307–331, 316.

14. Seol Seonggyeong, *Hong Gildong jeon ui bimil* (The secret of *The Story of Hong Gildong*) (Seoul: Seoul daehakgyo chulpanbu, 2004), 203–214.

15. Seol, *Hong Gildong jeon ui bimil*, 206–207.

16. Seol, *Hong Gildong jeon ui bimil*, 207–211.

17. Seol, *Hong Gildong jeon ui bimil*, 212–213.

18. Quoted in Lee, *"Hong Gildong jeon* wonbon hwakjeongeul wihan siron," 271.

19. Heo Gyeongjin, *Heo Gyun pyeongjeon* (Critical biography of Heo Gyun) (Seoul: Dolbaegae, 2002), 144–145.

20. See the introduction to "Kuunmong," in *Virtuous Women: Three Classic Korean Novels*, trans. Richard Rutt and Kim Chong-Un (Seoul: Kwang Myong, 1974), 3–15, esp. 6–7.

21. Kichung Kim, *An Introduction to Classical Korean Literature: From Hyangga to P'ansori* (Armonk, NY: M. E. Sharpe, 1996), 148.

22. Jae-Yung So, "The Life of Hŏ Kyun and the Features of His Literary Works," *Journal of Social Sciences and Humanities* 52 (1980): 1–17, 3.

23. Kim, *An Introduction to Classical Korean Literature*, 156.

24. Tai-jin Kim, *A Bibliographical Guide to Traditional Korean Sources* (Seoul: Asiatic Research Center, Korea University, 1976), 290.

25. Heo, *Heo Gyun pyeongjeon*, 297–374.

26. See Lee Yoon Suk, "Hong Gildong jeon jakja nonui ui gyebo" (The genealogy of the controversy over the authorship of *The Story of Hong Gildong*), *Yeolsanggojeong yeongu* 36 (December 30, 2012): 381–414, 390–391. For the English-language works that feature the misconception, see the article "Hong-Giltong-Jŏn" in *Korea: A Historical and Cultural Dictionary*, ed. Keith Pratt and Richard Rutt (Surrey: Curzon, 1999), 168; and Robert J. Fouser, "'Translations,' of Hong Kildong: From Story to Classic to Icon and Beyond," *Transactions of the Royal Asiatic Society, Korea Branch* 75 (2000): 25–41, 30. Also, Cyris H. S. Moon has incorrectly claimed that Heo Gyun came from the secondary-status class of *jungin*; see Cyris H. S. Moon, "A Korean Minjung Perspective: The Hebrews and the Exodus," in *Voices from the Margin: Interpreting the Bible in the Third World*, ed. R. S. Sugirtharajah (Maryknoll, NY: Orbis, 1995), 228–243, 237.

27. See Yang-hi Choe-Wall, "The Sino-Korean Poetic Tradition of the Late Sixteenth Century: Background to a Study of the Poetry of Hŏ Nansŏrhŏn," *Papers on Far East History* 33 (January 1986): 139–157.

28. Heo, *Heo Gyun pyeongjeon*, 154–156.

29. Heo, *Heo Gyun pyeongjeon*, 227–234.

30. Heo, *Heo Gyun pyeongjeon*, 268–278.

31. Seonjo 35 (1602), 5/17.

32. Gwanghae 9 (1617), 1/20.

33. Gwanghae 10 (1618), 8/21.

34. Gwanghae 10 (1618), 8/24.

35. Gwanghae 10 (1618), 8/24.

36. Gwanghae 10 (1618), 8/21.

37. Gwanghae 5 (1613), 6/17.

38. See *Hong Gildong jeon / Heo Gyun sanmunjip* (*The story of Hong Gildong* / Collection of Heo Gyun's writings) (Seoul: Hanyang chulpan, 1996), 110–113, 120–123.

39. Paik Sung-Jong has made a similar argument. See Paik, "Goseoseol *Hong Gildong jeon* ui chohak e daehan jaegumpto," 318–320.

40. Kim, *An Introduction to Classical Korean Literature*, 149.

41. So, "The Life of Hŏ Kyun and the Features of His Literary Works," 12.

42. *Hong Gildong jeon / Heo Gyun sanmunjip*, 131–177.

43. *Hong Gildong jeon / Heo Gyun sanmunjip*, 140.

44. *Hong Gildong jeon / Heo Gyun sanmunjip*, 142–146.

45. *Hong Gildong jeon / Heo Gyun sanmunjip*, 173–177.

46. *Hong Gildong jeon / Heo Gyun sanmunjip*, 147–172.

47. Michael Edson Robinson, *Cultural Nationalism in Colonial Korea, 1920–1925* (Seattle: University of Washington Press, 1988), 43–47.

48. For details on the early history of Korean communism, see Robinson, *Cultural Nationalism in Colonial Korea*, 109–133; and two full-length books on the topic: Dae-Sook Suh, *The Korean Communist Movement, 1918–1948* (Princeton, NJ: Princeton University Press, 1967); and Robert A. Scalapino and Chong-Sik Lee, *Communism in Korea*, part 1: *The Movement* (Berkeley: University of California Press, 1972).

49. For a full biography of Kim Taejun, see Kim Yong-jik, *Kim Taejun pyeongjeong: jiseong gwa yeoksajeok sanghwang* (Biography of Kim Taejun: intellectual and historical context) (Seoul: Iljisa, 2007).

50. Robinson, *Cultural Nationalism in Colonial Korea*, 19–24.

51. Kim Taejun, *Joseon soseolsa* (Seoul: Doseo chulpan, 1989), 10.

52. Kim, *Joseon soseolsa*, 16–17.

53. Kim, *Joseon soseolsa*, 17.

54. Hyung Il Pai, *Constructing "Korean" Origins: A Critical Review of Archaeology, Historiography, and Racial Myth in Korean State-Formation Theories* (Cambridge, MA: Harvard University Asia Center, 2000), 35–41.

55. Pai, *Constructing "Korean" Origins*, 257–261.

56. Kim, *Joseon soseolsa*, 72.

57. Kim, *Joseon soseolsa*, 72. In 1939, when Kim Taejun published a new version of the work under the title of *Enlarged History of Joseon Fiction* (*Jeungbo Joseon soseolsa*), he reduced the passage to one sentence with less flamboyant language. "Following the Japanese Invasion of the Imjin year, as the *yangban*'s extortion of wealth and appropriation of land became particularly serious, the nation's tax revenue was reduced in half, resulting in the weakening of the central government's authority and the lives of the common people falling into misery—a state that any wise man would regard with pity." Kim Taejun, *Jeungbo Joseon soseolsa* (Seoul: Hangilsa, 1990), 82.

58. Kim, *Joseon soseolsa*, 76.

59. Kim, *Joseon soseolsa*, 74.

60. Kim, *Joseon soseolsa*, 74–75.

61. Kim, *Joseon soseolsa*, 75.

62. Kim, *Joseon soseolsa*, 77–78.

63. Benedict Anderson, *Imagined Communities* (London: Verso, 2006), 192–199.

64. Anderson, *Imagined Communities*, 195.

65. Anderson, *Imagined Communities*, 193.

66. Lee Yoon Suk, "Hong Gildong jeon jakja nonui ui gyebo" (The genealogy of discussion on the authorship of *The Story of Hong Gildong*), *Yeolsang gojeong yeongu* 36 (December 30, 2012): 381–414.

67. Quoted in Lee, "Hong Gildong jeon jakja nonui ui gyebo," 403. For the original Japanese, see 404.

68. Yi Myeongseon, *Yi Myeongseong jeonjip* (Complete works of Yi Myeongseon) (Seoul: Bogosa, 2007), 3:244.

69. Kim, *Joseon soseolsa*, 77.

Chapter 3: The Imagined Hong Gildong at the Twilight of a Dynasty

1. Judith Butler, *Gender Trouble: Feminism and the Subversion of Identity* (New York: Routledge, 1999), xxi.

2. Ki-baik Lee, *A New History of Korea*, trans. Edward W. Wagner and Edward J. Shultz (Seoul: Ilchokak, 1984), 244.

3. Martina Deuchler, "'Heaven Does Not Discriminate': A Study of Secondary Sons in Chosŏn Korea," *Journal of Korean Studies* 6 (1988–1989): 121–163; JaHyun Kim Haboush, *A Heritage of Kings: One Man's Monarchy in the Confucian World* (New York: Columbia University Press, 1998), 94–95.

4. Kim Taejun, *Joseon soseolsa* (History of Joseon fiction) (Seoul: Doseo chulpan, 1989), 82.

5. W. E. Skillend, *Kodae Sosŏl: A Survey of Korean Traditional Style Popular Novels* (Old Woking: Unwin Brothers, 1968), 242.

6. Tai-jin Kim, *A Bibliographical Guide to Traditional Korean Sources* (Seoul: Asiatic Research Center, Korea University, 1976), 292.

7. Keith Pratt and Richard Rutt, *Korea: A Historical and Cultural Dictionary* (Richmond: Curzon, 1999), 168.

8. Peter H. Lee, *A History of Korean Literature* (Cambridge: Cambridge University Press, 2003), 275. Lee used the word "utopia" in his brief introduction to Marshall R. Pihl's translation of *The Story of Hong Gildong*. Peter H. Lee, ed., *Anthology of Korean Literature: From Early Times to the Nineteenth Century* (Honolulu: University of Hawai'i Press, 1981), 119.

9. Kim Yong-bok, "Messiah and Minjung: Discerning Messianic Politics over against Political Messianism," in *Minjung Theology: People as the Subjects of History*, ed. Kim Yonkbok (Maryknoll, NY: Orbis, 1981), 183–193, 188.

10. Sang Taek Lee, *Religion and Social Formation in Korea: Minjung and Millenarianism* (Berlin: Mouton de Gruyter, 1996), 56.

11. *Borderland Roads: Selected Poems of Hŏ Kyun*, trans. Ian Haight and T'ae-yŏng Hŏ (Buffalo, NY: White Pine, 2009), 17.

12. Kyung Moon Hwang, *A History of Korea* (Houndmills: Palgrave Macmillan, 2010), 110.

13. *The Story of Hong Gildong*, trans. Minsoo Kang (New York: Penguin, 2016), 70.

14. Yao (traditionally c. 24th–23rd centuries BCE) and Shun (traditionally c. 23rd–22nd centuries BCE) were two of the semimythical Three Sovereigns and Five Emperors of the earliest period of Chinese history, who were revered by Kongzi (Confucius) and countless others throughout the centuries as ideal monarchs under whose rule their realms enjoyed perfect peace and harmony. In the *Analects*, Kongzi says, "Sublime was the way Shun and Yu held possession of the empire" (book 8, 18), and "Great was Yao as a ruler!" (book 8, 19). Confucius, *The Analects*, trans. Annping Chin (New York: Penguin, 2014), 125–126.

15. *Hong Gildong jeon*, ed. Lee Yoon Suk (Seoul: Yonsei daehakgyo daehakchulpan munhwawon, 2014), 46.

16. *Hong Gildong jeon*, 49.

17. *Hong Gildong jeon*, 51.

18. *The Story of Hong Gildong*, 58.

19. *Hong Gildong jeon*, 49.

20. Jamie K. Taylor, *Fictions of Evidence: Witnessing, Literature, and Community in the Late Middle Ages* (Columbus: Ohio State University Press, 2013), 108–114.

21. See "Fouke le Fitz Waryn," in *Robin Hood and Other Outlaw Tales*, ed. Stephen Knight and Thomas Ohlgren (Kalamazoo: Western Michigan University, 1997), 687–623.

22. Taylor, *Fictions of Evidence*, 109.

23. Taylor, *Fictions of Evidence*, 110.

24. Stephen Knight, *Robin Hood: A Complete Study of the English Outlaw* (Oxford: Blackwell, 1994), 164.

25. Knight, *Robin Hood*, 81.

26. Kim, *Joseon soseolsa*, 61–62.

27. Kim Hŭnggyu and Peter H. Lee, "Chosŏn Fiction in Korean," in *A History of Korean Literature*, ed. Peter H. Lee (Cambridge: Cambridge University Press, 2003), 273.

28. Kim, *Joseon soseolsa*, 63–64.

29. On the Chinese genre of military romance, see C. T. Hsia, "The Military Romance: A Genre of Chinese Fiction," in *C. T. Hsia on Chinese Literature* (New York: Columbia University Press, 2004), 135–170.

30. Lee Pok-kyu, "Chogi gukmunsoseol ui jonjae yangsang" (The mode of existence of early Korean novels), *Gukjeeomun* 21 (2000): 25–44, 35.

31. Lee, "Chogi gukmunsoseol ui jonjae yangsang," 41.

32. Ian Watt, *The Rise of the Novel: Studies in Defoe, Richardson, and Fielding* (Berkeley: University of California Press, 1967), 35–59. For more recent assessments of the subject, see J. Paul Hunter, "The Novel and Social/Cultural History," in *The Cambridge Companion to the Eighteenth-Century Novel*, ed. John Richetti (Cambridge: Cambridge University Press, 1996), 9–40; and Deidre Lynch, *The Economy of Character: Novels, Market Culture, and the Business of Inner Meaning* (Chicago: University of Chicago Press, 1998).

33. For an excellent assessment of such activities during the reign of King Yeongjo, see JaHyun Kim Haboush, *A Heritage of Kings: One Man's Monarchy in the Confucian World* (New York: Columbia University Press, 1988).

34. Haboush, *A Heritage of Kings*, 87.

35. Haboush, *A Heritage of Kings*, 88.

36. For details on the market system of popular literature in the late Joseon period, see Lee Yoon Suk, *Joseonsidae sangeopchulpan* (Commercial publishing in the Joseon period) (Seoul: Minsokwon, 2016).

37. Lee Yoon Suk, "*Hong Gildong jeon* wonbon hwakjeongeul wihan siron" (Essay on the determination of the original text of *The Story of Hong Gildong*), *Tongbang hakji* 85 (January 1994): 247–285, 271–272.

38. For an English translation of this work, see *The Record of the Black Dragon Year*, trans. Peter H. Lee (Seoul: Institute of Korean Culture, Korea University, 2000).

39. Quoted in Lee, "*Hong Gildong jeon* wonbon hwakjeongeul wihan siron," 271.

40. The printed *gyeongpan* 30 text gives no date of publication, but it was definitely produced sometime before February 1892. Maurice Courant (1865–1935) was a French diplomat who was stationed in Korea from May 1890 to February 1892. After his return to France, he became a renowned professor of Asian languages at the University of Lyon. From 1894 to 1896, he published the monumental work *Bibliographie coréene*, a pioneering study of Korean literature, in which he references *The Story of Hong Gildong*, describing the

text he consulted as a printed work of thirty sheets. Given the time of his stay in Korea, the latest possible date of the text's publication is very early in 1892, but probably earlier. See Maurice Courant, *Bibliographie coréenne: tableau littéraire de la Coree* (New York: Burt Franklin, 1894), 1:441.

41. *Hong Gildong jeon / Jeon Uchi jeon* (The story of Hong Gildong / The story of Jeon Uchi) (Seoul: Munhak dongne, 2010), 84–90. A condensed and bowdlerized version of the story in English can be found in Zŏng In-sŏb, "The Legend of Zŏn U-Czi," in *Folk Tales from Korea* (Seoul: Hollym, 1982), 224–234.

42. For his works in English translation, see *The Novels of Park Jiwon*, trans. Emanuel Pastreich (Seoul: Seoul National University Press, 2011).

43. *The Novels of Park Jiwon*, 101–121.

44. For detailed discussions of evidence to this fact, see Lee, *Joseonsidae sangeopchulpan*.

45. Jang Hyo-hyon, *Hanguk gojeon soseolsa yeongu* (Research on the history of classic Korean fiction) (Seoul: Goryeo daehak chulpanbu, 2002), 157–178.

46. Hong Manjung and Hwang Yunseok, *Jeongbo haedong ijeok* (Enlarged edition of extraordinary events of Haedong), ed. Sin Haejin and Kim Seontek (Seoul: Gyeongin munhwasa, 2011), 223.

47. Hong and Hwang, *Jeongbo haedong ijeok*, 223.

48. Jang, *Hanguk gojeon soseolsa yeongu*, 163.

49. Jang, *Hanguk gojeon soseolsa yeongu*, 164.

50. Sejong 10 (1428), 10/28.

51. *The Record of the Black Dragon Year*, 57–58. I made slight adjustments to Peter H. Lee's translation.

52. *The Story of Hong Gildong*, 3.

53. *Yu Chungryeol jeon, Jeong Bi jeon* (The story of Yu Chungryeol / The story of Queen Jeong) (Seoul: Ihoe munhwasa, 2005), 28.

54. *Yu Chungryeol jeon, Jeong Bi jeon*, 31–32.

55. *Hong Gildong jeon / Jeon Uchi jeon*, 72.

56. *Hong Gildong jeon / Jeon Uchi jeon*, 76.

57. *Hong Gildong jeon / Jeon Uchi jeon*, 105–110.

58. Kim, *Joseon soseolsa*, 79.

59. *The Record of the Black Dragon Year*, 96—translation slightly adjusted.

60. *The Story of Hong Gildong*, 31.

61. *Hong Gildong jeon*, 16.

62. *Hong Gildong jeon*, 88–89.

63. Horace Newton Allen, *Korean Tales* (New York: G. P. Putnam's Sons, 1889), 178.

64. Kim Youg-kol, *Brave Hong Kil-dong / The Man Who Bought the Shade of a Tree* (Elizabeth, NJ: Hollym, 1990), 4.

65. Anne Sibley O'Brien, *The Legend of Hong Kil Dong: The Robin Hood of Korea* (Watertown, MA: Charlesbridge, 2008), no page numbers.

66. *Hong Gildong jeon*, 105.

67. *The Story of Hong Gildong*, 66.

68. *The Story of Hong Gildong*, 66.

69. *Hong Gildong jeon*, 43.

70. *Hong Gildong jeon*, 105.

71. *Hong Gildong jeon, Im Janggun jeon, Jeong Eulseon jeon, Yi Daebong jeon* (The story of Hong Gildong, the story of General Im, the story of Eulseon, the story of Yi Daebong) (Seoul: Gyeongin munhwasa, 2007), 53.

72. Allen, *Korean Tales*, 192.

73. Zŏng, *Folk Tales from Korea*, 222.

74. Kim, *Brave Hong Kil-dong*, 28.

75. O'Brien, *The Legend of Hong Kil Dong*, no page numbers.

76. Jeong Jongmok and Yi Gwangik (illus.), *Hong Gildong jeon* (Seoul: Changbi, 2003), 130.

77. See, for instance, Anton Blok, "The Peasant and the Brigand: Social Banditry Reconsidered," *Comparative Studies in Society and History* 14, no. 4 (September 1972): 494–503; and Richard E. Slatta, "Eric J. Hobsbawm's Social Bandit: A Critique and Revision," *A Contracorriente* 1, no. 2 (Spring 2004): 22–30.

78. See Hobsbawm's reply to Anton Blok's critique: Eric Hobsbawm, "Social Bandits: Reply," *Comparative Studies in Society and History* 14, no. 4 (September 1972): 503–505. Hobsbawm elaborates on his response in the postscript to the 2000 edition of *Bandits*; see Eric Hobsbawm, *Bandits* (New York: The New Press, 2000), 167–199.

79. For some examples, see Paul Kooistra, *Criminals as Heroes: Structure, Power, and Identity* (Bowling Green, OH: Bowling Green State University Popular Press, 1989), 28–29; Knight, *Robin Hood*, 61; and Graham Seal, *The Outlaw Legend: A Cultural Tradition in Britain, America, and Australia* (Cambridge: Cambridge University Press, 1996), 2–3.

80. Hobsbawm, *Bandits*, 47–48.

81. *The Story of Hong Gildong*, 46.

82. *The Story of Hong Gildong*, 41.

83. *Hong Gildong jeon*, 23.

84. Quoted in Knight, *Robin Hood*, 37.

85. Quoted in Knight, *Robin Hood*, 69; see also 79–80.

86. Knight, *Robin Hood*, 74.

87. *The Story of Hong Gildong*, 60.

88. *The Story of Hong Gildong*, 45.

89. Knight, *Robin Hood*, 56–57.

90. The religion is extant today in South Korea, now known primarily by its alternate name Cheondogyeo (religion of the Heavenly Way). There is now a substantial literature in English on the Donghak movement. The pioneering work on the subject is Benjamin Weems, *Reform, Rebellion, and Heavenly Way* (Tucson: University of Arizona Press, 1964). The most recent book-length works are Carl Young, *Eastern Learning and the Heavenly Way: The Tonghak and Ch'ŏndogyo Movements and the Twilight of Korean Independence* (University of Hawai'i Press, 2014); and George L. Kallander, *Salvation through Dissent: Tonghak Heterodoxy and Early Modern Korea* (Honolulu: University of Hawai'i Press, 2013). Kallender asserts that it is important to look at the difference between the original religion of the 1860s and the political movement that it became in the 1890s under different historical circumstances.

91. Young Ick Lew, "The Conservative Character of the 1894 Tonghak Peasant Uprising: A Reappraisal with Emphasis on Chŏn Pong-jun's Background and Motivation," *Journal of Korean Studies* 7 (1990–1991): 149–180.

92. Lew, "The Conservative Character of the 1894 Tonghak Peasant Uprising," 167.

93. Quoted in Lew, "The Conservative Character of the 1894 Tonghak Peasant Uprising," 168.

94. See, for instance, Suh Nam-dong, "Historical References for a Theology of Minjung," in *Minjung Theology: People as the Subjects of History* (Maryknoll, NY: Orbis, 1983), 155–182, 171. In a different essay in the same collection, the same author calls the members of Hwalbindang the "Korean Robin Hoods of late Yi Korea." Suh Nam-dong, "Towards a Theology of Han," in *Minjung Theology*, 55–69, 69.

Chapter 4: The Colonial Period, 1921–1936

1. "Golem: Between Magic and Metaphor," Los Angeles, UCLA, June 3, 2004.

2. E. Taylor Atkins, *Primitive Selves: Koreana in the Japanese Colonial Gaze, 1910–1945* (Berkeley: University of California Press, 2010), 1–12.

3. Atkins, *Primitive Selves*, 147–186.

4. See Sven Saaler and Christopher W. A. Szpilman, *Pan-Asianism: A Documentary History*, vol. 2: *1920–Present* (Lanham, MD: Rowman & Littlefield, 2011), 115–122; and Mark Caprio, *Japanese Assimilation Policies in Colonial Korea, 1910–1945* (Seattle: University of Washington Press, 2009), 116–119.

5. Quoted in Caprio, *Japanese Assimilation Policies*, 117.

6. Serk-Bae Suh, *Treacherous Translation: Culture, Nationalism, and Colonialism in Korea and Japan from the 1910s to the 1960s* (Berkeley: University of California Press, 2013), 18–45. Suh points out that Hosoi denigrated *The Story of Hong Gildong* as derivative of the tales of Nezumi Kozō (1797–1831), the righteous outlaw figure of Japan. Although there is no evidence that the legends of the Japanese hero influenced the writing of the Hong Gildong story, Suh dismissed Hosoi's claim on the basis of the "fact that the Korean tale preceded the famous early 19th-century Japanese thief by more than two hundred years" (that is, assuming Heo Gyun's authorship of the work). Suh, *Treacherous Translation*, 27.

7. *Ko Kichido den*, trans. Shiraishi Shigeru (Tokyo: Jiyu Tokyusa, 1921).

8. I am grateful to Hiroko Washizu and Yayoi Shinoda for providing me with an English translation of Hosoi Hajime's introduction.

9. *Ko Kichido den*, 1.

10. *Ko Kichido den*, 3.

11. *Ko Kichido den*, 4.

12. Lee Young-il and Choe Young-chol, *The History of Korean Cinema*, trans. Richard Lynn Greever (Seoul: Jimmundang, 1998), 19–20.

13. Lee and Choe, *The History of Korean Cinema*, 25–28.

14. Brian Yecies and Ae-Gyung Shim, *Korea's Occupied Cinemas, 1893–1948* (New York: Routledge, 2011), 90.

15. Yecies and Shim, *Korea's Occupied Cinemas*, 90–92.

16. Yecies and Shim, *Korea's Occupied Cinemas*, 115–140.

17. The two English-language works on Korean film that mention them in passing are Lee and Choe, *The History of Korean Cinema*, 61; and Yecies and Shim, *Korea's Occupied Cinemas*, 111–112.

18. Chon Pom-song, ed., *Hanguk yeonghwa chongseo* (Collection of Korean cinema) (Seoul: Hanguk Yeonghwa Jinheung Johap, 1972), 186.

19. Chon, ed., *Hanguk yeonghwa chongseo*, 186.

20. "Sinjak Joseon yeonghwa *Hong Gildong jeon*" (New Joseon film *The Story of Hong Gildong*) *Donga ilbo* (April 9, 1935): 3.

21. Mun Young Joo, "Ilje malgi gwanbyeon jabji 'Gajeong jiu' (1936. 12–1941. 03) wa 'saeroun buin'" (Late Japanese colonial-period government-sponsored journal *Friend of the Household* (Dec. 1936–Mar. 1941) and *New Wife*), *Yeoksa munjae yeongu* 17 (2007): 179–200.

22. Theodore Q. Hughes, *Literature and Film in Cold War South Korea: Freedom's Frontier* (New York: Columbia University Press, 2012), 26–34. Such serialized scripts and film fiction from 1925 to 1940 have been collected in four volumes: see Kim Sunam, ed., *Joseon sinario seonjip* (Collection of Joseon scripts) (Seoul: Jipmundang, 2003). See also Jina E. Kim, "Intermedial Aesthetics: Still Images, Moving Words, and Written Sounds in Early Twentieth-Century Korean Cinematic Novels (*Yeonghwa Soseol*)," *Review of Korean Studies* 6. no. 2 (December 2013): 45–79.

23. "Hong Gildong jeon," *Gajeong Jiu* 1, no. 2 (February 1937): 48–56.

24. "Hong Gildong jeon," 51–52.

25. "Hong Gildong jeon,"56.

26. Yecies and Shim, *Korea's Occupied Cinemas*, 87–88.

27. Lee and Choe, *The History of Korean Cinema*, 52–53.

28. Michael Robinson, "Mass Media and Popular Culture in 1930s Korea: Cultural Control, Identity, and Colonial Hegemony," in *Korean Studies: New Pacific Currents*, ed. Dae-Sook Suh (Honolulu: University of Hawai'i Press, 1994), 59–82, 60.

29. Chon, ed., *Hanguk yeonghwa chongseo*, 200.

30. Kim Gwan, "Sinyeong yeonghwa Hong Gildong jeon eul bogo" (After seeing the new version of the film *The Story of Hong Gildong*), *Choson ilbo* (June 25, 1936): 5.

Chapter 5: North and South Korea, 1947–1986

1. On the Group of Nine and KAPF, see Theodore Q. Hughes, *Literature and Film in Cold War South Korea: Freedom's Frontier* (New York: Columbia University Press, 2012), 20–49. Christopher Hanson has recently complicated the view of the Group of Nine as essentially apolitical and subjective in aesthetic orientation by demonstrating that their struggle with the problem of linguistic representation constituted an intimate engagement with the condition of the colonial subject. Christopher P. Hanscom, *The Real Modern: Literary Modernism and the Crisis of Representation in Colonial Korea* (Cambridge, MA: Harvard University Asia Center, 2013); for a detailed analysis of Bak Taejun's modernist works, see 38–77.

2. On the situation of Korean writers, including Park Taewon, during the war mobilization period, see Janet Poole, *When the Future Disappears: The Modernist Imagination in Late Colonial Korea* (New York: Columbia University Press, 2014), esp. 130–148.

3. Hughes, *Literature and Film in Cold War South Korea*, 66.

4. Park Baesik, "Park Taewon ui yeoksa soseolgwan" (Park Taewon's theory of the historical novel) *Gubo hakbo* 2 (December 31, 2007): 33–51.

5. Park Taewon, *Hong Gildong jeon* (Seoul: Joseon geumyung johap yeonhaphoe, 1947), 83.

6. Park, *Hong Gildong jeon*, 86–87.

7. Park, *Hong Gildong jeon*, 153–154.

8. Park, *Hong Gildong jeon*, 154.

9. Park, *Hong Gildong jeon*, 118.

10. Park, *Hong Gildong jeon*, 16–18.

11. Park, *Hong Gildong jeon*, 52.

12. Park, *Hong Gildong jeon*, 98–110.

13. Park, *Hong Gildong jeon*, 140–148.

14. Park, *Hong Gildong jeon*, 158–160.

15. Park, *Hong Gildong jeon*, 166.

16. Park, *Hong Gildong jeon*, 172.

17. Park, *Hong Gildong jeon*, 173.

18. Robert Fouser claims that the ending "depicts a battle between Hong Kildong and his followers as they head for Kyongbok Palace to take on the corrupt rulers." No such battle takes place in the novel. Robert J. Fouser, "'Translations' of Hong Kiltong: From Story to Classic to Icon and Beyond," *Transactions of the Royal Asiatic Society, Korea Branch* 75 (2000): 25–41, 33.

19. On Shin Dong Wu's life and career, see Yi Yongcheol, "'Hong Gildong gwa Chadolbawi' ro wangguk eul seun manhwaga, Shin Dong Wu" (The comic book artist Shin Dong Wu who built his kingdom with "Hong Gildong and Chadolbawi"), in *Shin Dong Wu Collection* (Seoul: Bucheon manhwa jeongbo center, 2007), 8–15.

20. Part of Shin Dong Wu's comic version of *Hong Gildong* has been reproduced with the dialogue in English translated by myself and edited by Heinz Insu Fenkl. See "Shin Dong Wu's *Hong Gildong*," *Azalea: Journal of Korean Literature and Culture* 6 (2013): 328–355.

21. *Shin Dong Wu Collection*, 71–84.

22. *Shin Dong Wu Collection*, 37.

23. *Shin Dong Wu Collection*, 32.

24. *Shin Dong Wu Collection*, 68–69.

25. *Shin Dong Wu Collection*, 104.

26. The film was thought to have been lost, but recently a copy that was exported to Japan has been found and is now available for viewing at the Korean Film Archive in Seoul.

27. The 1995 film can be viewed in full on YouTube: https://www.youtube.com/watch?v=ltov57P0CYE.

28. Brian Yecies and Ae-Gyung Shim, *Korea's Occupied Cinemas, 1893–1948* (New York: Routledge, 2011), 100.

29. On the position of literary writers under the regime of Park Chung-hee, see Youngju Ryu, *Writers of the Winter Republic: Literature and Resistance in Park Chung Hee's Korea* (Honolulu: University of Hawai'i Press, 2016).

30. For a detailed analysis of the story and the affair of Nam's prosecution, see Hughes, *Literature and Film in Cold War South Korea*, 153–158. For another excellent discussion of the work in the context of sexual labor in South Korea, see Jin-kyung Lee, *Service Economies: Militarism, Sex Work, and Migrant Labor in South Korea* (Minneapolis: University of Minnesota Press, 2010), 134–137.

31. Nam Jeonghyeon, *Bunji* (Land of excrement) (Seoul: Hangyeore, 1987), 314. This edition of Nam's representative works also contains essential documents of his trial.

32. Nam, *Bunji*, 319.

33. Nam, *Bunji*, 323.

34. Nam, *Bunji*, 337.

35. Kelly Y. Jeong, *Crisis of Gender and the Nation in Korean Literature and Cinema* (Lanham, MD: Lexington Books, 2011), 74. For a similar study of the theme of masculine crisis in Korean cinema of the 1970s and 1980s, see Kyung Gyun Kim, *The Remasculinization of Korean Cinema* (Durham, NC: Duke University Press, 2004).

36. Han Seungwon, "Sin Gildong jeon," in *Arirang byeolgok* (Song of Arirang) (Seoul: Munidang, 1999), 172–191.

37. Han, "Sin Gildong jeon," 712.

38. Han, "Sin Gildong jeon," 181.

39. Han, "Sin Gildong jeon," 187.

40. Han, "Sin Gildong jeon," 186.

41. Han, "Sin Gildong jeon," 191.

42. See Je-Hun Ryu, "Kyeryong Mountain as a Contested Place," in *Sitings: Critical Approaches to Korean Geography*, ed. Timothy R. Tangherlini and Sallie Yea (Honolulu: University of Hawai'i Press, 2008), 121–140.

43. Park Yangho, *Seoul Hong Gildong woe* (*Hong Gildong of Seoul* and other works) (Seoul: Beom Han, 1985), 11.

44. Park, *Seoul Hong Gildong woe*, 11.

45. Park, *Seoul Hong Gildong woe*, 19.

46. Park, *Seoul Hong Gildong woe*, 43.

47. Park, *Seoul Hong Gildong woe*, 58–59.

48. Park, *Seoul Hong Gildong woe*, 21.

49. Park, *Seoul Hong Gildong woe*, 29.

50. Park, *Seoul Hong Gildong woe*, 31.

51. Park, *Seoul Hong Gildong woe*, 33.

52. Park, *Seoul Hong Gildong woe*, 33.

53. Park, *Seoul Hong Gildong woe*, 83–85.

54. Park, *Seoul Hong Gildong woe*, 91.

55. Park, *Seoul Hong Gildong woe*, 102.

56. Park, *Seoul Hong Gildong woe*, 47.

57. Park, *Seoul Hong Gildong woe*, 136.
58. Park, *Seoul Hong Gildong woe*, 180.
59. For more on this work, see Hughes, *Literature and Film in Cold War South Korea*, 119–128.
60. Jeong Biseok, *Soseol Hong Gildong* (Hong Gildong the novel) (Seoul: Goryeowon, 1985), 1:8–9.
61. Park, *Hong Gildong jeon*, 12.
62. Jeong, *Soseol Hong Gildong*, 1:21.
63. Park, *Hong Gildong jeon*, 105–108.
64. Park, *Hong Gildong jeon*, 113; Jeong, *Soseol Hong Gildong*, 1:127.
65. Park, *Hong Gildong jeon*, 92–94, 118; Jeong, *Soseol Hong Gildong*, 1:147.
66. Park, *Hong Gildong jeon*, 94.
67. *Shin Dong Wu Collection*, 105.
68. Jeong, *Soseol Hong Gildong*, 1:85.
69. Jeong, *Soseol Hong Gildong*, 2:195.
70. Jeong, *Soseol Hong Gildong*, 2:196.
71. Jeong, *Soseol Hong Gildong*, 1:36.
72. Jeong, *Soseol Hong Gildong*, 2:116.
73. Jeong, *Soseol Hong Gildong*, 2:258–269.
74. Jeong, *Soseol Hong Gildong*, 2:270.
75. Jeong, *Soseol Hong Gildong*, 2:271.
76. Johannes Schönherr, *North Korean Cinema: A History* (Jefferson, NC: McFarland, 2012), 43–71.
77. The text is available in English translation. See Kim Jong Il, *On the Art of the Cinema* (Honolulu: University Press of the Pacific, 1989).
78. For a full account of the kidnapping story, see Paul Fisher, *A Kim Jong-Il Production: The Extraordinary True Story of a Kidnapped Filmmaker, His Star Actress, and a Young Dictator's Rise to Power* (New York: Flatiron, 2015). On Shin Sang-ok's cinematic works, see Steven Chung, *Split-Screen Korea: Shin Sang-ok and Postwar Cinema* (Minneapolis: University of Minnesota Press, 2014).
79. On the films they produced in North Korea, see Schönherr, *North Korean Cinema*, 72–90. See also Suk-Young Kim, *Illusive Utopia: Theater, Film, and Everyday Performance in North Korea* (Ann Arbor: University of Michigan Press, 2010), 19–41.
80. Schönherr, *North Korean Cinema*, 101; Kim, *Illusive Utopia*, 62–65. The film is available for viewing on YouTube: http://www.youtube.com/watch?v=UVnXAuaFY_s.
81. *Shin Dong Wu Collection*, 81–82.

Chapter 6: South Korea, 1994–Present

1. Yi Munyol, *Auwaeui manam oe* (An appointment with my brother and other stories) (Seoul: Doseo chukpan dungji, 1994), 205–206.
2. Yi, *Auwaeui manam oe*, 116.
3. Yi, *Auwaeui manam oe*, 119–120.
4. Yi, *Auwaeui manam oe*, 5.
5. Seo Hajin, *Hong Gildong*, trans. Leif Olsen and Janet Hong (Seoul: Jimoondang, 2007).
6. Seo, *Hong Gildong*, 30.
7. Seo, *Hong Gildong*, 7–8.
8. Seo, *Hong Gildong*, 40–41.
9. Seo, *Hong Gildong*, 41.
10. For full-length works on the *hallyu* phenomenon, see Beng Chua Huat and Koichi Iwabuchi, *East Asian Pop Culture: Analysing the Korean Wave* (Hong Kong: Hong Kong Uni-

versity Press, 2008); Mark James Russell, *Pop Goes Korea: Behind the Revolution in Movies, Music, and Internet Culture* (Berkeley, CA: Stone Bridge, 2008); Kyung Hyun Kim, *Virtual Hallyu: Korean Cinema in the Global Era* (Durham, NC: Duke University Press, 2011); Sun Jung, *Korean Masculinities and Transcultural Consumption: Yonsama, Rain, Oldboy, K-Pop Idols* (Hong Kong: Hong Kong University Press, 2011); and Euny Hong, *The Birth of Korean Cool: How One Nation Is Conquering the World through Pop Culture* (New York: Picador, 2014).

11. The DVD set of the show that I obtained through Amazon.com was released by a company in Singapore for a Chinese audience, with both Chinese and English subtitles.

12. For another comparison of the North Korean film and *Sharp Blade Hong Gildong*, see Hwang Mija and U Sangryeol, "Joseon yeonghwa <Hong Gildong jeon> gwa hanguk drama <Kwaedo Hong Gildong jeon> bigyo yeongu" (North Korean movie *The Story of Hong Gildong* and the South Korean drama *The Story of Sharp Blade Hong Gildong* comparison and analysis) *Hanjung inmunhak yeongu* 32 (April 2011): 207–221.

13. Robert J. Fouser, "'Translations' of Hong Kildong: From Story to Classic to Icon and Beyond," *Transactions of the Royal Asiatic Society, Korean Branch* 75 (2000): 25–41, 35.

14. Suk-Young Kim, *Illusive Utopia: Theater, Film, and Everyday Performance in North Korea* (Ann Arbor: University of Michigan Press, 2010), 332n4.

15. Hong Manjung and Hwang Yunseok, *Jeongbo haedong ijeok* (Enlarged edition of the extraordinary events of Haedong), ed. Sin Haejin and Kim Seontek (Seoul: Gyeongin munhwasa, 2011), 223.

16. Seol Seonggyeong and Jeong Cheol, *Siljon inmul Hong Gildong* (The real-life Hong Gildong) (Seoul: Jungang M & B, 1998), 21.

17. Sejong 10 (1428), 10/28.

18. Seol and Jeong, *Siljon inmul Hong Gildong*, 34–35.

19. Seol and Jeong, *Siljon inmul Hong Gildong*, 33–34.

20. Seol and Jeong, *Siljon inmul Hong Gildong*, 153–159.

21. Seol and Jeong, *Siljon inmul Hong Gildong*, 153–155.

22. See George H. Kerr, *Okinawa: The History of an Island People* (Rutland, VT: Charles E. Tuttle, 1958), 121.

23. Seol and Jeong, *Siljon inmul Hong Gildong*, 165–173.

24. Seol and Jeong, *Siljon inmul Hong Gildong*, 187–195.

25. Seol and Jeong, *Siljon inmul Hong Gildong*, 200–201.

26. Seol Seonggyeong, *Hong Gildong jeon ui bimil* (Secret of the story of Hong Gildong) (Seoul: Seoul daehak chulpanbu, 2004), 270–285.

27. Kang Cheolgeun, *Saramui nara* (Country of humanity) (Seoul: Iji chulpan, 2010), 13.

28. Kang, *Saramui nara*, 26.

29. Kang, *Saramui nara*, 165–166.

30. Kim Changyeop, "Character sijang tteugeoun 'Hong Gilong jeon,'" (Heated character market for "The Story of Hong Gildong"), *Jungang ilbo* (July 2, 1998), http://pdf.joinsmsn.com/article/pdf_article_prv.asp?id=DY01199807020147.

31. Ju-Hyun Ryu and Hyun Hyo Kim have written a study of what they call "storytelling tourism" comparing Spain's Don Quixote tourism in Castile–La Mancha and Hong Gildong tourism in Jangseong. Unfortunately, they present the ideas of Seol Seonggyeong uncritically as historical discoveries. See Ju-Hyun Ryu and Hyun Hyo Kim, "A Comparative Study of Storytelling Tourism Based on Literary Contents: The Case of Don Quixote and Hong, Gil-Dong," *Advances in Information Sciences and Service Sciences* 5, no. 15 (October 2013): 362–371.

32. Yu Hyeongjae, "Gangneungsi Hong Gildong character ilbu sayong bulga" (The city of Gangneung prohibited from the use of Hong Gildong character), *Yeonhap news* (September 7, 2009), http://news.naver.com/main/read.nhn?mode=LSD&mid=sec&sid1=102&oid=001&aid=0002850920.

33. Won Seonyeong, "Gangneungsi 'Hong Gildong character' Janseonggun e ppaet-gyeotda" (The city of Gangneung lost its Hong Gildong character to Janseong County), *Gang-won ilbo* (September 7, 2009), http://www.kwnews.co.kr/nview.asp?s=501&aid=209090600123.

34. Okpyo Moon, "Tourist Commoditization of Confucian Cultural Heritage in Korea," in *Consuming Korean Tradition in Early and Later Modernity: Commodification, Tourism, and Performance*, ed. Laurel Kendall (Honolulu: University of Hawai'i Press, 2011), 88–104, 33.

35. Timothy R. Tangherlini, "Chosŏn Memories: Spectatorship, Ideology, and the Korean Folk Village," in *Sitings: Critical Approaches to Korean Geography*, ed. Timothy R. Tangherlini and Sallie Yea (Honolulu: University of Hawai'i Press, 2008), 61–82, 63.

36. Nelson H. H. Gradburn, "Tourism, Modernity, and Nostalgia" in *The Future of Anthropology: Its Relevance to the Contemporary World*, ed. Akbar S. Ahmed and Cris N. Shore (London: Athlone, 1995), 158–178, 167.

Appendix

1. Lee Yoon Suk, "*Hong Gildong jeon* wonbon hwakjeongeul wihan siron" (An essay on the determination of the original text of *The Story of Hong Gildong*), *Tongbang hakji* 85 (January 1994): 247–285; Lee Yoon Suk, *Hong Gildong jeon yeongu: seoji wa haeseok* (Research on *The Story of Hong Gildong*: texts and interpretation) (Seoul: Gyemyeong daehakgyo chulpanbu, 1997).

Bibliography

SOURCES IN ENGLISH

Ahn Junghyo. *White Badge: A Novel of Korea*. New York: Soho Press, 1989.

Allen, Horace Newton. *Korean Tales*. New York: G. P. Putnam's Sons, 1889.

Anderson, Benedict. *Imagined Communities*. London: Verso, 2006.

The Annals of King T'aejo: The Founder of Chosŏn Dynasty. Translated by Byonghyon Choi. Cambridge, MA: Harvard University Press, 2014.

Atkins, E. Taylor. *Primitive Selves: Koreana in the Japanese Colonial Gaze, 1910–1945*. Berkeley: University of California Press, 2010.

Blok, Anton. "The Peasant and the Brigand: Social Banditry Reconsidered." *Comparative Studies in Society and History* 14, no. 4 (September 1972): 494–503.

Breuker, Remco. "Korea's Forgotten War: Appropriating and Subverting the Vietnam War in Korean Popular Imaginings." *Korean Histories* 1, no. 1 (2009): 36–59.

Butler, Judith. *Gender Trouble: Feminism and the Subversion of Identity*. New York: Routledge, 1999.

Caprio, Mark. *Japanese Assimilation Policies in Colonial Korea, 1910–1945*. Seattle: University of Washington Press, 2009.

Chandra, Vipan. *Imperialism, Resistance, and Reform in Late Nineteenth-Century Korea: Enlightenment and the Independence Club*. Berkeley: Institute of East Asian Studies, 1988.

Ch'ên Shou-yi. *Chinese Literature: A Historical Introduction*. New York: Ronald Press Co., 1961.

Cho'oe, Yŏng-ho. "An Outline History of Korean Historiography." *Korean Studies* 4 (1980): 1–27.

Choe-Wall, Yang-hi. "The Sino-Korean Poetic Tradition of the Late Sixteenth Century: Background to a Study of the Poetry of Hŏ Nansŏrhŏn." *Papers on Far East History* 33 (January 1986): 139–157.

Chung, Steven. *Split-Screen Korea: Shin Sang-ok and Postwar Cinema*. Minneapolis: University of Minnesota Press, 2014.

Confucius. *The Analects*. Translated by Annping Chin. New York: Penguin, 2014.

Courant, Maurice. *Bibliographie coréenne: Tableau littéraire de la Coree*. Vol. 1. New York: Burt Franklin, 1894.

Dau-Lin, Hsu. "The Myth of the 'Five Relations' of Confucius." *Monumenta Serica* 29 (1970): 27–37.

Deuchler, Martina. *The Confucian Transformation of Korea: A Study of Society and Ideology*. Cambridge, MA: Harvard University Asia Center, 1992.

———. "'Heaven Does Not Discriminate': A Study of Secondary Sons in Chosŏn Korea." *Journal of Korean Studies* 6 (1988–1989): 121–163.

———. *Under the Ancestors' Eyes: Kinship, Status, and Locality in Premodern Korea*. Cambridge, MA: Harvard University Asia Center, 2015.

Duncan, John. *The Origins of the Chosŏn Dynasty*. Seattle: University of Washington Press, 2000.

Fisher, Paul. *A Kim Jong-Il Production: The Extraordinary True Story of a Kidnapped Filmmaker, His Star Actress, and a Young Dictator's Rise to Power*. New York: Flatiron, 2015.

"Fouke le Fitz Waryn." In *Robin Hood and Other Outlaw Tales*, edited by Stephen Knight and Thomas Ohlgren. Kalamazoo: Western Michigan University, 1997.

Fouser, Robert J. "'Translations' of Hong Kildong: From Story to Classic to Icon and Beyond." *Transactions of the Royal Asiatic Society, Korea Branch* 75 (2000): 25–41.

Gradburn, Nelson H. H. "Tourism, Modernity, and Nostalgia." In *The Future of Anthropology: Its Relevance to the Contemporary World*, edited by Akbar S. Ahmed and Cris N. Shore, 158–178. London: Athlone, 1995.

Haboush, JaHyun Kim. *The Great East Asian War and the Birth of the Korean Nation*. New York: Columbia University Press, 2016.

———. *A Heritage of Kings: One Man's Monarchy in the Confucian World*. New York: Columbia University Press, 1998.

Hanscom, Christopher P. *The Real Modern: Literary Modernism and the Crisis of Representation in Colonial Korea*. Cambridge, MA: Harvard University Asia Center, 2013.

Hawley, Samuel. *The Imjin War: Japan's Sixteenth-Century Invasion of Korea and Attempt to Conquer China*. Berkeley: Institute of East Asian Studies, 2005.

Hŏ Kyun. *Borderland Roads: Selected Poems of Hŏ Kyun*. Translated by Lan Haight and T'ae-yŏng Hŏ. New York: White Pine, 2009.

———. "The Tale of Hong Kil-tong." Translated by Marshall R. Pihl Jr. *Korea Journal* (July 1, 1968): 4–21.

Hobsbawm, Eric. *Bandits*. New York: The New Press, 2000.

———. "Social Bandits: Reply." *Comparative Studies in Society and History* 14, no. 4 (September 1972): 503–505.

Hong, Euny. *The Birth of Korean Cool: How One Nation Is Conquering the World through Pop Culture*. New York: Picador, 2014.

Hong Kil-tong chon / The Story of Hong Gil Dong. Seoul: Baekam, 2000.

Hsia, C. T. "The Military Romance; A Genre of Chinese Fiction." In *C. T. Hsia on Chinese Literature*, 135–170. New York: Columbia University Press, 2004.

Huat, Beng Chua, and Koichi Iwabuchi. *East Asian Pop Culture: Analysing the Korean Wave*. Hong Kong: Hong Kong University Press, 2008.

Hughes, Theodore Q. *Literature and Film in Cold War South Korea: Freedom's Frontier*. New York: Columbia University Press, 2012.

Hunter, J. Paul. "The Novel and Social/Cultural History." In *The Cambridge Companion to the Eighteenth-Century Novel*, edited by John Richetti, 9–40. Cambridge: Cambridge University Press, 1996.

Hwang, Kyung Moon. *Beyond Birth: Social Status in the Emergence of Modern Korea.* Cambridge, MA: Harvard University Asia Center, 2004.

———. *A History of Korea.* Houndmills: Palgrave Macmillan, 2010.

Hwang Sok-yong. *The Shadow of Arms.* Translated by Chun Kyung-Ja. Ithaca, NY: Cornell East Asia Series, 1994.

Hyegyŏng. *The Memoirs of Lady Hyegyŏng.* Translated by JaHyun Kim Haboush. Berkeley: University of California Press, 1996.

Jeong, Kelly Y. *Crisis of Gender and the Nation in Korean Literature and Cinema.* Lanham, MD: Lexington, 2011.

Jung, Sun. *Korean Masculinities and Transcultural Consumption: Yonsama, Rain, Oldboy, K Pop Idols.* Hong Kong: Hong Kong University Press, 2011.

Kallander, George L. *Salvation through Dissent: Tonghak Heterodoxy and Early Modern Korea.* Honolulu: University of Hawai'i Press, 2013.

Kerr, George H. *Okinawa: The History of an Island People.* Rutland, VT: Charles E. Tuttle Co., 1958.

Kim Hŭnggyu and Peter H. Lee. "Chosŏn Fiction in Korean." In *A History of Korean Literature*, edited by Peter H. Lee, 273–287. Cambridge: Cambridge University Press, 2003.

Kim Jeongsu. *The History and Future of Hangeul, Korea's Indigenous Script.* Translated by Ross King. Folkestone: Global Oriental, 2005.

Kim, Jina E. "Intermedial Aesthetics: Still Images, Moving Words, and Written Sounds in Early Twentieth-Century Korean Cinematic Novels (*Yeonghwa Soseol*)." *The Review of Korean Studies*, 6. no. 2 (December 2013): 45-79.

Kim Jong Il. *On the Art of the Cinema.* Honolulu: University Press of the Pacific, 1989.

Kim, Kichung. *An Introduction to Classical Korean Literature: From Hyangga to P'ansori.* Armonk, NY: M. E. Sharpe, 1996.

Kim, Kyung Gyun. *The Remasculinization of Korean Cinema.* Durham, NC: Duke University Press, 2004.

Kim, Kyung Hyun. *Virtual Hallyu: Korean Cinema in the Global Era.* Durham, NC: Duke University Press, 2011.

Kim-Renaud, Young-Key, ed. *King Sejong the Great: The Light of Fifteenth-Century Korea.* Washington, DC: International Circle of Korean Linguistics, 1992.

———, ed. *The Korean Alphabet: Its History and Structure.* Honolulu: University of Hawai'i Press, 1997.

Kim, Suk-Young. *Illusive Utopia: Theater, Film, and Everyday Performance in North Korea.* Ann Arbor: University of Michigan Press, 2010.

Kim, Tai-jin. *A Bibliographical Guide to Traditional Korean Sources.* Seoul: Asiatic Research Center, Korea University, 1976.

Kim Yong-bok. "Messiah and Minjung: Discerning Messianic Politics over against Political Messianism." In *Minjung Theology: People as the Subjects of History*, edited by Kim Yong-bok, 183–193. Maryknoll, NY: Orbis, 1981.

Kim Youg-kol. *Brave Hong Kil-dong / The Man Who Bought the Shade of a Tree.* Elizabeth, NJ: Hollym, 1990.

Knight, Stephen. *Robin Hood: A Complete Study of the English Outlaw.* Oxford: Blackwell, 1994.

Kooistra, Paul. *Criminals as Heroes: Structure, Power, and Identity.* Bowling Green, OH: Bowling Green State University Popular Press, 1989.

Ledyard, Gary K. *The Korean Language Reform of 1446.* Seoul: Singu munhaksa, 1998.

Lee, Jin-kyung. *Service Economies: Militarism, Sex Work, and Migrant Labor in South Korea*. Minneapolis: University of Minnesota Press, 2010.

Lee, Ki-baik. *A New History of Korea*. Translated by Edward W. Wagner and Edward J. Schultz. Seoul: Ilchokak, 1984.

Lee, Ki-Moon. "The Inventor of the Korean Alphabet." In *The Korean Alphabet*, edited by Young-Key Kim-Renaud, 11–30. Honolulu: University of Hawai'i Press, 1997.

Lee, Peter H, ed. *Anthology of Korean Literature: From Early Times to the Nineteenth Century*. Honolulu: University of Hawai'i Press, 1981.

———. *A History of Korean Literature*. Cambridge: Cambridge University Press, 2003.

Lee, Sang Taek. *Religion and Social Formation in Korea: Minjung and Millenarianism*. Berlin: Mouton de Gruyter, 1996.

Lee Young-il and Choe Young-chol. *The History of Korean Cinema*. Translated by Richard Lynn Greever. Seoul: Jimmundang, 1998.

Lew, Young Ick. "The Conservative Character of the 1894 Tonghak Peasant Uprising: A Reappraisal with Emphasis on Chŏn Pong-jun's Background and Motivation." *Journal of Korean Studies* 7 (1990–1991): 149–180.

Li, Way-yee. "Full-Length Vernacular Fiction." In *The Columbia History of Chinese Literature*, edited by Victor H. Mair, 620–658. New York: Columbia University Press, 2001.

Long, William J. *English Literature: Its History and Its Significance for the Life of the English Speaking World*. Boston: Ginn and Co., 1909.

Lynch, Deidre. *The Economy of Character: Novels, Market Culture, and the Business of Inner Meaning*. Chicago: University of Chicago Press, 1998.

McCune, George M. "The Yi Dynasty Annals of Korea." *Transactions of the Korea Branch of the Royal Asiatic Society* 29 (1939): 87–82.

Moon, Cyris H. S. "A Korean Minjung Perspective: The Hebrews and the Exodus." In *Voices from the Margin: Interpreting the Bible in the Third World*, edited by R. S. Sugirtharajah, 228–243. Maryknoll, NY: Orbis, 1995.

Moon, Okpyo. "Tourist Commoditization of Confucian Cultural Heritage in Korea." In *Consuming Korean Tradition in Early and Later Modernity: Commodification, Tourism, and Performance*, edited by Laurel Kendall, 88–104. Honolulu: University of Hawai'i Press, 2011.

Nguyen, Viet Thanh. *Nothing Ever Dies: Vietnam and the Memory of War*. Cambridge, MA: Harvard University Press: 2016.

O'Brien, Anne Sibley. *The Legend of Hong Kil Dong: The Robin Hood of Korea*. Watertown, MA: Charlesbridge, 2008.

Pai, Hyung Il. *Constructing "Korean" Origins: A Critical Review of Archaeology, Historiography, and Racial Myth in Korean State-Formation Theories*. Cambridge, MA: Harvard University Asia Center, 2000.

Park, Eugene Y. *Between Dreams and Reality: The Military Examination in Late Chosŏn Korea, 1600–1894*. Cambridge, MA: Harvard University Press, 2007.

Park, Jiwon. *The Novels of Park Jiwon*. Translated by Emanuel Pastreich. Seoul: Seoul National University Press, 2011.

Plaks, Andrew H. *The Four Masterworks of the Ming Novel*. Princeton, NJ: Princeton University Press, 1987.

Poole, Janet. *When the Future Disappears: The Modernist Imagination in Late Colonial Korea*. New York: Columbia University Press, 2014.

Pratt, Keith, and Richard Rutt eds. *Korea: A Historical and Cultural Dictionary*. Surrey: Curzon, 1999.

The Record of the Black Dragon Year. Translated by Peter H. Lee. Seoul: Institute of Korean Culture, Korea University, 2000.

Robinson, Michael Edson. *Cultural Nationalism in Colonial Korea, 1920–1925.* Seattle: University of Washington Press, 1988.

———. "Mass Media and Popular Culture in 1930s Korea: Cultural Control, Identity, and Colonial Hegemony." In *Korean Studies: New Pacific Currents,* edited by Dae-Sook Suh, 59–82. Honolulu: University of Hawai'i Press, 1994.

Russell, Mark James. *Pop Goes Korea: Behind the Revolution in Movies, Music, and Internet Culture.* Berkeley: Stone Bridge, 2008.

Ryu, Je-Hun. "Kyeryong Mountain as a Contested Place." In *Sitings: Critical Approaches to Korean Geography,* edited by Timothy R. Tangherlini and Sallie Yea, 121–140. Honolulu: University of Hawai'i Press, 2008.

Ryu, Ju-Hyun, and Hyun Hyo Kim. "A Comparative Study of Storytelling Tourism Based on Literary Contents: The Case of Don Quixote and Hong, Gil-Dong." *Advances in Information Sciences and Service Sciences* 5, no. 15 (October 2013): 362–371.

Ryu, Youngju. *Writers of the Winter Republic: Literature and Resistance in Park Chung Hee's Korea.* Honolulu: University of Hawai'i Press, 2016.

Saaler, Sven, and Christopher W. A. Szpilman. *Pan-Asianism: A Documentary History,* vol. 2: *1920–Present.* Lanham, MD: Rowman & Littlefield, 2011.

Scalapino, Robert A., and Chong-Sik Lee. *Communism in Korea,* part 1: *The Movement.* Berkeley: University of California Press, 1972.

Schmid, Andre Schmid. *Korea Between Empires, 1895–1919.* New York: Columbia University Press, 2002.

Schönherr, Johannes. *North Korean Cinema: A History.* Jefferson, NC: McFarland & Co., 2012.

Schultz, Edward. *Generals and Scholars: Military Rule in Medieval Korea.* Honolulu: University of Hawai'i Press, 2000.

Seal, Graham. *The Outlaw Legend: A Cultural Tradition in Britain, America, and Australia.* Cambridge: Cambridge University Press, 1996.

Seo Hajin. *Hong Gildong.* Translated by Leif Olsen and Janet Hong. Seoul: Jimoondang, 2007.

Shapiro, James. *Contested Will: Who Wrote Shakespeare?* New York: Simon & Schuster, 2010.

Shin Dong Wu. "Shin Dong Wu's *Hong Gildong.*" Translated by Minsoo Kang and Heinz Insu Fenkl. *Azalea: Journal of Korean Literature and Culture* 6 (2013): 328–355.

Skillend, W. E. *Kodae Sosŏl: A Survey of Korean Traditional Style Popular Novels.* Old Woking: Unwin Brothers, 1968.

Slatta, Richard E. "Eric J. Hobsbawm's Social Bandit: A Critique and Revision." *A Contracorriente* 1, no. 2 (Spring 2004): 22–30.

So, Jae-Yung. "The Life of Hŏ Kyun and the Features of His Literary Works." *Journal of Social Sciences and Humanities* 52 (1980): 1–17.

"The Story of Hong Gildong." Translated by Minsoo Kang. *Azalea: Journal of Korean Literature & Culture* 6 (2013): 220–320.

The Story of Hong Gildong. Translated by Minsoo Kang. New York: Penguin, 2016.

Suh, Dae-Sook. *The Korean Communist Movement, 1918–1948.* Princeton, NJ: Princeton University Press, 1967.

Suh Nam-dong. "Historical References for a Theology of Minjung." In *Minjung Theology: People as the Subjects of History,* edited by Kim Yong-bok, 155–182. Maryknoll, NY: Orbis, 1983.

———. "Towards a Theology of Han." In *Minjung Theology: People as the Subjects of History*, edited by Kim Yong-bok, 55–69. Maryknoll, NY: Orbis, 1983.

Suh, Serk-Bae. *Treacherous Translation: Culture, Nationalism, and Colonialism in Korea and Japan from the 1910s to the 1960s*. Berkeley: University of California Press, 2013.

Tangherlini, Timothy R. "Chosŏn Memories: Spectatorship, Ideology, and the Korean Folk Village." In *Sitings: Critical Approaches to Korean Geography*, edited by Timothy R. Tangherlini and Sallie Yea, 61–82. Honolulu: University of Hawai'i Press, 2008.

Taylor, Jamie K. *Fictions of Evidence: Witnessing, Literature, and Community in the Late Middle Ages*. Columbus: Ohio State University Press, 2013.

Virtuous Women: Three Classic Korean Novels. Translated by Richard Rutt and Kim Chong Un. Seoul: Kwang Myong, 1974.

Wagner, Edward Willett. *The Literati Purges: Political Conflict in Early Yi Dynasty*. Cambridge, MA: Harvard University Press, 1974.

Watt, Ian. *The Rise of the Novel: Studies in Defoe, Richardson, and Fielding*. Berkeley: University of California Press, 1967.

Weems, Benjamin. *Reform, Rebellion, and Heavenly Way*. Tucson: University of Arizona Press, 1964.

Wilkins, Warren Wilkins. *Grab Their Belts to Fight Them: The Viet Cong's Big-Unit War Against the U.S., 1965–1966*. Annapolis, MD: Naval Institute Press, 2011.

Yecies, Brian, and Ae-Gyung Shim. *Korea's Occupied Cinemas, 1893–1948*. New York: Routledge, 2011.

Yi, Kil J. "The Making of Tigers: South Korea's Military Experience." In *The Australian Army and the Vietnam War 1962–1972*, edited by Peter Dennis and Jeffrey Grey, 152–179. Canberra: Army History Unit, 2002.

Yi Sŏngmu. "The Influence of Neo-Confucianism on Education and the Civil Service Examination System in Fourteenth- and Fifteenth-Century Korea." In *The Rise of Neo-Confucianism in Korea*, edited by Wm. Theodore de Bary and JaHyun Kim Haboush, 125–160. New York: Columbia University Press, 1985.

Young, Carl. *Eastern Learning and the Heavenly Way: The Tonghak and Ch'ŏndogyo Movements and the Twilight of Korean Independence*. Honolulu: University of Hawai'i Press, 2014.

Zŏng In-sŏb, "The Legend of Zŏn U-Czi." In *Folk Tales from Korea*, 224–234. Seoul: Hollym, 1982.

SOURCES IN KOREAN AND JAPANESE

Chon Pom-song, ed. *Hanguk yeonghwa chongseo* [Collection of Korean cinema]. Seoul: Hanguk Yeonghwa Jinheung Johap, 1972.

Han Seungwon. "Sin Gildong Jeon." In *Arirang byeolgok* [Song of arirang], 172–191. Seoul: Munidang, 1999.

Heo Gyeongjin. *Heo Gyun pyeongjeon* [Critical biography of Heo Gyun]. Seoul: Dolbaegae, 2002.

Heo Gyun. *Hong Gildong jeon / Heo Gyun sanmunjip* [The story of Hong Gildong / Collection of Heo Gyun's writings]. Seoul: Hanyang chulpan, 1996.

———. *Seongso bubugo* [Minor writings of Seongo]. Vol. 2. Seoul: Minjok munhwa chujinhoe, 1985.

"Hong Gildong jeon" [The story of Hong Gildong]. *Gajeong Jiu* 1, no. 2 (February 1937): 48–56.

Hong Gildong jeon [The story of Hong Gildong]. Seoul: Yonsei daehakgyo daehakchulpan munhwawon, 2014.

Hong Gildong jeon, Im Janggun jeon, Jeong Eulseon jeon, Yi Daebong jeon [The story of Hong Gildong, the story of General Im, the story of Jeong Eulseon, the story of Yi Daeebong]. Seoul: Gyeongin munhwasa, 2007.

Hong Gildong jeon / Jeon Uchi jeon [The story of Hong Gildong / The story of Jeon Uchi]. Seoul: Munhak dongne, 2010.

Hong Manjung and Hwang Yunseok. *Jeongbo haedong ijeok* [Enlarged edition of extraordinary events of Haedong]. Seoul: Gyeongin munhwasa, 2011.

Hwang Mija and U Sangryeol, "Joseon yeonghwa <Hong Gildong jeon> gwa hanguk drama <Kwaedo Hong Gildong jeon> bigyo yeongu" [North Korean movie <The Story of Hong Gildong> and the South Korean drama <The Story of Sharp Blade Hong Gildong> comparison and analysis]. *Hanjung inmunhak yeongu* 32 (April 2011): 207–221.

Jang Hyo-hyon, *Hanguk gojeon soseolsa yeongu* [Research on the history of classic Korean fiction]. Seoul: Goryeo daehak chulpanbu, 2002.

Jeong Biseok. *Soseol Hong Gildong* [Hong Gildong the novel]. Vol. 1. Seoul: Goryeowon, 1985.

Jeong Jongmok and Yi Gwangik (illus.). *Hong Gildong jeon* [The story of Hong Gildong]. Seoul: Changbi, 2003.

Kang Cheolgeun. *Saramui nara* [Country of humanity]. Seoul: Iji chulpan, 2010.

Kim Changyeop, "Character sijang tteugeoun 'Hong Gilong jeon.'" [Heated character market for "The Story of Hong Gildong"]. *Jungang ilbo* (July 2, 1998). http://pdf.joinsmsn.com/article/pdf_article_prv.asp?id=DY01199807020147.

Kim Gwan. "Sinyeong yeonghwa Hong Gildong Jeon eul bogo" [After seeing the new version of the film *The Story of Hong Gildong*]. *Choson ilbo* (June 25, 1936): 5.

Kim Ki-dong. *Hanguk godae soseol gaeron* [Survey of classic Korean fiction]. Seoul: Daechang munhwasa, 1956.

Kim Sunam, ed. *Joseon sinario seonjip* [Collection of Joseon scripts]. Seoul: Jipmundang, 2003.

Kim Taejun. *Jeungbo Joseon soseolsa* [Enlarged history of Joseon fiction]. Seoul: Hangilsa, 1990.

———. *Joseon soseolsa* [History of Joseon fiction]. Seoul: Doseo chulpan, 1989.

Kim Yong-jik. *Kim Taejun pyeongjeong: jiseong gwa yeoksajeok sanghwang* [Biography of Kim Taejun: intellectual and historical context]. Seoul: Iljisa, 2007.

Ko Kichido den. Translated (from Korean to Japanese) by Shiraishi Shigeru. Tokyo: Jiyu Tokyusa, 1921.

Lee Pok-kyu. "Chogi gukmunsoseol ui jonjae yangsan" [The mode of existence of early Korean novels]. *Gukjae eomun* 21 (2000): 25–44.

Lee Yoon Suk. "Hong Gildong jeon jakja nonui ui gyebo" [The geneaology of the controversy over the authorship of *The Story of Hong Gildong*]. *Yeolsanggojeong yeongu* 36 (December 30, 2012): 381–414.

———. *Hong Gildong jeon pilsabon yeongu* [Research into the handwritten manuscripts of *The Story of Hong Gildong*]. Seoul: Kyung-in, 2015.

———. "*Hong Gildong jeon* wonbon hwakjeongeul wihan siron" [An essay on the determination of the original text of *The Story of Hong Gildong*]. *Tongbang hakji* 85 (January 1994): 247–285.

———. *Hong Gildong jeon yeongu: seoji wa haeseok* [Research on *The Story of Hong Gildong*: texts and interpretation]. Seoul: Gyemyeong daehakgyo chulpanbu, 1997.

————. *Joseonsidae sangeopchulpan* [Commercial publishing in the Joseon period]. Seoul: Minsokwon, 2016.

————. "Kim Taejun 'Joseon soseolsa' geomto" [An examination of Kim Taejun's "History of Joseon Fiction"]. *Dongbak hakji* 161 (March 2013): 403–442.

Mun Young Joo. "Ilje malgi gwanbyeon jabji 'Gajeong jiu' (1936. 12–1941. 03) wa 'saeroun buin'" [Late Japanese colonial-period government-sponsored journal *Friend of the Household* (Dec. 1936–Mar. 1941) and *New Wife*]. *Yeoksa munjae yeongu* 17 (2007): 179–220.

Nam Jeonghyeon, *Bunji* [Land of excrement]. Seoul: Hangyeore, 1987.

Paik Sung-Jong. "Gososeol *Hong Gildong jeon* ui chohak e daehan jaegumpto" [Some problems of *The Tale of Hong Kiltong*, an old novel]. *Chindan Hakhoe* 80 (December 1995): 307–331.

Park Baesik. "Park Taewon ui yeoksa soseolgwan" [Park Taewon's theory of the historical novel]. *Gubo hakbo* 2 (December 31, 2007): 33–51.

Park Song-ui. *Hanguk godae soseollon gwa sa* [Theory and history of classical Korean fiction]. Seoul: Jimundang, 1992.

Park Taewon. *Hong Gildong Jeon* [The story of Hong Gildong]. Seoul: Joseon geumyung johap yeonhaphoe, 1947.

Park Yangho. *Seoul Hong Gildong woe* [*Hong Gildong of Seoul* and other works]. Seoul: Beom Han, 1985.

Shin Dong Wu. *Shin Dong Wu collection*. Seoul: Bucheon manhwa jeongbo center, 2007.

"Sinjak Joseon yeonghwa *Hong Gildong jeon*" [New Joseon film *The Story of Hong Gildong*]. *Donga ilbo* (April 9, 1935): 3.

Seol Seonggyeong. *Hong Gildong jeon ui bimil* [The secret of *The Story of Hong Gildong*]. Seoul: Seoul daehakgyo chulpanbu, 2004.

Seol Seonggyeong and Jeong Cheol. *Siljon inmul Hong Gildong* [The real-life Hong Gildong]. Seoul: Jungang M & B, 1998.

Won Seonyeong. "Gangneungsi 'Hong Gildong character' Janseonggun e ppaetgyeotda" [The city of Gangneung lost its Hong Gildong character to Janseong County]. *Gangwon ilbo* (September 7, 2009). http://www.kwnews.co.kr/nview .asp?s=501&aid=209090600123.

Yi Ik. *Seongho saseol* [Essays of Seongho]. Seoul: Minjok munhwa chu jinhwoe, 1995.

Yi Munyol. *Auwaeui manam oe* [An appointment with my brother and other stories]. Seoul: Doseo chukpan dungji, 1994.

Yi Myeongseon. *Yi Myeongseong jeonjip* [Complete works of Yi Myeongseon]. Vol. 3. Seoul: Bogosa, 2007.

Yi Sik. *Gukyeok Taekdang Jip* [Translated collected writings of Taekdang]. Vol. 6. Seoul: Minjok munhwa chujinhoe, 1996.

Yi Yongcheol. "'Hong Gildong gwa Chadolbawi' ro wangguk eul seun manhwaga, Shin Dong Wu" [The comic book artist Shin Dong Wu who built his kingdom with "Hong Gildong and Chadolbawi"]. In *Shin Dong Wu collection*, 8–15. Seoul: Bucheon manhwa jeongbo center, 2007.

Yu Chungreyol jeon, Jeong Bi jeon [The story of Yu Chungryeol / The story of Queen Jeong]. Seoul: Ihoe munhwasa, 2005.

Yu Hyeongjae. "Gangneungsi Hong Gildong character ilbu sayong bulga" [The city of Gangneung prohibited from the use of Hong Gildong character]. Yeonhap news (September 7, 2009). http://news.naver.com/main/read.nhn?mode=LSD&mid=sec &sid1=102&oid=001&aid=0002850920.

Index

About the Author

Minsoo Kang is associate professor of history at the University of Missouri–St. Louis. He is the author of *Sublime Dreams of Living Machines: The Automaton in the European Imagination* and the coeditor of *Visions of the Industrial Age: Modernity and the Anxiety of Representation, 1830–1914*. He is also a translator, most notably of the Penguin Classic *The Story of Hong Gildong*, the first book in the series to be rendered from Korean, and the author of a book of short stories, *Of Tales and Enigmas*.

Made in the USA
Coppell, TX
15 December 2021

68652785R00152